cey's
querade

80

Internationale Forschungen zur
Allgemeinen und
Vergleichenden Literaturwissenschaft

herausgegeben von

Alberto Martino
(Universität Wien)

Redaktion: Ernst Grabovszki

Anschrift der Redaktion:
Institut für Vergleichende Literaturwissenschaft, Berggasse 11/5, A-1090 Wien

De Quincey's Gothic Masquerade

Patrick Bridgwater

Rodopi

Amsterdam - New York, NY 2004

Cover:
L'accident,
Robert Hubert (1733-1808)
Paris, Musée Connacq-Jay

Le papier sur lequel le présent ouvrage est imprimé remplit les prescriptions de "ISO 9706:1994, Information et documentation - Papier pour documents - Prescriptions pour la permanence".

The paper on which this book is printed meets the requirements of " ISO 9706:1994, Information and documentation - Paper for documents - Requirements for permanence".

ISBN: 90-420-1813-5

Printed in The Netherlands

Contents

Preface

Variously dubbed Gothic Hero, Gothic Parasite, and author of a Gothick sport, De Quincey is the dark horse of Gothicism, for while his work has, increasingly, been associated with Gothic, not one of the recent companions to Gothic so much as mentions his name.[1] There will be more than one reason for this state of affairs. One is the fact that, while definitions of what is meant by 'Gothic' have changed, and are still evolving, claiming more territory all the time, even Gothic specialists have their blind spots, of which De Quincey is one. This is shown by the fact that the editor of the recent and generally excellent *Cambridge Companion to Gothic Fiction* felt able to write that 'several features of the Gothic [...] eventually became a basis for Sigmund Freud's *fin de siècle* sense of the unconscious as a deep repository of very old, infantile, and repressed memories or impulses, the archaic underworld of the self',[2] without mentioning De Quincey's *Confessions*, and that Alison Milbank's essay on 'Victorian Gothic in English Novels and Stories, 1830-1880' included the anonymous 'The Iron Shroud' (*Blackwood's*, August 1830), but not *The Avenger* (*Blackwood's*, August 1838) or any other tale by De Quincey, who is not mentioned, despite the fact that he had featured in a recent study of Victorian Gothic.[3]

Another reason for this neglect will be the fact that in his work the Gothic is interwoven with the German. Gothic, as he knew and loved it, had a German dimension in that it was regarded, and for a time disparaged, as largely German-inspired, and these days English studies tend to ignore German literature or betray unfamiliarity with the language and its literature by the serial mistakes that mar so much Gothic criticism (e.g. by treating *Romantik* as though it meant Romantic, when its real meaning is Romanticism; by the same token, *Schauerromantik* means Dark Romanticism, not its practitioners). That it was not always so, is, of course, shown by De Quincey's generation. The present study, which is concerned with his knowledge of German literature only insofar as it impinges on or illuminates his gothicity, shows that his knowledge of German Gothic/Romantic literature (as opposed to his very wide knowledge of the secondary literature in German on all manner of subjects) and his indebtedness to it have both been exaggerated.

What makes him an interesting figure in this context is (i) the way in which he epitomizes Gothic in both ancient and modern definitions, and (ii) the way in which focusing on the Gothic takes one to the heart of his literary masquerade, and more especially to the heart of his masked autobiographical enterprise, in other words, to the heart of the matter so far as De Quincey as a writer is concerned. His life and work are alike shot through with Gothic motifs, while his fiction in the narrower sense is entirely Gothic in today's terms. The texts examined here are those on which, for better or worse, his reputation as a writer both of autobiography and of fiction depends. What will probably come as the greatest

---

1 Viz. *The Handbook to Gothic Literature,* ed. Marie Mulvey-Roberts (Basingstoke: Macmillan Press, 1998); *A Companion to the Gothic*, ed. David Punter (Oxford: Blackwell, 2000); *The Cambridge Companion to Gothic Fiction,* ed. Jerrold E. Hogle (Cambridge: Cambridge University Press, 2002).

2 *Cambridge Companion*, 3.

3 *Victorian Gothic*, ed. Ruth Robbins & Julian Wolfreys (Basingstoke: Palgrave, 2000), xi, xii-xiii, 33, 36, 53ff.

surprise to many readers are the manifold parallels between De Quincey and Kafka, a writer separated from him in time, place, race, religion, and language, but who proves, in all sorts of interesting ways, to be a literary descendant.

For help with problems along the way I am indebted to the staff of the Bodleian, Taylorian, and English Faculty Libraries, Oxford, the Special Collections of the Brotherton Library, Leeds, and the Deutsche Bücherei, Leipzig. It is a pleasure to acknowledge their invariable helpfulness.

Abbreviations

De Quincey's Works (ed. Masson) are quoted by volume and page number only, in the form 1: 234.

WTDQ *The Works of Thomas De Quincey*, ed. Grevel Lindop et al.

E Eaton (reference in text)

L Lindop (reference in text)
All other references appear in the footnotes, in full on the first occasion, thereafter in the shortest intelligible form. To avoid confusion, *Thomas De Quincey. Bicentenary Studies*, ed. Robert Lance Snyder (Norman & London: University of Oklahoma Press, 1985) is shortened to *Bicentenary Studies.*

1. Early Gothic Reading

1.1. Infant Literature

De Quincey's encounter with the Gothic goes back to what he calls 'The Affliction of Childhood'. In this part of the original *Suspira de Profundis* he describes the 'sudden revelation that all is lost' (13: 338) following the tragically early death in 1792, at the age of nine (he was himself seven at the time), of his sister Elizabeth, with whom he lost the 'central security which belong[s] to love that is past all understanding' (1: 29), to say nothing of losing the lively, intuitive companion of his early reading.[1] From that time onwards, with the twin pillars of his life in ruins and his mind clouded by darkness, the idea, and ultimately the metaphysics, of loss, one of the key features of Gothic, never left his mind.[2] 'Happy the man,' the artist Hubert Robert wrote in 1806, 'who can live philosophically in the memory of what he has been.'[3] De Quincey, for one, found it extremely difficult to do so. He grew up in a Gothic inner world, a fractured personality, afraid that he was nothing but a phantom self, a second identity projected from his consciousness, and therefore a non-ens. The 'real' Thomas De Quincey died with his sister Elizabeth. As a writer he is a phantom, a ghost crab living in the house of others' words, of any available pre-text.

The awareness of a 'hideous incubus' bearing down on him turned into a wider awarenesss of the chasm dividing self and other, God and the absence of God, faith and recusancy, possession and loss, reality and dream (so much more real than 'reality'), truth and illusion, truth and untruth, the moral and the aesthetic. He was haunted by those he lost in the course of his life (notably his sister Elizabeth, Ann the Outcast, and Kate Wordsworth, but also his father, his elder brother, his sister Jane, and, later, his wife Margaret and two sons). Spurred by a subconscious wish to bridge the inner divide, things come together in his mind. He possesses the poet's awareness that 'all things appear to be related to all' (10: 115), but the gift 'for feeling in a moment the secret analogies or parallelisms that connect things else apparently remote' (3: 332) is in reality a curse, for it leads him astray, making him unable to concentrate on the here-and-now, unable to surrender to the moment. All that is left are the past and the future, both of which belong to Death. His very digressiveness is doubly Gothic, for it is by nature transgressive, a matter of 'going too far', of continually crossing lines in the sand of the text. Gothic is all about liminalities, boundaries of all kinds transgressively crossed.

---

1 The depth of De Quincey's lack of self-confidence was illustrated in 1898, when Friedrich Christoph showed that his description of his sister's deathbed scene was indebted to the description of Liana's death in Jean Paul's novel *Titan*, which he is thereby known to have read (Friedrich Christoph, *Über den Einfluß Jean Paul Richters auf Thomas De Quincey* (Hof: no publisher named, 1898), 28.

2 See J. Hillis Miller, *The Disappearance of God: Five Nineteenth-Century Writers* (Cambridge, Mass. & London: Harvard University Press, The Belknap Press, 1975], 17-80.

3 Quoted from W. Gaunt, *Bandits in a Landscape* (London: The Studio, 1937), 108.

So far as the literary expression of aspects of what is now called Gothic is concerned, it is two 'fairy tales' – the Arabian tale of Aladdin, and the *Lügenmärchen* (tall story) in the form of the mendacious tales falsely attributed to Baron Münchhausen – on which we need to focus, and two or three years later there was the appeal first of the fabulist Phaedrus and then of Lucian. The attraction of the fabulous was instant; it never left him. He was fascinated by 'the world of dreams and fable' (3: 328). The reference in the *Autobiography* to 'a cruel Bluebeard' (1: 388), and the references to a 'Bluebeard room' in the Greek Street house, can safely be taken as evidence that he read Perrault's fairy tales (*Mother Goose Tales*, tr. R. Samber, 1729) and/or the collection *Fairy Stories* (*c.* 1750), which contains 'The Blue Beard'. He may also have known Joseph Ritson's *Fairy Tales Selected from the Best Authors* (2 vols, 1788). *Tabart's Collection of Popular Stories* (4 vols, 1804-9), on the other hand, came out too late to be relevant. He was probably also familiar with Mme d'Aulnoy's *Tales of the Fairies*, 1707), which influenced Ann Radcliffe, and Musäus's *Volksmärchen der Deutschen* (5 vols, 1782-87), which came into the domain of the Gothic novel when it was translated into English, supposedly by William Beckford, but in reality by Thomas Beddoes (1760-1808, the father of the Gothic poet), as *Popular Tales of the Germans* (2 vols) in 1791. He may have known Horace Walpole's *Hieroglyphic Tales* (privately published in 1785 in an edition of just six copies, but reprinted in his *Works* of 1798), a 'fairy-tale' anthology drawing on Arabian, Celtic and Oriental fantasy.

The *Arabian Nights Entertainments* (translated from Antoine Galland's French, 6 vols, in print throughout the century from 1717) was a particular childhood favourite of the young Thomas (see 'Infant Literature' in the *Autobiography* [1: 127-30]), as it was of many other young writers-to-be at the time. Wordsworth read the *Arabian Night*s as a child and later made a collection of different versions of the *Nights* that De Quincey will no doubt have been shown,[4] and Coleridge left accounts of the 'obscure dread and intense desire' that he himself associated with the *Arabian Nights.*[5] Some years before De Quincey's first immersion in the thousand and one tales, John and Laetitia Aikin had written that 'The old Gothic [medieval] romance and the Eastern tale, with their genii, giants, enchantments, and transformations, however a refined critic may censure them as absurd and extravagant, will ever retain a most powerful influence on the mind', and had added that 'In the *Arabian Nights* are many most striking examples of the terrible joined with the marvellous'.[6] It is to this that De Quincey is alluding when he writes of Mrs Barbauld (née Aikin) – mistakenly in his view, although it is she who has been vindicated by history – insisting on 'Aladdin' and 'Sinbad' as the two jewels of the collection (1: 127). He and Elizabeth, for their part, pronounced 'Aladdin' to be 'pretty nearly the worst' of the tales on the grounds that 'after possession of the lamp has once been secured by [...] accident, the story ceases to move', but this magisterial judgment of the very young is belied by the fact that he proceeds to retell the story in a way that shows how much it meant to him. Imagery from the tale spans his work, his concept of the sublime goes back to the story of Aladdin, and it was his love

4 For details, see *The Arabian Nights in English Literature*, ed. Peter L. Caracciolo (Basingstoke: Macmillan, 1988), 7, 64 n. 21.

5 See Richard Holmes, *Coleridge: Early Visions* (London: Hodder & Stoughton, 1989), 10f.; also, *Collected Letters of Samuel Taylor Coleridge,* ed. E. L. Griggs, 6 vols (Oxford: Clarendon Press, 1956-71), I, 208.

6 Quoted from *Gothic Documents,* ed. E. J. Clery & Robert Miles (Manchester & New York: Manchester University Press, 2000), 128, 129.

of the *Arabian Nights* in general, and the story of Aladdin in particular, that led directly to his enthusiastic reading of Gothic novels and tales a few years later, there being many bridges between the two, including the idea of 'live burial in subterraneous chambers', and the forbidden chamber (Bluebeard room), which are leitmotifs of the *Arabian Nights*. He never forgot the *Arabian Nights*: in 1854 he told Hogg that he was planning a volume of 'Arabian Tales', and while the plan was hardly serious, his continued attachment to the *Nights* certainly was.

The passage in the tale of Aladdin that most held his attention (see 1: 383, 388; 7: 181) as exemplifying sublimity is that at the beginning of the tale in which a magician from the central depths of Africa is introduced to the reader. The secret art of an enchanted lamp imprisoned in subterraneous chambers (his use of this phrase may or may not reflect his reading of Ann Radcliffe's *The Italian* [Vol. I, ch. 9]), the mighty labyrinth of sounds, the sorcerer with his demoniac gifts and murderous intention, the phantoms of the brain, and the idea that the least things in the universe can be secret mirrors of the greatest, such ideas fascinated De Quincey and are constantly reflected in his work. As he grew up and experienced a traumatic fall not just into adult self-awareness, but into the awareness of guilt, *rifacimento* and the incorporation of others' work into his own became just such a 'secret mirror' by means of which he, the pariah, might secretly emulate the greatest, borrowing the emperor's clothes at will. It was much the same idea that he drew from Phaedrus, who was so important to him because the 'apotheosis of the slave' gave him his 'first grand and jubilant sense of the moral sublime', and from Lucian, another early favourite, who wandered around Ionia in the garb of a slave before settling in Athens, where he wrote the works that brought him fame. Aladdin was a comparable figure, initially little better than a street Arab, who became a king. Aladdin's 'enchanted lamp' became identified in De Quincey's mind with that 'lamp of Paradise [...] which burned so steadfastly' in his sister Elizabeth (1: 36), and therefore came to symbolize the enchanted childhood that came to an abrupt end on her death, which 'turn[ed] his heaven into hell, and reveal[ed] the abysmal depths of human life',[7] following which he became fixated on the underworld of death. Into those abysmal, abyssal depths he would descend in search of his lost paradise, reason enough in itself to account for his later devotion to Milton. That he seems to have seen Elizabeth at the moment of his death confirms that his whole life had been a quest for the lost paradise of early childhood.

It is the all too early experience of 'the horror of life' (13: 350) that underlies the gothicity of his work. The subterraneous chamber was to be transformed into the 'secret chambers' of the mind (in which that tragic knowledge was stored) and the secret 'mirrors of darkness' (on which his eye 'traced the plots 'of his dreams), and in *Suspira* there is a related description of a walled garden, a *hortus occlusus*. 'Open sesame!', he writes:

> Behold a lawn islanded with thickets! How perfect is the verdure; how rich the blossoming shrubberies that screen with verdurous walls from the possibility of intrusion, whilst by their wandering line of distribution they shape, and umbrageously embay, what one might call lawny saloons and vestibules, sylvan galleries and closets! Some of these recesses, which unlink themselves as fluently as snakes, and unexpectedly as the shyest nooks, watery cells, and crypts, among the shores of a forest-lake, being formed by the mere caprices and ramblings of the luxuriant shrubs, are so small and so quiet that one might fancy them meant for *boudoirs*.

7 Hillis Miller, 18.

> Here is one that in a less fickle climate would make the loveliest of studies for a writer of breathings from some solitary heart, or of *suspira* from some impassioned memory! And, opening from one angle of this embowered study, issues a little narrow corridor, that, after almost wheeling back upon itself in its playful mazes, finally widens into a little circular chamber; out of which there is no exit (except back again by the entrance) (13: 357)

This is the apparently idyllic scene from a writer's study, a harmless-looking mirror-image of the enclosed spaces of Gothic, which underlie it. That 'little circular chamber, out of which there is no exit' is a version of the 'subterraneous chamber' in the tale of Aladdin, but at the same time it can be read as a description of the mind, of consciousness and its imprisoning spaces, in which De Quincey spent his life, unable (and indisposed) to escape from the central trauma of childhood.

Another childhood favourite was *The Travels and Surprising Adventures of Baron Munchausen,* which greatly impressed the young Thomas, a fact that can be extrapolated from his own later penchant for exaggeration to the point of untruth, which ultimately has a psychological explanation. The *Lügenmärchen*, the genre to which Munchausen belongs, goes back via Swift's *Gulliver's Travels* to the mendacious *Vera historia* of Lucian. De Quincey was enthusiastic about Lucian, whose work he described as containing 'passages of more terrific effect, more German [= Gothic in today's terminology] and approaching to the sublime, than anywhere else in Greek literature' (10: 322), and was delighted by *Gulliver's Travels* (11: 12ff.). The *Vera historia* contains some early versions of stories that are also found in the *Arabian Nights*. *Gulliver's Travels*, like Defoe's *Robinson Crusoe* before it, spawned a host of imitators, including Raspe's *Baron Munchausen's Narrative of his Marvellous Travels and Campaigns in Russsia* (1785), of which *The Travels and Surprising Adventures* is an expanded version. *The Travels* are, of course, part of the stream of whimsical and fantastical fictions that fed into the Gothic romance. The cheeky advertisement for (of all things) the book's veracity signed by Gulliver, Sinbad and Aladdin speaks for itself. In his imaginative work De Quincey will internalize the imaginary voyage or journey which so fascinated him in Lucian, the *Arabian Nights, Gulliver's Travels*, Ludvig Holberg's *Nicolai Klimii Iter Subterraneum*, and the tall stories attributed to Baron Münchhausen.

If the tale of Aladdin first acquainted De Quincey with Gothic imagery (scattered references in the works show that he never forgot that 'murderous subterraneous chamber' embodying the sublime of terror, which his imagination endlessly elaborated), Munchausen is no less important, for the idea of 'spiritual transfigurations of a word or a sentence' became an abiding concern. What is in question is the aesthetic idea of a sublimity that can be attained through words, for instance by the non-sublime means of exaggeration – hyperbole was a constant temptation – and the disregard of truth; but words also embellish, enabling the lowest to vie with the highest, the outcast with the king, by putting sublimity within the reach of both. De Quincey is, of course, less interested in writing than in rewriting, rewriting his own life and bolstering his own ego in the process by correcting others' work, putting them right, putting himself in the right. By such means the nobody becomes, in his own estimation, somebody of consequence. We shall return to the psychological, notably in connexion with the dream-texts, but in literary terms there is no doubt that the 'prelapsarian idyll'[8] of De Quincey's childhood at Greenhay was marked by his discovery first, at about the age of six, of the *Arabian Nights Entertainments* and the *Travels [...] of Baron Munchausen*, and then, two or three years later, of the work of the fabulist Phaedrus, an early role model, who started life as a slave and made his name and gained his freedom by translating and imitating Aesop. From these he acquired not only a taste for the fabulous and a sense of the sublime, but also the first inklings of his destiny as a writer and what it might mean to him From Phaedrus he took the seductive, subversive idea that it was possible to achieve fame by translating and imitating others: the roots of *rifacimento* lie this far back in De Quincey's development.

It is appropriate that of the three literary works that most deeply impressed De Quincey in mid-childhood, one (the imitations of Aesop by Phaedrus) is a *rifacimento*, while the other two are forgeries. *The Arabian Nights Entertainments* was an English version of what was less a French adaptation of a collection of Indian, Persian and Arabic tales, than a work of Galland's own creation, concocted by deleting, adding to, and altering a 14th-century Syrian text.[9] So successful was Galland's collection of 1704-17[10] that by 1800 there were in all some eighty translations, pseudo-translations and imitations of it. Moreover, the story of 'Aladdin and the Magic Lamp' is non-canonical, having been written down only in the early eighteenth century; in scholarly terms it is a forgery, as is *Baron Munchausen's Narrative of his Marvellous Travels and Campaigns in Russia*, which appeared in 1785 after earlier versions of the first seventeen tales had appeared in a disreputable Berlin periodical, the *Vade Mecum für lustige Leute*, in 1781 and 1783. This was a forgery in the sense that it was the work not of Hieronymus Karl Friedrich, Freiherr von Münchhausen (1720-97),[11] but of an unscrupulous German expatriate scholar-embezzler on the run in England, Rudolf Erich Raspe (1737-94), who, not wishing to reveal his own whereabouts, attributed his tall stories to Münchhausen, a famous raconteur with a reputation for gilding the lily. This English-language forgery then became the basis for a German *rifacimento* brought out in 1786 by the poet Bürger of *Lenore* fame. Many of Raspe's stories are of ancient date, some going back to Lucian; a number of them appeared under the title 'Mendacia Ridicula' in the third volume of *Deliciae Academicae* (Heilbron, 1665). While De Quincey will not have known all these facts, some of them not available in his day, they prefigure his later penchant for appropriating the work of others. He will, however, have known the basic facts, and will also have discovered a few years later that Raspe was the author of a Gothic novel of banditti (*Räuberroman*) narrated by 'Baron Munchausen', *Königsmark der Räuber; oder, Der Schrecken aus Böhmen* (1790), which was adapted by J. H. Sarratt, whose *rifacimento* (*Koenigsmark the Robber; or, The Terror of Bohemia*, 1803) then became the basis for a pirated chapbook purporting to be by M. G. Lewis.

---

8 Snyder, in *Thomas de Quincey. Bicentenary Studies*, ed. Robert Lance Snyder (Norman & London: University of Oklahoma Press, 1985), 350.

9 At this point I am indebted to Husain Haddawy's Introduction to his recent translation of *The Arabian Nights* (London: Davis Campbell, 1992). The motif of putting one's ear to the ground to listen for distant sounds is found in other Arabian 'Nights', but not in *Aladdin.*

10 By 1711 Shaftesbury, in his 'Advice to an Author', remarked that 'Monsters and monsterland' had never been more popular (Shaftesbury, *Characteristics of Men, Manners, Opinions, Times*, ed. J. M. Robertson (New York: Bobbs-Merrill, 1964), I, 221-5.

11 English translations drop the *Umlaut* and the second h in the good Baron's name.

1.2. Thomas de Quincey and Charles de Moor

In a letter to Wordsworth written in March 1804 De Quincey said, not entirely wisely, that between the ages of twelve and sixteen he had modelled his conduct and aims on characters from legend or the German drama, until he came to feel himself 'unfettered by any ties of common restraint' (L 117). By 'characters from legend' he probably meant Odysseus (see L 29) and other heroes of Greek legend, men in possession of that elixir of life, heroic stature, which he was missing at the time. He gives no sign of having heard Hannah More's view that the German drama of the time was 'hostile alike to the principles of Religion and Morality',[12] but if he had heard of it, he would, provided he had been reading the fourth edition (1800) of A. F. Tytler's translation of *The Robbers*, as he most likely had, have been amused and persuaded by the translator's assurance that

> He wishes earnestly [...] that he had *left undone* what he *has done* [...] But [...] it is some alleviation of this unavailing regret, that he cannot, upon the strictest revision of this particular piece, and the most attentive consideration of its scope and tendency, judge it in any degree subversive either of *Religion* or of *Morality* [...] If the *German Theatre* had inculcated no lessons of morality more faulty, no pictures more corrupting than those of the *Tragedy of the Robbers*, its Translator should have no cause at this day to lament that any labour of his should have promoted the taste for its productions.

It is entirely possible that he took up German drama because his mother had warned him off it. In saying this, I have in mind the fact that Willibald Alexis, author of the German *Walladmor*, on his own admission took to reading German 'Gothic' novels only when he was expressly forbidden to do so, and that E. T. A. Hoffmann too read in his youth the 'Gothic' books he had been forbidden to read. De Quincey's mother was at this time a friend of Hannah More, whose views she espoused. When De Quincey later wrote an essay on Hannah More, whom he came to know well after first meeting her in 1809, he attacked 'Holy Hannah's' 'unctuous morality'. In 1800-04 he was under the very different influence of the 'Female Infidel', Mrs R. F. A. Lee. He probably read Goethe's *Götz von Berlichingen* (translated by Scott in 1799 as *Goetz of Berlichingen with the Iron Hand*),[13] and certainly read Schiller's *The Ghost-Seer* and *The Robbers* at this early age, in English, for he only learnt German while at Oxford, and may have been led by them to the Gothic novel (and to the *Schauerroman* and *Räuberroman* in translation) that was appearing in all the libraries, for all three works contain elements of the Gothic.

Die Räuber first appeared in English in 1795. De Quincey probably first read it in 1800, and was, inevitably, greatly impressed, this being shown by the terms in which he later wrote of 'this demoniac drama' in his entry on Schiller for the seventh (1838) edition of the *Encyclopaedia Britannica*:

---

[12] Hannah More, *Strictures on the Modern System of Female Education*, 2 vols (London: T. Cadell Jun. & W. Davies,1799), I, 39ff.

[13] Scott's translation was reprinted in Zwickau in 1829. De Quincey refers to the play (4: 411), but remarks only that the original was pirated. He read the translation of Goethe's *Die Geschwister* (*The Sister*, tr. Henry Mackenzie or Alexander Thompson) as part of a volume of *Dramatic Pieces from the German* [Edinburgh: W. Creech, & London: T. Cadell, 1792] in 1803.

> Under the oppression of this detested system [of personal discipline], and by pure reaction against its wearing persecutions, we learn from Schiller himself that in his nineteenth year he undertook the earliest of his surviving plays, *The Robbers,* beyond doubt the most tempestuous, the most volcanic [...] of all juvenile productions anywhere recorded. He himself calls it 'a monster', and a monster it is; but a monster which has never failed to convulse the heart of young readers with the temperament of intellectual enthusiasm and sensibility [...] it possesses a power to agitate and convulse, which will always obliterate its great faults to the young, and to all whose judgment is not too much developed. (4: 435f.)

However, the very fact that he was obviously sincere in his enthusiasm for *Die Räuber,* which influenced him profoundly, makes it all the more extraordinary that when he goes on to quote what Schiller himself says about the play, he does so in a re-make of Carlyle's translation of the German playwright's words that, far from betokening a lack of confidence in his own ability as a translator at that time, shows just how inveterate a method and crucial a psychological need *rifacimento* had by then become:

> To escape from the formalities of a discipline which was odious to my heart, I sought a retreat in the world of ideas and shadowy possibilities, while as yet I knew nothing at all of that human world from which I was harshly secluded by iron bars. Of men, the actual men in this world below, I knew absolutely nothing at the time when I composed my *Robbers*. Four hundred human beings, it is true, were my fellow-prisoners in this abode [a military academy]; but they were mere tautologies and reiterations of the self-same mechanic creature, and like so many plaster casts from the same original statue. Thus situated, of necessity I failed. In making the attempt, my chisel brought out a monster, of which (and that was fortunate) the world had no type or resemblance to show.

These words, as Peter Michelsen has pointed out,[14] are simply a slightly altered version of Carlyle's translation. As such, they bear out his conclusion that De Quincey's knowledge of Schiller's work in the wider sense is essentially superficial.

Although it is a tragedy rather than a Gothic drama, *The Robbers* includes many 'Gothic' features. Coleridge described it as being linked by mysterious villains, ruined castles, dungeons, trap-doors, skeletons, flesh-and-blood ghosts and perpetual moonshine with *The Castle of Otranto,* translations of which were about that time [the late 1790s] beginning to make as much noise in Germany as their original was making in England.[15] *The Castle of Otranto* was first translated into German (*Seltsame Begebenheiten im Schloße Otranto, eine gotische Geschichte*) in 1768, but attracted little attention at that time; Coleridge had presumably seen F. L. W. Meyer's translation (*Die Burg von Otranto. Eine Gothische Geschichte*), which was published in 1794. It was in 1797 that T. J. Matthias declared that 'Otranto Ghosts have propagated their species with unequalled fecundity. The spawn is in every novel shop'.[16]

Other Gothic features of *The Robbers* include the Count and his Castle; 'live burial' in the form of incarceration in an underground dungeon; something rather like the Gothic hero-villain in the person of Karl Moor; the outcast as Gothic hero in the mould of Milton's Satan; the robber-band and the desperate captain of banditti; the Bohemian forest in which they operate; dispossession and disinheritance; usurpation; purloined/forged letters; the

---

14 Peter Michelsen, 'Thomas De Quincey und Schiller', *German Life & Letters*, 9 (1956), 98, and Thomas Carlyle, *The Life of F. Schiller* (London: Chapman & Hall, n.d.), 16.

15 *Biographia Literaria* , new edn (London: George Bell, 1876), 276.

16 *The Pursuit of Literature*, 6th edn, 1798, 343.

effect on the reader (cf. Coleridge: 'I tremble like an aspen leaf'); and the motif of revenge, though this is a feature of the literature of the time, not just of Gothic. Such lists can, however, be misleading (no reader would recognize the play from Varma's inaccurate list of 'dramatis personae': 'banditti, monks, inquisitors, tortures and prison, haunted towers and yelling ghosts, dungeons and confessionals'[17]), and the tragedy is in any case diminished by the Gothic epithet, for its dialectic of virtue and villainy, vengeance and regeneration, freedom and order goes way beyond Gothic as such.

If De Quincey is to be believed – and there is no reason to disbelieve him on this score – it would seem that his rebellious behaviour during his early teenage years of exile in Bath, culminating in running away from Manchester Grammar School in 1802 at the age of seventeen, was in part prompted by his reading of *Die Räuber,* which could thus be said to have had a deleterious effect on him in existential/moral terms. In literary terms it was a different matter, for this passionately idealistic, dramatically Gothic work was to prove an inspiration in more ways than one. He read it, as he had read *Der Geisterseher,* in English, for it was not until 1805 that his German would enable him to read Schiller in the original, and even then he read *Wallenstein* in Coleridge's translation (1800), from which he quoted (without acknowledgment) in *Suspira.*[18] Coleridge had read *Die Räuber* some years earlier, with dramatic effect:

> Coleridge at Cambridge in 1794 read *Die Räuber* one dark November evening at midnight, and an hour or so later threw down the book trembling like an aspen leaf and seizing a pen to pour out his heated fancies in a letter: 'My God, Southey, who is this Schiller, this convulser of the heart ? [...] Upon my soul, I write to you because I am frightened [...] Why have we ever called Milton sublime?'[19]

Shelley, who in his teens shared De Quincey's fascination with the Gothic novel, was similarly affected, *Die Räuber* being, according to Peacock, one of the works that had the strongest influence in the formation of his character; the same goes for De Quincey, and *The Robbers* (for she read it in English) was one of Ann Radcliffe's favourite books. It has been said that Shelley translated 'A volume of [Gothic] tales from the German', his *St Irvyne* being made up of two German romances of unknown authorship.[20] This dubious, if not entirely implausible, claim, unsupported by any evidence, needs to be explored. What seems more certain is that Shelley came across a trashy, long forgotten German Gothic tale by Friedrich Christian Laukhard (1758-1822), *Franz Wolfstein oder Begebenheiten eines dummen Teufels* (1799), which gave him the name of his Wolfstein and Mary the name of her Frankenstein (Franz → Frank[en] + stein). In addition Shelley was influenced by Charles Brockden Brown, who also worked, in part, from German models.

Die Räuber first impinged on the English-speaking world in Edinburgh on 21 April 1788, when Henry Mackenzie delivered to the Royal Society of Edinburgh a lecture that focussed on '*Les Voleurs*, a tragedy by Mr. Schiller', 'one of the most uncommon

---

17 Devendra P. Varma, *The Gothic Flame* (Metuchen, N.J. & London: The Scarecrow Press, 1987), 33.

18 The words 'in to-day already walks to-morrow' (13: 350) come from Coleridge's *The Death of Wallenstein* (V, i, 102).

19 Montague Summers, *The Gothic Quest* (New York: Russell & Russell, 1964), 121, quoting from *Letters of S. T. Coleridge*, ed. E. H. Coleridge, 2 vols (London: Heinemann , 1895), I, 96f.

20 V. Stockley, *German Literature as Known in England, 1750-1830* (London: Routledge, 1929), 218 n. 5.

productions of untutored genius that modern times can boast'. Mackenzie, having no German at the time, was obliged to read the tragedy in French, but within a few years his enthusiasm had led to the appearance of the best of four different English translations of the play,[21] that by Alexander Fraser Tytler, in 1792 (four editions by 1800). Mackenzie's description of Karl Moor as having 'a soul of fire and a heart of sensibility':

> The intrinsic force of this dramatic character (the hero of the piece) is heightened by the singular circumstance in which it is placed. Captain of a band of inexorable and sanguinary banditti, whose furious valour he wields to the most desperate purposes, living with those associates amidst woods and desarts [sic], terrible and savage as the wolves they have displaced, this presents to the fancy a kind of preternatural personage, wrapped in all the grandeur of visionary beings[22]

leads, in the present context, to De Quincey's somewhat hubristic description of himself, in the same 1804 letter to Wordsworth, as being 'led on by high aims [and] the hope of elevating my name in authority & kingly splendour over every name that is named upon earth'.[23] In the text of *The Robbers* the word 'king' appears only in tandem with the word 'outcast', thus underlining the idea that De Quincey had already gleaned from the cases of Aladdin and Phaedrus. That the youthful De Quincey's enthusiasm was fired by *The Robbers* to the point of identification with its lawless hero, the outcast in the 'Hercynian' forests of Bohemia, is clear. There was no way in which young Thomas de Quincey (he began by writing de with a lower-case d), who identified with Charles de Moor, as Karl Moor became in the 1795 translation, was going to drop the apparent cachet of (intellectual) nobility, one of the earliest of his masks, adopted in emulation of Charles de Moor and Daniel De Foe.[24] Karl Moor is the ultimate model for all De Quincey's heroic avenger-figures, and for the related figures in Maturin's *Bertram*, Byron's *Werner* and the work by which it was inspired, Harriet Lee's *Kruitzner*.[25]

More important, however, is the fact that Karl Moor is also the model for De Quincey's Gothic hero (see 4. 2 below) as such. Presented by Schiller in much the same way that Satan is presented by Milton, he is associated with the Devil in the text: he appears in his father's castle in disguise, as Count de Braund, the pseudonym indicating not only that he is sunburnt from living in the wilds, but also that he is the Dark Count (in seventeenth-century German *braun* meant dark) of Gothic convention, the Dark Lord of fantasy. By extension he represents De Quincey's Gothic self. Presently he characterizes himself: 'the Exterminating Angel is my name', and when Herman says 'As soon could Satan force the gates of heaven, as thou that door', he promptly opens the door. When the castle is stormed, Switzer is heard saying 'It is the devil come from hell to seize him. Where's Blackman with his troop?' Blackman is, of course, one of the Devil's appellations. Karl invokes the God of vengeance ('my trade is the *lex talionis*', 'vengeance is my trade'). When he proclaims 'Vengeance belongs exclusively to me', it becomes clear that he is being presented, like the

---

21 See L. A. Willoughby, 'English Translations and Adaptations of Schiller's Robbers', *MLR*, 16 (1921), 297-315.

22 Henry Mackenzie, in his 'Account of the German Theatre', *Transactions of the Royal Society of Edinburgh,* Vol. II (1790), pt. 2.

23 Cf. the childhood games in which De Quincey was king of the fantasy realm of Gombroon.

24 Readers will also think of Ferdinand De Fathom.

25 See Margaret W. Cooke, 'Schiller's „Robbers" in England', *Modern Language Review*, 11 (1915), 166.

hero of *The Avenger,* as an uncanny amalgam of the vengeful God of the Old Testament and the fallen Angel, Lucifer. De Quincey, as High Churchman and recusant in one, is not so different.

Given that De Quincey identified both with 'Charles de Moor' and also, though without ever consciously admitting it, with Satan as the personification of his own guilt, it is difficult to overstate the significance of *The Robbers* in his development: it was as formative an influence for him as it was for Shelley. In a metaphorical sense De Quincey sees himself, with Karl Moor, as 'The companion of murderers – of viperous fiends'. The attraction of Karl Moor is clear: here is the outcast as hero (Schiller has Amelia proclaim 'Outcasts are kings, and kings are outcasts'), so that being one of 'heaven's outcasts', as Karl Moor is, and as De Quincey felt himself to be, can be seen as a lot that can be overcome, a lot through which sublimity can be attained. De Quincey adopts the public pose of the Tory High Churchman while inwardly proclaiming with the role-model of his teens: 'I am myself my heaven or my hell'.[26] Henry Mackenzie wrote of Karl Moor and his banditti being as savage as the wolves they had displaced; if De Quincey had read his Schopenhauer, he would have found the *homo homini lupus* theme fully orchestrated. Even the 'treacherous crocodile', 'the crocodile's foul form', in Schiller's tragedy left its mark on his imagination, and the extraordinary image of the 'great tube through which man communicates with the shadowy' (13: 335) goes back to his memory of the words 'this little tube [a pistol] unites Eternity to time' in Tytler's translation of *Die Räuber*. In addition there are links between *Klosterheim* and *The Robbers*: the hero of *Klosterheim* bears the name of Karl Moor's father (Maximilian Count de Moor), and Maximilian, who, like Karl Moor, is the avenger of his father, similarly enters his father's castle in disguise.

1.3. Teenage Gothic Reading

De Quincey's reading of choice in 1803,[27] while he was in Everton waiting to be allowed to go up to Oxford, was the Gothic novel. At this time he read Schiller's *The Ghost-Seer, or Apparitionist* (tr. 1795), Grosse's *The Dagger* (tr. 1795; he was inclined to think it a translation from the German, but was not sure since the title-page of the copy he borrowed had been torn out), Ann Radcliffe's *The Castles of Athlin and Dunbayne* (1789) and *The Italian* (1797), Sophia Lee's *The Recess* (1783-85), William Parnell's *Julietta; or, The Triumph of Mental Acquirements over Personal Defects* (1802), Mary Pilkington's *The Accusing Spirit, or: De Courcy and Eglantine* (1802), Clara Reeve's *Memoirs of Sir Roger de Clarendon* (1793), Mary Robinson's *Angelina* (1796; whether he knew her – Perdita's – previous Gothic novel, *Vancenza, or The Dangers of Credulity* [1792], which is said to have sold out in a day, I do not know); Jane West's *The Infidel Father* (1802); and M. G. Lewis's *Tales of Wonder* (poems, 1801), Anne Bannerman's *Tales of Superstition and Chivalry* (poems, 1802), and Southey's 'Thalaba'.

After Ann Radcliffe, 'the enchantress of that [1790s] generation' (3: 282), and Harriet Lee, whom he also greatly admired, his favourite Gothic novelist was Charlotte Smith,

---

[26] Schiller, *The Robbers*, [tr. Tytler], 2nd edn (London: Robinson, 1795) 108 (Act IV, sc. 4).

[27] At the same time his contemporary Arthur Schopenhauer was languishing in Mr Lancaster's academy at Wimbledon while his parents, like the slightly older Achim von Arnim, were travelling around Scotland.

which means that, in addition to *Emmeline, The Orphan of the Castle* (1788), he is likely to have read *Ethelinde* (1789), *The Old Manor House* (1793) and *The Wanderings of Warwick* (1794), *The Banished Man* (1794), and *Marchmont* (1796; he read her *Letters of a Solitary Wanderer* [poems, 1801] in 1802). He also read (though not necessarily in 1803) Lewis's *Romantic Tales*, and no doubt also knew his *The Monk*, and some of the many Gothic novels published in 1802,[28] including Charles Lucas, *The Infernal Quixote,* and T. J. Horsley Curties, *Ethelwina, or: The House of Fitz-Auberne* (which probably gave him the name of Count Fitz-Hum). In addition to Schiller's *The Ghost-Seer*, he also came to know, perhaps via his Oxford friend Schwartzburg, who came from Dresden, Tieck's *Phantasus,* and some of the work of Friedrich August Schulze (Friedrich Laun), including the *Gespensterbuch* of Johann August Apel and Friedrich Laun, the first two volumes of which contained the stories that prompted Mary Shelley's *Frankenstein* and John Polidori's *The Vampyre*; but it was only later, through R. P. Gillies and J. H. Bohte, that he got to know Laun's work well. How many of the trend-setting German *Schauerromane* (Kahlert, *The Necromancer*; Naubert, *Herman of Unna*; Tschink, *The Victim of Magical Delusion*; Weber, *The Sorcerer*; Grosse, *The Genius* and *Horrid Mysteries*) he knew, is unlikely to be established with any certainty. He had the opportunity to read (in German) *The Sorcerer* and *The Genius*, and a version of *Herman of Unna*, when staying with the Bohtes in 1821, although it cannot be taken for granted that he did so.

Apart from confessing that 'the latter part of *[The] Recess*' reduced him to tears, he did not comment on most of these titles, which, collectively, suggest that he had, partly as a result of growing up in a predominantly female world, and partly in consequence of his own sense of invaded space, a penchant for female, sentimental Gothic. He must have relished the 'imposture and extensive confederacy' of *The Ghost-Seer,* which was written, in A.F. Tytler's words, 'with the view of exposing to contempt and detestation the artifices of those impostors in Germany, who distinguished themselves, and their disciples, or dupes, by the epithet of *The Illuminated.*'[29] This fed into his later interest in Freemasonry and secret societies in general, but I imagine it was because he was shocked by Schiller's view of the Church as a force for evil that he never commented on the content of Schiller's novel. There is a parallel here with his silence on the subject of Hoffmann's *The Devil's Elixir*.

Given his age in 1803, it is reasonable to suppose that he was attracted by titles that held out the promise of relevance to his problematical and, in the long run, increasingly burdensome self-consciousness. One can, for instance, imagine him being attracted to Parnell's book by the title, which amounted to a summary of his own existential and literary enterprise, and several of these novels left their mark on his work in one way or another. Thus Grosse's *The Dagger* features the dissipated court of a German petty prince, divided into the prince and his circle of sychophants on the one hand, and on the other Baron St.--- and his wife Albertina of F., which contains the germ of *Klosterheim,* although I hasten to add that *The Dagger,* unlike *Klosterheim,* is a novel of passion and intrigue. The subterranean passage in *Klosterheim* may or may not owe something to the subterranean cavern in Sophia Lee's *The Recess,* for this is a Gothic stock motif that reappears in Gillie

28 See Frederick S. Frank, *The First Gothics* (New York & London: Garland 1987), 461; and *The English Novel 1779-1829*, ed. Peter Garside, James Raven & Rainer Schöwerling, 2 vols (Oxford: Oxford University Press, 2000), II, 145-61.

29 'Advertisement', in *The Robbers.*

Godber's subterraneous grotto in *Walladmor*. Be this as it may, the typically Gothic word 'recess' is found throughout De Quincey's work, testimony to the profound effect on him of Sophia Lee's novel.

Mary Pilkington's *The Accusing Spirit*, for its part, includes both the conflict between Protestantism and Catholicism of *Klosterheim* and the freeing of the beloved from imprisonment in a monastery or whatever, that is a Gothic commonplace, but it is with another Gothic novel, Jane West's *The Infidel Father*, to which he will have been drawn by the title, which probably led him to dub Mrs R. F. A. Lee 'the Female Infidel', that we come to a remarkable parallel between letters and life, to which Alina Clej has rightly drawn attention, writing of *The Infidel Father*:

> *The Infidel Father* describes the case of a reckless lord who seduces an innocent seamstress, only to abandon her and her child. After remarrying unlawfully and losing his wife, he is afflicted with melancholia, remorse, and a whole array of symptoms, among them stomach pains, that he alleviates with laudanum, seeking the 'feverish repose of forced forgetfulness.' While under the power of the opiate, 'imagination [...] released from the curb of reason, recall[s] some of the forms which he had withered into shapeless dust beneath the pressure of his neglect, his perfidy, or his revenge.' These images bear an uncanny resemblance to De Quincey's later opium visions, to their forgetfulness haunted by compunctive visitings of remorse. It may be difficult to determine what made De Quincey identify with an old rake and his guilty conscience, or whether he had abandoned Ann on Oxford street the way Lord Glanville abandoned Sophia, the seamstress from Oxford, as De Quincey himself was abandoned by an 'infidel father', his own, whose untimely death deprived him of a needed paternal figure. However, in his later work De Quincey certainly assumes the role of the male deserter and the female derelict, as if reenacting a previous, traumatic scene.[30]

It is as though De Quincey, his imagination out of control, comes to react to his reading to the point of trauma. It is as though fiction and reality have become confused in a simulacrum of the 'world of sensibility encouraged and heightened into unreality' inhabited by Goethe's Werther.[31] Perhaps this is why he objected to the way in which Defoe passed false historical records (see 6: 84). It is as though he is using his reading to generate not only his writing, but his life as well. All this is speculative. The one thing that is certain is that Jane West's novel struck a deep chord: Lord Glanville is, with Karl Moor, a model for De Quincey's avengers.

It is revealing to find De Quincey reading *Tales of Superstition and Chivalry* (London: Vernor & Hood, 1802) by the Edinburgh poet Anne Bannerman (1765-1829), who had published her *Poems* (including a series of ten 'Sonnets from Werter') in 1800. Exactly what drew him to this collection of 'ballads of ghosts and female prophets, exclamatory in style, with scholarly historical notes',[32] one can only surmise, but a note in 'My Brother Pink' suggests that he was, as so often, searching for his own past self, and thereby for his present self, identifying with one who was

---

30 Alina Clej, *A Genealogy of the Modern Self* (Stanford: Stanford University Press, 1995), 143, and Jane West, *The Infidel Father*, 3 vols (London: Longman, 1802), I, 293; II, 97]

31 J. W. von Goethe, *The Sorrows of Werter*, tr. Daniel Malthus, introd. Jonathan Wordsworth (Oxford & New York: Woodstock, 1991), [iii].

32 *The Feminist Companion to Literature in English*, ed. V. Blain, I. Grundy & P. Clements (New Haven & London: Yale University Press, 1990), 56f.

> chased away to the Antipodes from one early home by his sense of wounded honour, and from his immediate home by superstitious fear, recalled to my mind an image and a situation that had been beautifully sketched by Miss Bannerman in 'Basil', one of [her] striking [...] metrical tales [...] Basil is a 'rude sea-boy', desolate and neglected from infancy, but with feelings profound from nature, and fed by solitude. He dwells alone in a rocky cave; but, in consequence of some supernatural terrors connected with a murder [...] he leaves it in horror, and rushes in the grey dawn to the sea-side rocks; seated on which, he draws a sort of consolation for his terrors, or of sympathy for his wounded heart, from that mimicry of life which goes on for ever among the raving waves. (1: 308)

Behind Basil he perceives Pink, and behind Pink, himself. Though he proceeds to criticize Defoe for locating the shipwreck of Robinson Crusoe on the wrong side of the American continent, it is clear that he, like his brother, and like Kafka, identified with the legendary castaway. It was for this reason, and because he identified with Defoe as a literary 'coiner', that he used Defoe's name as a pseudonym in 1825.

He probably opened *Tales of Superstition and Chivalry* expecting to find further 'Gothic' ballads of the kind to be found in M.G.Lewis's *Tales of Terror* (Kelso, 1799) and *Tales of Wonder* (Kelso, 1800), collected as *Tales of Wonder* (2 vols, London, 1801), which he had just been reading, and which mostly concern ghosts and witches. Be this as it may, what he actually found was something at once similar and very different, for Anne Bannerman possessed a piety that Lewis lacked, and her ballads had a twist that his lacked in the form of a kind of messianic proto-feminism and an emphasis on female prophets, the sibyls of classical antiquity and Coleridge's later *Sibylline Leaves* (1817), which included 'The Ballad of the Dark Ladie' (written in 1798). Written in the same ballad form, her 'The Dark Ladie' appears to be a continuation of the 'Introduction to the Tale of the Dark Ladie' (published in the *Morning Post*, 21 December 1799) in which Coleridge ended:

> I promis'd thee a sister tale
>   Of Man's perfidious cruelty:
> Come, then, and hear what cruel wrong
>   Befel the Dark Ladie.

Anne Bannerman supplied a sister tale. Both poets are haunted by the Dark Ladie, the *mater tenebrarum*, Love's twin sister Death. Responding to Anne Bannerman's sensitivity, which matched his own, De Quincey was evidently most impressed by this, the very first poem in her volume, for 'The Dark Ladie' was to lead, via the High-Church liturgy to which he was so attached, to his 'Our Lady of Darkness' in *Suspira de Profundis*, which shows that his reaction to the 'Dark Ladie', as to the *Infidel Father*, went way beyond a surface reaction to a text read in his teens. It may be that Our Lady of Darkness is an anima-figure, as Andriano has argued, but her roots are in classical mythology rather than Jungian psychology. As the Dark Ladie of all our nameless fears, the 'suggestress' who placed the idea of suicide in Werther's mind,[33] she shows again that De Quincey was deeply affected by his 'trashy' reading, some of which, coming on top of his feelings of guilt and insecurity, and inability to grieve for those he loved, left him radically confused.

---

33 When he wrote that 'Of human suicides, the most affecting I have seen recorded is one which I met with in a German book' (8: 402), De Quincey probably had in mind not Werther but an actual suicide recorded on C. H. Spieß's *Biographien der Selbstmörder* (4 vols, Leipzig, 1790), which he evidently read at Bohte's in 1821.

Harriet Lee (1757-1851), author of De Quincey's favourite 'Gothic novel', *Kruitzner*, 'a novel of the free adventurous type set in fashion by *Die Räuber*',[34] to which we are coming, is sometimes confused (as in L 51) with Mrs Rachel Fanny Antonina Lee (1774-1829), the 'female infidel' of De Quincey's autobiographic sketches, who serves to link two of the most memorable events of his childhood and undergraduate days with the essay *On Murder Considered as one of the Fine Arts.* Mrs R. F. A. Lee was the colourful natural daughter of a notoriously colourful father, Sir Francis Dashwood (1708-1781, fifteenth Baron Le Despencer, 1763) who famously lived a riotous life on the Continent before entering the household of Frederick Lewis, Prince of Wales, and eventually becoming Chancellor of the Exchequer in the Bute administration of 1762-63; he became archmaster of the Dilettanti Society in 1746, and in 1755 founded the Hell-Fire Club or Society of the Monks of Medmenham Abbey mentioned by De Quincey at the beginning of his essay *On Murder Considered as one of the Fine Arts,* a notorious fraternity of thirteen members who included John Wilkes (author of 'An Essay on Woman', to which was attached an obscene paraphrase of the 'Veni creator spiritus' by the wit Thomas Potter), the poet Charles Churchill, John Stuart third Earl of Bute (married to Mary, only daughter of Lady Mary Wortley Montagu), John Montagu fourth Earl of Sandwich, and the satirist Paul Whitehead, who acted as secretary and steward. Meeting in the ruins of Medmenham Abbey in Buckinghamshire, this bunch of rake-hells enacted their motto 'Fay ce que voudras' by reputedly indulging in debaucheries and profanities, mocking organized religion by the performance of blasphemous 'black masses'.

Mrs Lee would have found her father's reputation a difficult act to follow, had she not been a chip off the old block. Heroine of a criminal trial and subject of Chapter 4 of De Quincey's 'Autobiographic Sketches', she married Matthew Lee in 1794, but soon separated from him, separating him from half his fortune in the process. In 1804 she eloped with Loudoun Gordon, accompanied by his brother Lockhart, and appeared as a witness against the Gordons when they were brought to trial in Oxford in 1804 for her abduction. De Quincey, who was in court, wrote of her 'impressive appearance' and the 'appalling coolness' of her answers. The trial was abandoned when she was trapped into admitting her atheism, which meant that her oath was invalid and her evidence unsound. De Quincey went to her lodgings after the trial, just in time to see her carriage hooted out of town by a savagely baying mob. After this he heard nothing of her for many years, save that she was residing in the family of an English clergyman distinguished for his learning and piety. Then he saw that she had published a book 'connected with political or social philosophy'. This was her 'Essay on Government' of 1808 (De Quincey was vague about dates), which Wordsworth praised for its vigour and originality of thought. A scandalous and no doubt libellous account of her life, *Memoirs of R. F. A. Dashwood Lee* (London, n.d.), was suppressed after publication.

In 1794 Mrs Quincey made a serious mistake when, misled by Mrs Lee's reputation as 'a bold thinker [with] an astonishing command of theological learnings' (1: 136), she invited her to dinner, expecting evangelistic conversation. Had she known her for a daughter of the Hell-Fire Club, she would never have dreamed of inviting her to her sanctimonious table in genteel Bath. That the eight-year-old Thomas De Quincey would,

[34] Cooke, 166.

however, when he now met her, be bowled over by Mrs Lee, was inevitable. He was an impressionable young man and she not easily forgotten. The fifth chapter of his autobiography is devoted to this

> most eccentric young woman [...] with a face and a figure classically beautiful, and with the reputation of extraordinary accomplishments; these accomplishments being not only eminent in their degree, but rare and interesting in their kind. In particular, she astonished every person by her *impromptu* performances on the organ, and by her powers of disputation. These last she applied entirely to attacks upon Christianity; for she openly professed infidelity in the most audacious form.

One of her opponents in the doctrinal joust that followed at Greenhay was De Quincey's guardian, Rev. Samuel Hall, whose charge described him as 'dull, dreadfully dull', so that the encounter with Mrs Lee 'presented the distressing spectacle of an old, toothless, mumbling mastiff, fighting for the household to which he owes allegiance, against a young leopardess [...] every touch from [whose] velvety paw drew blood'. Mrs Lee's other opponent was Rev. John Clowes, Rector of St. John's, Manchester, who 'for any polemic service [...] wanted the taste, the training, and the particular sort of erudition required':

> Horror, blank horror, seized him upon seeing a woman, a young woman, a woman of captivating beauty, whom God had adorned so eminently with gifts of person and mind, breathing sentiments that to him seemed fresh from the mintage of hell. He could have apostrophised her (as long afterwards he himself told me) in the words of Shakspere's Juliet 'Beautiful tyrant! fiend angelical!' [...] it was in effect the lofty Lady Geraldine from Coleridge's 'Christabelle' that stood before him in this infidel lady. A magnificent witch she was, like the Lady Geraldine; having the same superb beauty; the same power of throwing spells over the ordinary gazer; and yet at intervals unmasking to some solitary, unfascinated spectator the same dull blink of a snaky eye.

This militant atheist and brilliant debater, who had read and endorsed *The Robbers,* and who breathed rebellion, trounced in argument both his sainted mother and her two clergymen in attendance, reducing his mother to hysterics in the process, a turn of events highly pleasing to young Thomas. From then until 1804 she could no wrong in his eyes. The 'Venetian' duplicity and malice of Adorni in *Klosterheim* belong to De Quincey's own dark or Gothic self, but Leigh Hunt's description of Wordsworth's eyes as being 'like fires, half burning, half smouldering, with a sort of acrid fixture of regard', quoted by John Beer,[35] is reminiscent of De Quincey's memorable description of the Female Infidel, her eyes ablaze with passion, yet 'at intervals unmasking [...] the dull blink of a snaky eye'. In the background here is Schiller's Armenian, a mysterious, Cagliostro-like figure wearing the dress of the Armenian clergy in Venice, with his 'penetrating look of grandeur and superiority'. So much for the 'Female Infidel' who sped meteor-like across the dark sky of young Thomas's childhood. From Mrs Lee we therefore pass to Miss Lee (no relation).

Harriet Lee, a less colourful, more important character in the present context – she too was a 'female infidel', but did not parade her atheism – was no less admired by Thomas De Quincey, albeit for quite different reasons. In 1798, put off by William Godwin's rigidity and condescension toward her in the course of arguments on the subject of religion, she turned down the opportunity to become Mary Shelley's stepmother. The Lee sisters were

---

35 In *Bicentenary Studies*, 182.

joint-heads of a fashionable Bath school, Mesdames Lees Ladies Boarding School, since 1786 at Belvidere House, Lansdown Road; one of their early pupils was Ann Ward, the later Ann Radcliffe. In 1852 Jacox heard De Quincey say 'I had believed Miss Lee to have been dead long since [she died in 1851], or I should certainly have called upon her in Bath, to offer her my intellectual respects and to express my gratitude at her intellectual prowess' (E 467). She owes her literary reputation to the *New Canterbury Tales,* in which she collaborated with her elder sister Sophia Lee (1750-1824), which De Quincey at one time intended to copy, the remnant of his intention being visible in *Klosterheim*; more particularly, she is the author of *Kruitzner*.

That De Quincey's projected *New Canterbury Tales* were to be modelled on Harriet and Sophia Lee's *Canterbury Tales* is shown by a letter to John Wilson of 14 January 1830: 'New Canterbury Tales' (i.e. on the model of Miss Lee's)' (E 327). That he writes of Miss Lee in the singular means that what he has in mind is Harriet's *The German's Tale: Kruitzner*. So emphatic is his praise of this tale as being 'almost unequalled in narrative skill, so artistic in the arrangement of the story, and so exquisite the delineation of Josephine's character' (E 467),[36] that it deserves to be quoted in full:

> The 'Canterbury Tales' of the Miss Lees are sufficiently well known, but not sufficiently appreciated; and one reason may be that the very inferior tales of Miss Sophia Lee are mingled with those of Miss Harriet. Two of those written by Harriet, viz *The Landlady's Tale* and *The German's [Tale]* are absolutely unrivalled as specimens of fine narration. With respect to the latter it is well known that Lord Byron travestied this inimitable tale into a most miserable drama; interweaving with the dialogue of his piece every word in the original conversations, unaltered nearly, and assuredly not bettered. And the very act of borrowing a plot from a tale in which so very much depends upon the plot, and where it is of a kind that will not bend to alterations or modifications of any kind, – this in itself bespoke a poor ambition and the servile spirit of a plagiarist [It is quite unknown to the world that Lord Byron's poem of 'Lara' had already contained a gross plagiarism from Miss H. Lee. The whole outline of the story, and many remarkable phrases, are borrowed from *The German's Tale*].

Particularly interesting here is the questionable distinction implicitly made – on aesthetic, not moral or legal grounds – between plagiarism, which is servile in spirit because it does not improve upon the original, and *rifacimento*, which is not, because it does. It is the self-justifying logic of the dyed-in-the-wool plagiarist. He then goes on to write of Wordsworth's reaction to *The German's Tale*:

> This most splendid tale I put into the hands of Wordsworth; and, for once, having, I suppose, nothing else to read, he condescended to run through it. I shall not report his opinion, which, in fact, was no opinion; for the whole colossal exhibition of fiendish grandeur in Conrad, the fine delineation of mixed power and weakness in Siegendorf, and the exquisite relief given to the whole by the truly Shaksperian portrait of feminine innocence and nobility in Josephine, he had failed so much as to guess at. All that he wondered at was the Machiavelian insight into motives, and the play of human character; with respect to which he said, coldly enough, that it left an uncomfortable impression of a woman as being too clever. (3: 204f.)

This is a bit rich – Thomas De Quincey, the High Tory, lumping together Byron and Wordsworth as male enemies of female Gothic, but it is also important, for De Quincey resolved to cultivate the Gothic partly as a way of maintaining his independence vis-à-vis

---

36 Eaton was quoting Jacox in 1852.

Wordsworth, on whom the popular form was generally wasted. *Kruitzner*, originally published in Vol. IV (1801) of the *Canterbury Tales,* was published as a separate volume in 1822, by Byron's publisher John Murray, on the occasion of the publication of *Werner,* which, as Byron himself stated, was 'taken entirely from *The German's Tale, Kruitzner*'. Reappearing in the course of what seems to have been De Quincey's most concentrated reading of Gothic novels and tales since 1802, perhaps under the influence of his reading of German 'Gothic' tales at Bohte's, it was, as we shall see, to leave its mark on *Klosterheim.*

Harriet Lee was a friend of the later Ann Radcliffe in her Bath days. De Quincey's daughter Emily, whose literary tastes were evidently not his, wrote in 1907 that

> no one will make much out of my father who does not take in the extreme mixture of childish folly joined to a great intellect. The novels of his youth were of the Mrs Radcliffe order full of mysteries, murders, highwaymen, mysterious people and dark corners [...] He never got beyond the Mrs Radcliffe stage and he was but a poor judge of a novel. He could make nothing of the modern novel with its pictures of real life. The heroes and heroines of his youth were all upon stilts. (E 223, 467)

Without knowing Ann Radcliffe personally, De Quincey revered her as 'the enchantress of that generation'. The two novels of hers that he read in 1802 both left their mark on his work in superficial ways, and in the longer run (see 4.2) she became a major influence in terms of his exploration of inner space. Alina Clej has pointed out that one of De Quincey's poetic exercises features a hero named Orellana who is presented as 'having lost a friend in addition to his other misfortunes', an idea borrowed from the lamentation of Earl Osbert of Dunbayne on the supposed loss of his friend Alleyn in *The Castles of Athlin and Dunbayne.*[37] *The Italian,* on the other hand, yielded the idea that Wordsworth, whose views on the sacramental significance of baptism differed from those of De Quincey, who preened himself on his knowledge of theology, 'had a natural resemblance to Mrs Ratcliffe's [sic] Schedoni and other assassins roaming through prose and verse' (8: 291). In other words, De Quincey sensed in Wordsworth a dark self that was normally repressed, but which surfaced in some surprisingly Gothic passages of his work, hence the way in which, in the essay on Wordsworth, De Quincey is able to transpose images from 'The Prelude' into 'a baffling succession of Gothic tableaux'.[38] What De Quincey apparently does not see is that he is himself in some ways Schedoni-like, and therefore, on this account, Wordsworth-like.

---

37 Clej, 145.

38 Clej, 179.

2. *Teutophilia*

2.1. Oxford, van Haren and Schwartzburg

When Carlyle, in 1827, wrote that German literature was 'thought to dwell with peculiar complacency among wizards and ruined towers, with knights, secret tribunals, monks, spectres and banditti',[1] he was summarizing a view of German literature that was almost exactly a generation out of date, but in the early years of the century 'German' and 'Gothic' were, for a time, popularly supposed to be more or less synonymous, for what the 'plague ship of German letters' denounced by Charles Maturin[2] carried in her hold was, implicitly, Gothic *Schauerromane,* in other words, what Coleridge, slating Maturin's *Bertram,* referred to as 'speaking Monsters imported from the banks of the Danube'.[3] Maturin wrote that

> The present style of novels is most piteously bewailed by those who are, or say they are, well affected to the cause of literature. *Diavolerie tales fit to frighten the nursery*, German horrors, are the best language they give us. Whatever literary articles have been imported in the plague ship of German letters, I heartily wish were pronounced contraband by competent inspectors. But I really conceive that the present subjects of novels and romances are calculated to unlock every store of fancy and feeling. I question whether there be a source of emotion in the mental frame so powerful or universal as *the fear arising from objects of invisible terror.*

Bram Stoker's schooner *Demeter* was presumably to be based on Maturin's 'plague ship'.

London with its German-speaking court and sizeable German colony was the main source of information about contemporary German letters, which meant not so much the lucubrations of the high-brow Romantics as the Gothic effusions of the popular writers of the day:

> In the last decade of the eighteenth century, the years of 'the revival of Gothic romanticism', the popularity of German literature was at its height, and the number of translations increased each year. The novel-reading public threw themselves eagerly on translations and adaptations of German novels [...], above all the 'Schauer- und Ritterromane', which provided English writers with rich materials for their own tales of horror and mystery.[4]

By the beginning of the new century *The German Museum or Monthly Repository of the Literature of Germany, the North and the Continent in General* (printed for C[onstantine] Geisweiler [of 42 Parliament Street, Westminster] and the Proprietors, 3 vols, January 1800

---

1 Thomas Carlyle, 'State of German Literature', in his *Critical and Miscellaneous Essays*, 4 vols in 2 (London: Chapman & Hall, n.d.), I, 28.

2 Quotation from the Preface to Maturin's *Fatal Revenge* (1807).

3 Coleridge, *Biographia Literaria,* new edn (London: Bell, 1876), 274. The Danube tends to be mentioned in such contexts because it is the Catholic south of 'Germany' that is important in the Gothic context.

4 Stockley, 6.

to June 1801), to which many of the German literati in London[5] briefly contributed, set out to 'make the English reader more intimately acquainted with the literary labours of Germany', an endeavour in which it must be deemed to have failed. The lingering predilection of the British at this time for 'trifling German novels' was a matter of comment. German visitors, overlooking the fact that the novels in question were German, were inclined see this as evidence of British shallowness. *The German Museum* failed because by 1800 the popularity of German literature had peaked, the years 1797-98 having seen a reaction against it. It was not until 1817 that Coleridge was instrumental in founding the 'Friends of German Literature'. That June, when Tieck was the Friends' first guest, De Quincey was in Westmorland, being plagued by terrifying dreams, and therefore missed an opportunity to meet a writer with whom he would have had much in common; but perhaps it was as well, for he would have been piqued on finding himself, here too, so much overshadowed by Coleridge.

That the traffic in Gothic novels was two-way is confirmed by the recently rediscovered library of Schloß Corvey[6] (Fürstliche Bibliothek Corvey) and the resultant bibliography (the second volume of Garside, Raven and Schöwerling, *The English Novel 1770-1829*, 2 vols [Oxford: Oxford University Press, 2000]) that contains many English Gothic novels no longer extant in this country. This two-way traffic included many translations, *rifacimenti,* plagiarisms and works seeking to cash in on fashion by purporting (in the target country) to be German or English respectively. Plagiarism, pastiche and sham translation are part and parcel of the Gothic novel. Ann Radcliffe's work, in particular, was much imitated and the subject of not a little fraudulence.[7] Willibald Alexis's *Walladmor,* famously refashioned by De Quincey, was only the most daring and, in literary terms, the most interesting, of such forgeries. In the Gothic novel and tale supposedly German names abound, many of them showing nothing more clearly than the author's ignorance of German onomastics, and German castles, forests full of banditti, and attendant horrors, are as de rigueur as Italian and Spanish villains and villainesses of a monkish or nunnish hue, all of them reflecting the long life (till 1834 in Spain, till 1859 in Italy) of the Inquisition, a fact that is easily overlooked.

Via, or despite, the Gothic novels, tales and chapbooks that he, like so many of his generation, devoured in huge numbers as a young man, De Quincey became an enthusiast for many things German; 'Grasmeriensis Teutonizans' or 'The German Student of Grasmere' he signed the best of his German essays, that on Jean Paul. In respect of German metaphysics he sided with Coleridge rather than Peacock, but he remained critical of German style (except that of Jean Paul, which he never tires of praising for its vitality and

5 One of whom, the Rev. Peter Will (1764-1839, Minister in charge of the Reformed German Congregation in the Savoy, and best known as translator of Grosse's landmark *Horrid Mysteries*), gave Peter Pindar's term 'pulpit terrorist' a new meaning.

6 See Rainer Schöwerling, *Die Wiederentdeckung der Corveyer Schloßbibliothek* (Paderborner Universitätsrede 4, 1986), and Christopher Skelton-Foord, '„Universalbibliothek der Trivialliteratur", 1800-1830: Castle Corvey and the Distribution of Circulating Library Fiction in English', *Library History,* 14 (Nov. 1998), 117-32.

7 On these 'confusing translations, adaptations and re-adaptations', see Daniel Hall, 'The Gothic Tide: *Schauerroman* and Gothic Novel in the Late Eighteenth Century', in *The Novel in Anglo-German Context,* ed. Susanne Stark (Amsterdam & Atlanta, GA: Rodopi, 2000), 51-60. On novels falsely attributed to Mrs Radcliffe, see James Trainer, *Ludwig Tieck. From Gothic to Romantic* (The Hague: Mouton, 1964), 24f.

wit), although this is as much a reflection of his reading as a reflection on German literature as such. He is inclined to be rather oldmaidish on the subject of German manners and, at times, of German letters. That he, to his chagrin, lacked Coleridge's knowledge of German transcendental philosophy is shown by the fact that he failed to write on the subject in any real depth. Much of his library consisted of German books (2: 191), of which Coleridge is, ironically, said to have borrowed 'as many as 500' at a time (E 190). In an equally ironic remark, worthy of his mother, De Quincey referred to his library as being 'rich in the wickedest of German [anti-Christian] speculations'.[8] That he was a gifted linguist is abundantly clear, but his (literary) reputation as an expert on German metaphysics in general and on Kant in particular is not entirely well-founded.[9] Nor is he in any sense an expert on German literature. There is a more general point here, for he did not merely crave credit for what he might have done rather than for what he did; to a considerable extent he has long been given credit for what he might – and should – have done. The credit he has been given for his essays on Goethe, Lessing and Schiller is a case in point. He is less a scholar than a journalist with a scholarly manner. He has a tenacious memory and a truly remarkable stock of miscellaneous knowledge – much of it gained from German criticism read in 1821 – that is, however, often out of date and incomplete. There are surprising gaps in the knowledge of this Polyhistor.

Now in a paper on *Walladmor* Frederick Burwick has written that

> In assuming his role as translator, mediator, interpreter, and popularizer of German literature and philosophy, De Quincey maintains a whimsical distance. Rather than delving deeply into Kantian metaphysics, as does Coleridge, De Quincey is more fond of calling attention, as does Friedrich Schlegel, to the 'transcendental buffoonery', making the pretensions of transcendentalism an occasion for jokes and games. To be sure, Coleridge too indulges his jests at the expense of Kant and Fichte, but he also goes on to grapple with the metaphysical problems on their own ground. De Quincey, by contrast, is more ready to reassert a traditional British perspective.[10]

While this is both true and perceptive, it is not the whole truth. Other factors enter into the equation, among them the fact that De Quincey is not equipped to delve into the subject as Coleridge does, for he lacks Coleridge's superior knowledge of the subject, the necessary time, and the necessary motivation. He has a psychologically explicable need to criticize the great, vis-à-vis whom he has an inferiority complex that sorely inhibited his development as a writer. On his own admission, his initial enthusiastic study of Kant lasted just six weeks, and his essay on 'Kant's Last Days', which, notwithstanding his disclaimers, implies (carelessly rather than dishonestly) that he attended Kant's lectures in 1773-4 and later became his amanuensis, is a fictionalized and thereby falsified *rifacimento* of Ernst Anton

---

8 Quoted from F. W. Stokoe, *German Influence in the English Romantic Period* (Cambridge: Cambridge University Press, 1926), 179.

9 See Peter Michelsen, 'Thomas De Quincey und die Kantische Philosophie', *Revue de Littérature Comparée,* 33 (1959), 356-75. For fuller discussion of De Quincey's understanding of Kant, see, especially, two books by René Wellek: *Immanuel Kant in England, 1793-1838* (Princeton, N.J.: Princeton University Press, 1931), 171-80, and *Confrontations: Studies in the Intellectual and Literary Relations between Germany, England and the United States During the Nineteenth Centur* (Princeton, N.J.: Princeton University Press, 1965), 114-52.

10 Frederick Burwick, 'How to Translate a Waverley Novel: Sir Walter Scott, Willibald Alexis, and Thomas De Quincey', *The Wordsworth Circle* (Spring 1994), 99. It may be his own indebtedness to Friedrich Schlegel in this respect that leads De Quincey to criticize him so fiercely.

Wasianski's *Immanuel Kant in seinen letzten Lebensjahren* (Königsberg, 1804). On the other hand his essay on 'German Studies and Kant in Particular' shows him to have studied the *Kritik der reinen Vernunft* to some point. Written for Hannah More, who had requested 'a general rude outline' of the 'purposes and machinery' of Kant's philosophical system, it is complemented by the fifth of the *Letters to a Young Man,* 'On the English Notices of Kant', that comprises a detailed, admirably well-informed discussion of the early literature on Kant in English. Unaccountably, De Quincey concentrated on Kant's epistemology, virtually ignoring the *Kritik der praktischen Vernunft* (but see 10: 160) and the *Kritik der Urteilskraft,* to say nothing of the Preface to the *Metaphysische Anfangsgründe zur Tugendlehre* (Metaphysical Elements of Ethics), which, with its account of the working of the internal tribunal of conscience that was to give Kafka a model for the Court in *Der Proceß,* would have been of abiding interest to De Quincey's Gothic self with its somewhat old-fashioned interest in secret societies, secret tribunals, imaginary prisons, and the rest of it. That a supposed expert on Kant and man with a sense of guilt that threatened at times to overwhelm him (in the *Confessions* he wrote of 'those anomalous practitioners in lower departments of the law, who [...] deny themselves all indulgence in the luxury of too delicate a conscience', adding that 'In many walks of life a conscience is a more expensive encumbrance than a wife or a carriage') has nothing to say on Kant's construct of Conscience spells either ignorance or evasiveness; in view of his claimed Kantian expertise, one must assume the latter. It joins his silences on the subject of Schiller's *The Ghost-Seer* and Hoffmann's *The Devil's Elixir*, all of them highly revealing.

Nor, surprisingly, has he anything worthwhile to say on the Kantian or Burkeyan Sublime, although 'sublimity' was an important concept for him, and *Walladmor* in particular shows him to be fully aware of the sublime of terror. This too is extraordinary. He had the highest opinion of Burke – 'All hail to Edmund Burke, the supreme writer of his century, the man of the largest and finest understanding' – yet this man who passes as an expert on literature and philosophy (particularly Kantian philosophy) alike, and who was fascinated by Gothic writing, has nothing to say of the '*delightful horror* which is [...] the truest test of the sublime' as seen in the Gothic novel (mountain crags, heart-stopping abysses, moonlit ruins, and the rest, all of them featured in abundance not in *Klosterheim*, but in the even more questionable, ironical context of *Walladmor*). He must have experienced those mixed sensations often enough, and one would have expected him to analyse them, as Kant does in the *Kritik der Urteilskraft,* and as Schiller does in his various writings on the sublime and on tragedy. Both Kant and Schiller see sublime objects as making us aware both of our physical inability to resist them, our puniness in comparison with them, and of our rational or moral or spiritual capacity to resist them on the supra-physical level; a true definition of humanity includes both. It therefore looks as though De Quincey, finding that the *Kritik der reinen Vernunft* would not accommodate even his High-Church Tory preconceptions – Carlyle dubbed De Quincey 'one of the most irreclaimable Tories now extant'[11] – did not bother, or was afraid, to look into other parts of the work of the *Alleszermalmer* (destroyer of everything, as Kant was known because of the number of illusions he shattered), which would, and should, have been of the greatest

[11] *The Collected Letters of Thomas and Jane Welsh Carlyle*, ed. C. R. Sanders et al., 21 vols (Durham, NC: Duke University Press, 1970-), VI, 371.

interest to him. He refers to Fichte, but, surprisingly, gives no sign that the German philosopher's attempt to reconcile the Kantian philosophy and Christianity held his attention. Hegel he was content to label 'that great master of the impenetrable', which is as good an indication as any of the inadequacy of his pretensions as an expert in the field of German metaphysics. The emperor's clothes, in this respect, seem distinctly threadbare.

With the exception of the essay on Jean Paul[12] and the essays on Kant in 'German Studies and Kant in Particular' and 'On the English Notices of Kant', his essays on German writers are for the most part made up of basic biographical knowledge, padded out with digressive material that reflects his reading of Jean Paul, who is forever sheering off into digressions on all manner of peripheral topics: rather than face up to the demands of his subject, De Quincey all too often heads for the nearest bolt-hole, only emerging in time to tack on a hasty conclusion. According to Friedrich Schlegel, the novel tends naturally towards *parekbasis* (digression): 'Parekbasis must be permanent in the fantastic novel'.[13] Given that *parekbasis* means 'a step to the side' (in German, *Seitensprung*, which actually means infidelity), this appears to underline my point that, in De Quincey's case at least, digression is transgressive. His real knowledge and real purpose are often revealed not in the highways of a subject, but in its byways or footnotes. Even in the essay on Schiller, who was, with Kant and Jean Paul, his favourite German writer, he shows real engagement only when writing on *Die Räuber*, which he linked with the Gothic novel. With Gothic it was a different matter, for much of his work is, especially on modern definitions, Gothic through and through. As Teutophile he is an historical curiosity; as Gothic he is more important than has yet been realized, in some ways the epitome of late-Romantic/post-Romantic Gothic.

He acquired his excellent reading knowledge of German, which has the same kind of tell-tale orthographic fallibility as Scott's, and his interest in contemporary German literature in two stages. In his wanderings in North Wales during what would now be called his pre-university 'gap year', he met 'Mr De Haren, an accomplished young German' who had been serving in the British Navy:

> I recollect with especial pleasure Mr. De Haren, an accomplished young German who held, or *had* held, the commission of lieutenant in our British navy, but now, in [the] interval of peace [established by the Peace of Amiens, a fourteen-month cessation of hostilities during the Napoleonic Wars lasting from April 1802 to June 1803], was seeking to extend his knowledge of England, and also of the English language; though in *that*, as regarded the fullest command of it colloquially, he had little indeed to learn. From him it was that I obtained my first lessons in German and my first acquaintance with German literature. Paul Richter I then first heard of, together with Hippel, a humourist admired by Kant, and Hamann, also classed as a humourist, but a nondescript writer, singularly obscure, whom I have never seen in the hands of any Englishman, except once of Sir William Hamilton. With all these writers Mr. De Haren had the means of making me fully acquainted in the small portable library which filled one of his trunks. (*Confessions*, 3: 333)

Steel's List of the Royal Navy for the period 1796-1802 does not include a De Haren or van Haren (or Vanharen) in its lists of lieutenants or Marine First- or Second-Lieutenants. If van Haren joined under an assumed name (such as John Dutch, 1796), he may be untraceable

12 On De Quincey and Jean Paul, see Frederick Burwick, 'The Dream-Visions of Jean Paul and Thomas De Quincey', *Comparative Literature*, 20 (1968), 1-26; Joel D. Black, 'Levana: Levitation in Jean Paul and Thomas De Quincey', *Comparative Literature*, 32 (1980), 42-62.

13 Friedrich Schlegel, *Literary Notebooks, 1799-1801*, ed. Hans Eichner (London: Athlone Press, 1957), 61.

via admiralty records. However, it seems highly likely that he is Pieter Willem van Haren (born Amsterdam 1774; died Aachen 1850), only surviving son of the Friesian nobleman Duco van Haren (1747-1801), who was the eldest son of the famous Dutch poet Onno Zwier van Haren (1713-1779). The van Harens are at this time a distinguished Dutch family of German origin and Hanoverian sympathies.[14] Duco van Haren retired to Weimar in 1797 and died there in 1801. Pieter Willem entered the Hanoverian service in the second half of the 1790s, transferring to the service of England shortly afterwards. He became a major (presumably of Marines) before retiring to Leeuwarden. Most of these facts suggest that Pieter Willem van Haren it was who first interested De Quincey in German literature: he is the right age, is the grandson of a poet (and nephew of the Dutch translator of Pope's *Essay on Man*, Jan Poppe Andrée van Haren, 1755-1818), and had, until shortly before De Quincey met him in 1802, a father living in Weimar. In late summer 1802 he was probably on extended leave from the Marines; he subsequently served in Canada. Made a baron in 1825, he never married.

This also serves as a reminder that one of the ways in which German literature was introduced into England in the latter part of the eighteenth century was via 'German' (especially Prussian) officers serving in the British army during the American War of Independence; the same holds for 'German' officers serving in the British army and navy during the Napoleonic wars. The smattering of German that van Haren taught De Quincey was soon forgotten, but not so the travelling library, which included work by Jean Paul, van Haren's admiration for whom De Quincey came to share as Jean Paul quickly became an influential favourite (and arguably a bad influence, if one thinks of his digressive technique, although one must remember that digression was a common feature of the novel at the time). His 1821 essay on Jean Paul, which appeared six years before Carlyle's, is his most original and substantial on a German literary subject, and he was rightly proud of the fact that he was the first to translate work by Jean Paul into English.

In 1804, at Oxford, De Quincey, by then 'immersed in metaphysics',[15] it being this philosophical interest that drew him (as it was later to draw Pater) to the study of German, took up the study of the language in earnest, enlisting as tutor a shadowy German student from Dresden named Schwar(t)zburg, with whom he also studied Hebrew, and who, judging by his name, may have been another aristocrat. Dresden was, from the turn of the eighteenth century, a focal point for high- and low-brow literature alike, but also for painting and the nascent opera. Presumably Schwar(t)zburg gave him some account of the burgeoning cultural activity there, which, though different in kind, was comparable to that of Edinburgh. De Quincey later told Woodhouse that it had been his intention at this time to travel in Germany, and while this came to nothing, he now persevered with the German language to the point of becoming able to read Kant.

Initially he was 'fascinated by the riches to which his budding knowledge of German promised to be the key' (E 117), and while in the short term he was soon disenchanted with Kant, he remained interested in all things German, about which he became increasingly opinionated, and indeed in some respects distinctly anti-German. Nor does his disenchantment with Kant in his undergraduate days mean that he never returned to the

---

14 See J. H. Halbertsma, *Het geslacht der van Haren's. Fragmenten* (Deventer: Lange, 1829).

15 'Of German literature apart from philosophy, he [...] in his college days knew next to nothing' (E 115). As we shall see, most of his knowledge of German literature as such was acquired via R. P. Gillies and J. H. Bohte.

'sage of Königsberg', for he did, though not until his command of German was adequate. In the *Confessions* he wrote that 'in 1812 [...] as well as for some years previous. I have been chiefly studying German metaphysics, in the writings of Kant, Fichte, Schelling, &c.' (3: 397). If true, this, and the comparison with Coleridge's *Notebooks*, underlines how much he, and contemporary criticism, lost to opium. 1812 belongs to a somewhat obscure period in De Quincey's inner life, though one in which he did much miscellaneous reading. What is not clear is how much he chose, or was able, to concentrate on German metaphysics as such, for he was a man of many, but flawed, parts. The evidence of his writing shows that concentration was not his strong point, and the idea of him being immersed in German transcendental idealism for years on end does not ring wholly true. At all events he has little to show for it. There is no reason to take at its face value Woodhouse's statement that De Quincey 'has gone very deep in the German metaphysics': the claim is most likely another 'mask', donned in order to boost his self-esteem vis-à-vis Coleridge, who had the knowledge De Quincey claimed to have. Of Fichte and Schelling little more is heard until the note on Tieck appended to 'The Love-Charm', and that is not the work of De Quincey.

Looking back, in 1836, on his 'German Studies and Kant in particular', he wrote of his 'first launching upon that vast billowy ocean of the German literature':

> *Ten thousand* new books [...] – *a literal myriad* – is considerably below the number annually poured from all quarters of Germany into the vast reservoir of Leipsic: spawn infinite, no doubt, of crazy dotage, of dreaming imbecility, of wickedness, of frenzy, through every phasis of Babylonian confusion; yet, also, teeming and heaving with life and the instincts of truth – of truth hunting and chasing in the broad daylight, or of truth groping in the chambers of darkness; sometimes seen as it displays its cornucopia of tropical fruitage; sometimes heard dimly, and in promise, working its way through diamond mines. Not the tropics, not the ocean, not life itself, is such a type of variety, of infinite forms, or of creative power, as the German literature in its recent motions (say for the last twenty years), gathering, like the Danube, a fresh volume of power at every stage of its advance. A banner it was, indeed, to me of miraculous promise, and suddenly unfurled. It seemed, in those days, an El Dorado as true and undeceiving as it was evidently inexhaustible. And the central object in this interminable wilderness of what then seemed imperishable bloom and verdure – the very tree of knowledge in the midst of this Eden – was the new or transcendental philosophy of Immanuel Kant. (2: 85f.)

This passage of autobiography, which first appeared in *Tait's Magazine* in June 1836, is vintage De Quincey, who later wrote that 'The German literature is at this time beyond all question, for science and philosophy properly so called, the wealthiest in the world. It is an absolute Potosi [...] a mine of which the riches are scarcely known by rumour in this country'.[16] He admitted to having 'lingered in painting that glad aura of my first pilgrimage to the fountains of the Rhine and of the Danube, in order[...] to shadow out the gloom and blight which soon afterwards settled upon the hopes of that golden dawn', thereby giving the misleading impression that he had visited Germany and Austria. Elsewhere he observed that 'Germany [...] found her new literature the mere creation and rebound of this great moral tempest [the French Revolution]. (2: 274).

One of the difficulties in the present context concerns De Quincey's reliability. He implies that he has visited the Rhine and the Danube, but has not; he seems to imply that he attended Kant's lectures and acted as his amanuensis, but did not, and by the same token, in a footnote taken over lock, stock and barrel from his source (13: 405), implies that he has

[16] Quoted from Stockley, 292. Potösi is a once famous silver mine in Bolivia.

visited the famous library at Wolfenbüttel, which he (unlike Coleridge, who was there in June 1799) has not; he claims to have taken lodgings 'at a German circulating library', and to have read there a matter of three thousand tales, long and short, but the long and the short of it is that the first claim is misleading and the second exaggerated; and so forth. In brief, it appears that for him, as later for George Moore, truth is an aesthetic category: true means what sounds best. He, who wrote of truth 'groping in the chambers of darkness' (2: 85), thereby implying that a magic lamp was needed to perceive it, privately regards as true things that contain some 'plausible or colourable truth', but which are 'not in an absolute and unconditional sense true' (10: 86). The word 'colourable' is the give-away. The reason(s) for this strange state of affairs, which must be psychological, probably lies partly in his diminutive stature, which drove him to prove himself, *coûte que coûte*, with the pugnacity of the pint-sized, and partly in his awareness that the secret art of the magic lamp is not always available. It is an odd coincidence that George Moore also, and a deal less plausibly, sought to prove his intellectual credentials via Kant, being dubbed 'Kant' Moore by an early lady friend because of the way in which he had taken to walking around with a copy of the *Critique of Pure Reason* in his pocket. It is highly likely that De Quincey felt challenged by Coleridge's knowledge of German literature, and that this is one reason why he often used his own knowledge of German to read up and subsequently 'translate' the German secondary literature on recondite, often non-literary subjects. His knowledge of German literature as such, as opposed to the critical literature in German on all manner of classical and historical subjects, is very limited.

Disillusionment came via the very source of his enthusiasm, the philosophy of Kant, or such of it as he became acquainted with in the course of six weeks, for six weeks' study, he insists, was 'sufficient to close my hope in that quarter for ever'. This claim too is not to be taken *au pied de la lettre*, for the best of his writings on Kant did not come about as a result of a mere six weeks' study of the most difficult of philosophers[17] read, in his teens, in a language barely acquired. He later regretted not having read Kant in Latin, which he would have found far easier. Disillusionment was all the more bitter because 'For two or three years before I mastered the language of Kant, it had been a pole-star to my hopes [...] the luminous guide to my future life – as a life dedicated and set apart to philosophy' (2: 89). He wrote of his 'shock' on being 'repelled from German philosophy' (2: 107), finding Kant 'a disenchanter, and a disenchanter the most profound', not least because his philosophy was at odds with the Church of England religion to which the conservative De Quincey was emotionally attached. The reason for his disenchantment with Kant can be found between the lines of what he writes of Shelley's 'Antichristian madness' (11: 359). Many young men of the time became disenchanted with Christianity as a result of reading Kant, who in 1794 was indicted for the 'Herabwürdigung mancher Haupt- und Grundlehren der Heiligen Schrift und des Christentums', that is, for setting at naught many of the basic tenets of the Bible and of Christianity. De Quincey, not prepared to jettison the religious faith which was the only sheet-anchor remaining to him at the time, proclaimed himself disenchanted with Kant, although he continued to study him in later years. In his early Oxford days, 'immersed in metaphysics', he had wanted to visit the home of German metaphysics – he

[17] Peacock refers to 'the sublime Kant, who delivers his oracles in language which none but the initiated can understand' (*Nightmare Abbey*, ch. 2).

meant Königsberg, where Kant held the Chair of Logic and Metaphysics from 1770 to 1804 – but he never got there. German transcendentalism quickly loses its first magic for him, and no sooner has he dismissed German philosophy from his mind *pro tempore* than he 'relaxed a little that spirit of German abstraction which had prompted it' (E 117). His subsequent 'Kantianism' was thus essentially a mask,[18] one of many.

His disenchantment with the once-powerful magic of Kant is of a piece with his view of Goethe's *Wilhelm Meister* as 'revolting to English good sense', which just happens to be the opposite of Carlyle's view. What is in some ways more surprising is that he knew little of the *Sturm und Drang,* and indeed of German Romanticism, although this has been exaggerated:

> Noch weniger hat Thomas De Quincey aus seiner Abneigung [gegenüber der deutschen Romantik] ein Geheimnis gemacht: aus dem langen Zeitalter der deutschen Romantik weiß er nur mit Jean Paul etwas anzufangen, während er der Erscheinung des von ihm als Romantiker interpretierten Goethe verständnislos gegenübersteht.[19]
> (Still less did Thomas De Quincey make a secret of his antipathy toward German Romanticism: of [the writers of] the whole long era of Romanticism, he was able to make something only of Jean Paul, being left cold by Goethe, whom he mistook for a Romantic)

What is true is that, if one excludes Goethe and Schiller (who, early English views on the subject notwithstanding, are not 'Romantics' as such, and on whom he did not, in any case, write at any critical length), Jean Paul is the only German 'Romantic' on whom De Quincey wrote in any detail. He knew some of the work of other writers of the Romantic period (Schelling and Fichte; Hoffmann, Fouqué, and Tieck; and Grosse, Laun, Alexis, and Tromlitz, all four of them, incidentally, men who chose to masquerade under a pseudonym), and made considerable use of the work of Laun in particular; but he dismissed Friedrich Schlegel as 'utterly worthless', and seems not to have known of Novalis, Brentano, Arnim, Hölderlin, Kleist, Eichendorff, and Heine. It is, on the face of it, an extraordinary gap in his knowledge. He never tired of speaking of the riches of German literature of the Romantic period, yet knew little of that period's real riches. There are several reasons for this relative ignorance. His interest was, for instance, in the ('sub-literary') *Schauerroman*[20] and in German imitators of Scott (Alexis, Tromlitz), rather than in writers whom he would perhaps have linked with the transcendental philosophy on which he had by then turned his back, and in any case poverty both prevented him from travelling to Germany and, more to the point, prevented him from keeping up with German literature to anything like the extent he would have wished, this despite the fact that he 'probably knew the book-shops of London – new and secondhand – better than any other man of his time' (E 146). Living mostly in

---

[18] Cf. the double mask worn by Charles Brockden Brown in his self-analysis as a writer of fiction, 'Walstein's School of History', said to be 'From the German of Krants of Gotha', in Charles Brockden Brown, *The Rhapsodist and other uncollected writings*, ed. Harry R. Warfel (New York: Scholars' Facsimiles and Reprints, 1943), xi, 145-56.

[19] H. Oppel, *Englisch-deutsche Literaturbeziehungen*, 2 vols (Berlin: Erich Schmidt, 1971), II, 28.

[20] The old German prejudice against 'popular' literature presumably lies behind Peter Michelsen's rather loose remark that 'Von Bedeutung sind freilich noch einige obskure Romanschreiber, denen De Quincey Stoff für seine Erzählungen entlehnte' (Not to be overlooked are a few obscure novelists, from whom De Quincey borrowed material for his tales) (Michelsen, *GLL* [1956], 98).

Edinburgh at a time when Gillies was in London and Bohte dead, he lost touch with German literature.

2.2. J. H. Bohte

It may seem surprising that De Quincey's stay with the renowned German bookseller J. H. Bohte in 1821, when there must have been endless discussion of German literature, the classics, and philosophy, in which Bohte specialized, does not seem to have given him any increased awareness of German Romantic literature. Part of the explanation must be the fact that German Romanticism, pronounced unwholesome by Goethe, was at the time completely overshadowed by Weimar Classicism, and, in England, by the *Schauerroman*. Bohte was, it is true, one of the first to stock the illustrated books associated with the German Romantics, but this is precisely the point: that he necessarily followed the market, and the market wanted, above all, (i) Goethe, (ii) the Grimm brothers' fairy tales, (iii) Gothic novels and tales, and (iv) illustrated books. It was not until the accession of Queen Victoria that German Romantic writing, in the form of less demanding writers like Chamisso, Fouqué and the Grimms, until then known mostly from translations in the literary magazines, became really popular in England. The British, ever conservative, ever pragmatic, were excited by the German Gothic Romantics for a time, as part of the craze for the Gothic, but so far as Teutonic idealism was concerned, they had their insular doubts, although there are honourable exceptions to the rule. Indeed, Kantian transcendental idealism became a popular stalking-horse, most amusingly so in Peacock's *Nightmare Abbey* (1818). The Germans, for their part, complained of the 'Gedanken- und Ideenarmuth' (conceptual poverty)[21] of English literature.

Now in the course of his review-article on 'Gillies's German Stories' in 1826, De Quincey wrote that 'Some years ago, we took lodgings at a German circulating library, and read „a matter" of three thousand tales, long and short' – an odd claim that the editor of the piece has recently passed over in silence. The claim may seem, at first glance, to be fictional, for while he was keenly interested in German literature and in the Gothic novel and tale that were, at the time, associated with it, and was powerfully attracted by bookshops and libraries, circulating or otherwise, there is no record of De Quincey having patronized a 'German circulating library', if indeed such a thing existed in this country at the time. He is clearly not thinking of van Haren's 'small portable library', which did no more than kindle his interest; to feed the flames something much more extensive (and therefore static and, normally, much more expensive) would have been required. Earlier, he had made heavy use of James Wright's circulating library in Everton, but was then reading Gothic novels rather than German ones. He always availed himself of any library to which he had access, but I have found no sign of a German circulating library or *Leihbibliothek* (as opposed to a 'Deutsche Lesebibliothek' or German Reading Room) among them. However, since most libraries in England at the time were circulating libraries, De Quincey has probably used the term as a translation of 'Lesebibliothek'.

---

21 The phrase is that of Willibald Alexis, author of the original *Walladmor*, in the context of an important survey of the romances of Walter Scott (*Wiener Jahrbücher*, 2 [1823], 1-75, phrase on p. 2), but the sentiment is general.

In 1802, when De Quincey, fresh from his meeting with van Haren and first introduction to the work of Jean Paul, a German traveller[22] said there were only three German booksellers in London, and that they, whom he does not name, but who were in fact Griffiths of Paternoster Row, Constantine Geisweiler of Parliament Street, who by 1805 had failed as a bookseller and publisher, and had transmogrified himself into a 'Dealer in Foreign Wines',[23] and Henry Escher of Gerrard Street,[24] were not worthy of notice; it was mainly 'trifling German novels' of the type devoured by De Quincey that found their way into the circulating libraries. By the mid-1790s mounting interest in 'vivid' and 'terrific' German novels was fuelled by translations such as Kahlert's *The Necromancer* (1794), Naubert's *Herman of Unna* (1794), Schiller's *The Ghost-Seer* (1795), Tschink's *The Victim of Magical Delusion* (1795), Veit Weber's *The Sorcerer* (1795), and Grosse's *Horrid Mysteries* (1796).[25] It was because of the popularity of such novels with 'a Gothic and sensationalist hue' that English novels began to masquerade as 'from the German'. The fact that Scott, as late as 1814, seriously considered subtitling Waverley 'A Romance from the German', speaks for itself. With such a title, Scott asks, 'what head so obtuse as not to image forth a profligate abbot, an oppresive duke, a secret and mysterious association of Rosycrucians and Illuminati, with all their properties of black cowls, caverns, daggers, electrical machines, trapdoors, and dark lanterns?'

By 1807 German booksellers/sellers of German books in London included Thomas Boosey (who issued *Catalogues of foreign books on sale*, 4 parts, London, 1807-16) and Henry Escher (see *A Catalogue of German Books and Prints now on sale at Henry Escher's*, 1807, in the British Library), and the father of H. G. Bohn (whom Lindop, following De Quincey, appears to mistake for Bohte: L 273), who will have been known to De Quincey as a secondhand bookseller, indeed, it is possible, though unlikely, that he was the royal bookbinder of De Quincey's acquaintance. John Henry Martin Bohn (1758-1843) of Münster settled in London in 1795, where he married a Scotswoman and worked as a bookbinder and secondhand bookseller; following his death his stock of some ten thousand books was sold by auction in 1847. His elder son Henry George Bohn (1796-1884) only began business on his own account, as a seller of new foreign books, in 1831, in Bohte's former premisses at 4 York Street; in 1824 he was working in his father's secondhand bookshop. When De Quincey wrote to Hessey 'Pray send if you can to Bohn's. They have promised to lend Sir W. Scott's copy [of *Walladmor*]' he presumably made a slip of the pen, explicable in terms of his penchant for secondhand books. It was Bohte, the leading seller of new German books in London, from whom Scott had ordered a copy of *Walladmor*. In 1834 the younger brother of H. G., James Stuart Burges Bohn (1803-1880), who had been educated at Winchester and Göttingen, opened a bookselling business in at 12 King William Street, Strand, which lasted until 1845. By 1812 Henry Escher had faded from the scene, and Thomas Boosey (who had originally dealt in French books, in which he continued to specialize, although his catalogues describe him as still dealing in 'Foreign

---

22 Stockley, 7f.

23 See Lieselotte Blumenthal, 'Geisweiler und Weimar', *Jahrbuch der deutschen Schillergesellschaft,* 11 (1969), 14-46.

24 *The Picture of London for 1802* (London: Phillips, [1802]), 28.

25 See James Raven, 'The Novel Comes of Age', in *The English Novel 1770-1829*, ed. Garside, Raven, and Schöwerling, I, 60-71.

Books' in 1816 (Coleridge was still dealing with him in 1817), and in 'Foreign Engravings and Woodcuts' in 1820) had been overtaken in the London trade in German books by Black, Young and Young, and by J. H. Bohte,[26] an important figure in the present context.

When he claimed to have lodged at a German circulating library and there read 'three thousand tales', De Quincey was evidently referring to June-December 1821, when he lodged, on and off, with the German bookseller Johann Heinrich Bohte (1779-1824; he was born in Bremen) and his wife Sarah, over the premises at 4 York Street, Covent Garden, of J. H. Bohte and Co., who in 1819 had stocked 2458 German titles, including Retzsch's outlines (engravings), to which De Quincey refers in his review of Gillies's *German Stories*. By 1821 Bohte's stock very likely amounted to 'a matter of three thousand' titles (as opposed to tales). The figures are too close for there to be any room for doubt in the matter, but as for De Quincey reading them all, one can only suppose that he had been re-reading Raspe's or Bürger's *Münchhausen*. Bohte, who was appointed Foreign Bookseller to George III in 1819, and was known to Carlyle, Coleridge and Scott, among others, all of whom dealt with him, was described by Carlyle as 'a very civil person'.

Bohte's catalogues can be seen in the British Library (*Verzeichniss deutscher Bücher [...] zu haben bei J. H. Bohte* [London: G. Schulze & J. Dean, 1814]), and in the Bodleian Library, Oxford, which has six of J. H. Bohte and Co.'s catalogues dating from 1816 to 1823, as well as the *Handbibliothek der deutschen Litteratur [...] welche [...] zu haben sind bei J. H. Bohte,* Part I [no more published] (London, 1825). Such catalogues provide valuable evidence concerning English knowledge of German literature in late Georgian and Regency England, as well as shedding light on an aspect of De Quincey's actual and likely German (and Gothic) reading that has hitherto gone unnoticed.

The first of the catalogues in the Bodleian, *A Catalogue of Books in various languages on sale [...] at J. H. Bohte, Bookseller and Importer of Classsics and German Books, No. 3* [sic] *York Street, Covent Garden* (1816), shows that Bohte stocked some 'Gothic' titles (Schiller, *Der Geisterseher* [3 vols, Leipzig, 1799] and *Der Räuber*; [C. H.] Spie[ß], *Klara von Hoheneichen, Ritterschauspiel* [n. p.]; [Graf von] Vargas [Karl Grosse], *Novellen* [2 vols, Berlin, 1792] and *Versuche* [2 vols, Meissen, 1799, not in Kosch]; Zschokke, *Abäl[l]ino der große Bandit, ein Trauerspiel* [Leipzig, 1796]), to which De Quincey presumably had accesss in 1821; he probably already knew M. G. Lewis's *rifacimento*, to which *Klosterheim* is much indebted. While he did not stock Laun's early Gothic novel, *Die grauen Brüder, oder Der Bund der Schrecklichen* (1795), which De Quincey seems not to have known, he did, perhaps because his contacts in Leipzig had 'puffed' a local author, rather specialize in Laun's work, stocking, in 1816, *Antonie, Das schauerliche Wort, Die Blendlaterne: Drei Erzählungen* (Leipzig, 1813), *Drei neue Erzählungen* (Leipzig, 1813), *Die Traumdeutung, Herr Blitz, Die Glückswürfel* (Leipzig, 1814), *Seifenblasen* (2 vols, Tübingen, 1810), *Freierei und Drangsal des Doctor Schwefellebers* (Leipzig, 1813), and *Der Polizeidirektor, Das geheimnißvolle Verhängniß, Das Abenteuer des Baron von **** (Leipzig, 1812). Material from two of these Laun titles was used by De Quincey.

Equally interesting is the Supplement to the 1816 Catalogue, which included Benedikte Naubert's *Graf Rosenberg, oder das enthüllte Verbrechen* (Vienna, 1810), which De

---

[26] For much of the detail on German bookshops in London I am indebted to William Vaughan's admirable *German Romanticism and English Art* (New Haven & London: Yale University Press, 1979), 25f., 130, 270.

Quincey may thus well have read, and a stage version of her important *Hermann von Unna* (Copenhagen, 1800), which, given his interest in secret societies, he may have known already, although he neither refers to it nor uses material gleaned from it. De Quincey's reference to 'a German Professor's novel' in the context of the Englishing of German novels (WTDQ, 6: 24), which has hitherto gone without comment, was probably to Professor Laurids Kruse (see 3.1. below), but he may also have known at least one of the novels of 'Professor Kramer', the male masque of bestselling Gothic/historical novelist Benedikte Naubert, author of what Scott called 'excellent romances', and translator of Sophia Lee's *The Recess (Ruinen, eine Geschichte aus den vorigen Zeiten von dem Verfasser des Kapitels der Zufälle*, 1786), which she no doubt recognized as resembling her own blending of fiction with historical events and characters. We have already seen that De Quincey, for all sorts of reasons, was drawn to female Gothic. In Naubert's *Graf Rosenberg, oder: Das enthüllte Verbrechen* (1791), which he very likely read at J. H. Bohte's bookshop in 1821, his favourite unmasking motif is combined with crime, to which he was also attracted. Benedikte Naubert wrote the kind of gothified history that is later seen in *Klosterheim*.

In the Supplement to the 1816 Catalogue there are, again, books by Laun: *Die Reise ins Schlaraffenland, ein Fastnachtsmärchen* (Leipzig, 1816), *Schloß Riesenstein, Roman mit und ohne Gespenster* (2 vols, Leipzig, 1807), *Die seltsame Ehe, ein Roman* (Leipzig, 1809), and *Die Fehdeburg* (2 vols, Leipzig, 1811). In addition there are books by C. H. Spieß, which Kosch mistakenly implies to be a pseudonym of Laun: *Biographien der Wahnsinnigen* (4 vols, Leipzig, 1795), *Reisen durch die Höhlen des Unglücks und Gemächer des Jammers* (4 vols, Leipzig, 1796), *Die zwölf schlafenden Jungfrauen* (3 vols, Leipzig, 1795), and *Die Löwenritter* (4 vols, Leipzig, 1796). The truth of the matter is that Schulze (Laun) was given to using other pseudonyms, and on one occasion used Spieß's name in a novel (*Die ganze Familie wie sie sein sollte, ein Roman, wie er sein kann, von Ch. H. Spieß, Geschwindschreiber in der Unterwelt*, 1801) that Bohte did not stock and De Quincey presumably did not know. Spieß and Laun are two writers, not one.

Bohte's 1819 Catalogue is the one that most reflects the contemporary English predilection for the Gothic that was even then rushing towards a climax. Titles include [Hoffmann], *Elixierre [sic] des Teufels* (2 vols, Berlin, 1816); the anonymous *Gräfin Pauline* (2 vols, Berlin, 1800), which may have given De Quincey the name of his Countess Paulina in *Klosterheim*; [Naubert], *Graf Rosenberg, oder das enthüllte Verbrechen* (Vienna, 1810); Grosse, *Erzählungen* (2 vols, Berlin, 1793); Joseph von Hammer, *Geschichte der Assassinen* (Stuttgart, 1818), which De Quincey almost certainly read at Bohte's in 1821 since it is most unlikely to have come his way in any other way; more works by Laun over and above the titles in the previous catalogue – *Drei Tage zu Pferde* (Dresden, 1816), *Darstellungen* (Berlin, 1818), *Die Gattin zweier Könige* (Berlin, 1817); [Vulpius], *Rinaldo Rinaldini, der Räuberhauptmann* (6 vols, Leipzig, 1802) and *Die Zigeuner* (Rudolstadt, 1812); Wächter, *Sagen der Vorzeit von Veit Weber* (4 vols, Berlin, 1789-93) and *Holzschnitte, oder die Betfahrt des heiligen Gramsalbus* (Berlin, 1794); *Sagen der österreichischen Vorzeit* (2 vols, Vienna, 1811); Spieß, *Biographien der Selbstmörder* (4 vols, Leipzig, 1790), which De Quincey evidently read (see 8: 402); *Die gerechten Vehmrichter oder der unglückliche Holger von Daneburg* (Leipzig, 1810), which he may have read; and the *Gespensterbuch*, ed. Apel & Laun, from which he translated two stories.

The Second Supplement to a Catalogue of Books (1821) also included a number of German 'Gothic' titles: *Aranzo der Räuberhauptmann, ein Schrecken in Spaniens Thälern und Gebirgen* (2 vols, Leipzig, 1820); Grosse, *Der Genius, aus den Papieren des Marquis C* von G**** (3 vols, Halle, 1791); Naubert, *Turmalin und Lazerta, eine Relique des 17ten Jahrhunderts* (2 vols, Leipzig, 1820); Spieß, *Reise und Abentheuer des Ritters Benno von Elsenburg* (3 vols, Leipzig, 1795); *Der Meuchelmörder, ein Roman* (2 vols, Quedlinburg, 1820). There are also further titles by Laun: *Der wilde Jäger* (Dresden, 1820), *Des Pastors Liebesgeschichte* (Dresden, 1820), *Der gute Genius and Die Braut, zwei Erzählungen* (Dresden, 1819), *Der Traum von vier Wochen und so weiter* (Leipzig, 1820), and *Das Hausleben, eine Charakterzeichnung* (Dresden, 1820).

The List of Select Books published on the occasion of the Leipzig Easter Fair 1823 includes Tieck's *Der Geheimnisvolle*, together with yet more titles by Laun: *Des Fürsten Geliebte. Eine Geschichte* (Frankfurt a. M.), *Neue Kleinigkeiten: Die Schlittenfahrt zur Hochzeit, Die Zwillingsschwestern* (Leipzig), *Die schwache Stunde* (Leipzig), *Der große Mann in Liebesnöthen. Ein komischer Roman* (2 vols, Berlin), and *Die Sache des Herzens. Roman* (Leipzig).

J. H. Bohte & Co's last catalogue, the *Handbibliothek der Deutschen Litteratur enthaltend eine Sammlung der vorzüglichsten Werke Deutscher Schriftsteller aus allen Fächern der Litteratur [...], 1ster Theil, mit einer Vorrede von August Wilhelm Schlegel* (1825) is a substantial catalogue of secondary literature on a variety of subjects; it does not include literature as such, which would have been listed in the second part that never appeared. What it does include is many of the works to which De Quincey refers in his essays, suggesting that what he read at Bohte's in 1821 was probably as much critical literature, to which he would for the most part have had no other access, as belles lettres. Among many other interesting titles it includes Gotthilf Heinrich Schubert's *Die Symbolik des Traumes* (Bamberg, 1821) and *Ansichten von der Nachtseite der Naturwissenschaft* (Dresden, 1817); unfortunately there is no way of telling whether De Quincey read them, and, if he did, what he made of them. On the face of it, Schubert's analysis of dreams (see 5) in *Die Symbolik des Traumes* would have been likely to interest De Quincey, so the assumption must be that he did not notice it, unless, that is, he chose to conceal his interest in it, or reacted against it for some personal reason.

In his Foreword to this final catalogue, A. W. Schlegel refers to 'the estimable collector and bookseller the late Mr. Bohte, whose premature death is a real loss to the literary commerce of the two countries' and 'a real loss to literary Germany as well as to England', while a grateful customer, the Germanophile John Hawkins, wrote to Bohte's friend, the antiquarian and librarian to the Saxon royal family, Karl August Boettiger, that 'He [Bohte] was intelligent and indefatigable in his professsion. His shop is the first in that line [...] there is no other German bookseller here who enjoys much credit, the dealers in German books being mostly German bookbinders; low-minded and imposing.'[27] The obituary in the *Gentleman's Magazine* for October 1824 is both more detailed and more fulsome:

> Mr. J. H. Bohte
> Sept. 2. In York-street, Covent Garden, in the 45th year of his age, Mr. J. H. Bohte, Foreign Bookseller to his Majesty – a man, of whom it is no exaggeration to assert, that by integrity of principle, kindness of disposi-

---

27 Quoted from Vaughan, 25. It sounds as though Hawkins is alluding to H. M. Bohn.

tion, and suavity of manners, he had conciliated the friendship and regard of all who knew him. He was a native of Bremen in Germany, and having settled young in this country, he showed, in the business which he created, and to the improvement of which he devoted all his energies, how much may be accomplished by industry and perseverance combined with probity and honour.

For the purpose of increasing his connexions, he had been in the habit, for several years past, of attending the great annual mart for German literature at Leipzig, where he had opportunities of becoming personally acquainted not only with the principal booksellers, but also with many of the most eminent scholars of the continent. The circle of English Literati also, with whom he was on terms of friendship, was not small; and many of them can, with the writer of these lines, attest from experience the cheerfulness with which he was ever ready to further their pursuits, and to facilitate their enquiries and researches to the utmost of his power. Amidst the enjoyment of vigorous health, which authorized the anticipation of many years of active life, he was almost suddenly snatched away, after an illnesss of only four days, the fatal termination of which was quite unexpected.

Mr. Bohte had long been one of the principal importers of German works, as well such as belong to the current literature, as the different editions and collections of the Classics printed abroad; and it will be gratifying to his friends to learn that his business will not suffer any interruption from his abrupt removal, but be continued for the benefit of his widow.

A number of conclusions can be drawn from Bohte's catalogues. In the first place, his interests were, like De Quincey's, as much classical and historical/critical as literary. He will have been a major influence, adding much to De Quincey's already impressive general knowledge, thereby helping to make good the failings of De Quincey's Oxford tutor. In terms of German literature, he will have added substantially to what De Quincey already knew from Gillies and elsewhere, but, although he carried the work of Musäus and the Grimms, and the odd title by Arnim, Novalis and Tieck, he did not stock much German Romantic literature as such, and is therefore implicated in De Quincey's relative ignorance on this score. Of the popular 'novelists' of the time he evidently preferred Caroline de la Motte Fouqué and Caroline Pichler, neither of whom was rated by De Quincey. So far as the German Gothic novelists are concerned, he stocked works by Veit Weber, Grosse, Spieß, Cramer, and Naubert, with the emphasis, rightly, on Veit Weber. He carried not everything, but most new titles by the genial but lightweight and only marginally Gothic Friedrich Laun, and is clearly the main source of De Quincey's enthusiasm for Laun in general, and for his knowledge of particular works and tales by Laun. When De Quincey wrote of reading some three thousand tales, he was exaggerating both the nature and the number of the books he read at Bohte's, although, as we have already seen, the figure was grounded in reality.

De Quincey's most significant contact so far as contemporary German literature is concerned, Bohte regularly made book-buying trips to Germany. By 1819 he had not only an office in Leipzig during the fair, but, in addition, a permanent representative there, so that his firm was, according to the list of *Fremde Buchhändler welche die Leipziger Messe besuchen* (*Foreign Booksellers in attendance at the Leipzig Book Fair*), one of those 'welche zwischen den Messen ausliefern lassen' (who supply books between fairs).[28] It was while attending the Leipzig Book Fair at Easter 1824 that he bought copies of a novel, *Walladmor,* purporting to be by Scott, which he exposed as a forgery on his return to London. In order to be able to write his review for the *London Magazine,* De Quincey appears to have borrowed from Bohte the copy of the book that Scott had ordered, and which De Quincey is

---

28 Quoted from Vaughan, 270, n. 118.

supposed to have read without cutting the pages, for fear of offending Scott. Unfortunately Bohte died, on 2 September, before the review had appeared. While I have yet to see any evidence that he ran a 'circulating library' as well as a bookshop, he certainly had, from 1814, a 'German reading-room' where German literary periodicals were to be found, this 'Deutsche Lesebibliothek' being available to subscribers for two guineas a year. It is inconceivable, given Bohte's later willingness to lend him Scott's copy of *Walladmor*, that De Quincey did not borrow many books from him when he was lodging with the Bohtes in 1821, a fact which would of itself be sufficient to account for De Quincey's use of the term 'circulating library'. Given that Bohte was prepared to lend books, at least to some customers, his establishment was, so far as De Quincey was concerned, tantamount to a *Leihbibliothek* or circulating library. We have seen De Quincey stretch many larger points.

It was probably in December 1821 that the young Thomas Hood, who had met De Quincey at dinner at Taylor and Hessey's on 6th December, called on his fellow-contributor to the *London Magazine*, and found him 'in the midst of a German Ocean of Literature', meaning an ocean of German literature. The word 'ocean' tallies with De Quincey's 'three thousand'. In 1821 Bohte was the latest of De Quincey's German friends and acquaintances; others included the Wrights' maid ('little Kitty') in Liverpool, van Haren, the Schreibers,[29] Schwar(t)zburg, and many others, one of the most interesting being the 'old German bookbinder, of great respectability, settled in London' (1: 169), who was employed to bind Admiralty records in Buckingham House, and who seems to have befriended young Thomas in spring 1800; assuming he was not Henry Martin Bohn, his name was probably Kaltoeber or Staggemeier (7: 188).

On 12 October 1823 De Quincey wrote to Hessey: 'On coming to London I shall stay about 6 weeks or 2 months [,]and shall then accompany a party of friends to Dresden [...] The library at Dresden will afford me advantages that I much want at this time'.[30] There is no reason to suppose that this visit ever took place.

Frederick Burwick has speculated (WTDQ, 6: 279) that De Quincey may have visited the Leipzig Book Fair of Easter 1825, in place of Bohte, in order to help Mrs Sarah Bohte in her attempt to keep the business going. This is unlikely to have been the case, given that Sarah Bohte, in a circular addressed to customers of her late husband's firm, acknowledges her indebtedness to the firm's representative in Leipzig, Adolph Bach, for seeing the firm through the 1826 (and, one assumes, the 1825) Easter Fair. The letter in question, dated from London on 29 June 1826, reads as follows:

> Da seit dem leider zu früh für mich erfolgten Ableben meines Gatten Herrn H. Bohte meine Gesundheitsumstände mir nicht erlauben wollen, mein Geschäft so fortzuführen als ich es gewünscht hätte, so sehe ich mich verbunden, dasselbe gänzlich aufzugeben. Zu dem Ende habe ich die Activa und Passiva desselben mit völliger Einstimmung der darin interessirten Partien in die Hände der Herren Wilson und Triphook, zweier hier allgemein geschätzten Männer gelegt, die sich erboten haben, die Liquidation desselben mit allem Eifer zu unternehmen, welches jedoch so wie der theilweise Verkauf des nicht unbedeutenden Lagers nur nach und nach geschehen kann.

---

29 Old Mr Schreiber De Quincey immortalized as 'an ancient German gentleman, to what century belonging I do not know, who had every possible bad quality known to European experience, and a solitary good one – viz, eight hundred pounds of sterling' (1: 352).

30 Quoted from Frederick Burwick, 'De Quincey and the Aesthetics of Violence', *The Wordsworth Circle*, XXVII/2 (Spring 1996), 78.

Damit nun aber durch diese gänzliche Unterbrechung meines Geschäfts, welches durch die gefälligen Bemühungen des Herrn Adolph Bach während der verflossenen Ostermesse geordnet und von neuem eingeleitet wurde, diejenigen meiner resp. Handelsfreunde, die meinen seligen Mannn seit einer langen Reihe von Jahren mit Ihrem [sic] so schätzbaren Zutrauen, und mich nach dessen Ableben mit der Fortsetzung desselben beehrten, in Hinsicht ihrer werthen Aufträge, durch keinen Verzug in Verlegenheit gesetzt werden mögen, so habe ich vom 1sten July an die etwa rückständigen Bestellungen, so wie auch die Liste der zu liefernden Fortsetzungen an die Herren Treuttel & Würtz, Treuttel jun. & Richter allhier zur Ausführung abgegeben, ein Haus, dessen Solidität und Rechtlichkeit, Ihnen ohne Zweifel durch dessen frühere Etablissementer in Paris und Strasburg schon hinlänglich bekannt ist, und von welchem Sie und ich erwarten dürfen, es werde dasselbe alles mögliche aufbieten, um sich seinerseits Ihr Zutrauen und Ihre Zufriedenheit durch Schnelligkeit und durch die möglichst billigen Bedingungen zu erwerben oder zu erhalten suchen; in der völligen Ueberzeugung hiervon, ersuche ich Sie dasselbe mit Ihren fernern Aufträgen zu beehren.

Es bleibt mir nur übrig Ihnen meinen herzlichen Dank für das für meinen seligen Gatten wie für mich gehabte Wohlwollen und die Freundschaft auszudrücken, von welcher er und ich so oft die schönsten Beweise erhielten, und von der die Erinnerung mich in jeder künftigen Lage meines Lebens begleiten wird.

Ihre dankbar ergebene Dienerinn Wittwe Sarah Bohte.[31]

(Since following the tragically early death of my husband H. Bohte my health has not permitted me to carry on my business in the way I would have wished, I now find myself obliged to give it up. To this end I have, with the agreement of interested parties, placed its assets and liabilities in the hands of Messrs Wilson and Triphook, who are held here in high esteem, and who have affered to undertake the liquidation of the business, something which, like the partial sale of the not inconsiderable stock, can only be done gradually.

However, in order that as a result of this cessation of my business, which throughout the last Easter Fair was in the capable hands of Herr Adolph Bach, those of my esteemed customers who for many years have entrusted their orders to my late husband (and, after his death, to myself) may not be embarrassed by any delay in the execution of their valued orders, I have, with effect from 1st July, placed all the outstanding business of J. H. Bohte & Co. in the hands of Messrs Treuttel & Würtz, trading in London as Treuttel Sohn & Richter, a long-established firm whose excellent reputation, which will be familiar to you from their existing establishments in Paris and Strasbourg, means that you and I may confidently expect that they will do everything in their power to gain or retain your trust and satisfaction by the speed and fairness with which they conducts their business;[32] confident that this will be the case, I beg you to entrust your further orders to them.

It only remains for me to express my sincere gratitude for the goodwill you have extended to my late husband and myself, and for the friendship of which he and I so often received proofs which I shall never forget.

I have the honour to be your most grateful servant, Sarah Bohte.)

This letter confirms that De Quincey's services would not have been required in Leipzig since Sarah Bohte's interests were, as might be expected, being looked after by the firm's permanant representative there. The fact that De Quincey was in London from January to July (or later) 1825, so that a window of opportunity was there, is neither here nor there. The *Handbibliothek* of 1825 was the last catalogue to be published by the firm, which went into liquidation on 29 June 1826, whereupon outstanding orders were taken over by the old Strasbourg firm of Treuttel and Würtz, who were duly granted the position of Foreign Bookseller to King George IV.

Then there is the draft letter to the Editor of *Blackwood's Magazine*, apparently written in April 1828, in which De Quincey makes his persona write: 'Several months ago, while travelling in Germany'. This can hardly be construed as meaning 'three years ago'. It is

31 Original ('Rundschreiben der Wittwe Sarah Bohte') in the Deutsche Bücherei, Leipzig (Signatur Bö-GR/B/1181), to which acknowledgment is made.

32 Sarah Bohte's circular to customers of J. H. Bohte & Co. was accompanied by a letter dated 1 July from Treuttel & Würtz, Treuttel Sohn & Richter, of 30 Soho Square, setting out their terms of business.

conceivable, of course, that he travelled to Germany both in 1825 and in 1827-8; indeed, it is even possible, while we are in such airy realms of speculation, that the 'German circulating library' at which he claimed, in 1826, to have taken lodgings 'some years ago', was in Germany, although the very fact that he could not possibly have read anything like three thousand titles in any such time available to him makes this extremely unlikely. However, I have no doubt that his travels, like the good Baron Munchausen's, were imaginary, and that the reference is to Bohte's establishment, at which De Quincey certainly lodged in June to late December 1821, while his friend R. P. Gillies was in Germany visiting Hamburg, Berlin, Dresden, Weimar, and Frankfurt. De Quincey also claimed to have been in Dresden in spring 1831, but that visit at least is a palpable fiction. Given all the background facts, it is tempting, but mistaken, to conclude that De Quincey may have visited Germany on at least one occasion, and maybe on several. While this would help to explain the way in which he pontificates about aspects of German life, he does so without claiming first-hand knowledge, presumably on the basis of conversations with van Haren, Schwar(t)zburg, Bohte, Gillies, and others.

Against this idea must be set his penury, which means that while a visit to Leipzig in 1825, funded by Mrs Bohte, is a possibility, any other visit is surely out of the question. Even a visit in 1825 seems most unlikely; there is no evidence for it, and in any case De Quincey could not have done much to help Sarah Bohte, who would naturally have preferred to deal with the firm's permanent representative in Leipzig in the normal way rather than through an inexperienced, unreliable intermediary. She will not have forgotten that debt had obliged De Quincey to flee his lodgings over the shop at 4 York Street four years earlier. Besides, if De Quincey, in the guise of bookseller's deputy, had visited the country about which he was a self-professed expert, and whose literature he so much admired, he would surely have written about it. As it is, the absence of such evidence, and the facts of the case, as we have just seen them to be, make it highly unlikely that he ever visited Germany. It would take incontrovertible evidence to disprove Eaton's categorical statement that:

> He wanted to go to Germany, because of the fascination of German metaphysics; and one of his few satisfactions at being at Oxford was that the name of having been at the university would be an introduction abroad as a scholar. To be sure, nothing came of his desire, and actually he never set foot on the continent. (E 117)

If it had been Thomas De Quincey (1785-1859), rather than Washington Irving (1783-1859), who spent 1822-3 in Dresden in the company of writers like Tieck and Laun, we may be sure that he would have made better literary use of the experience, although in fairness it has to be said that Irving , whose works were published in ten volumes , in Paris , as early as 1825, made far more productive use of his early life in general terms. As it is, De Quincey probably first heard of Tieck, Laun and the Dresden literary scene from Schwar(t)zburg, who came from Dresden. In 1821 he will have had further accounts of Dresden from Gillies, who was there while De Quincey was staying with the Bohtes, and from Bohte. The fact that De Quincey claimed to be planning a visit to Dresden in late 1821, and to have been there in spring 1831, shows only that he was fully aware of the cultural reputation of the Saxon capital.

3. Translations from the German

3.1. *Gillies's German Stories*

By far the most revealing document as regards De Quincey's knowledge of contemporary German literature, 'Gothic' writing emanating from German-speaking Europe, and the technique of *rifacimento*, which he uses to appropriate and colonize or 'vampirize' what he has read, is his review of 'R. P. Gillies's German Stories', which appeared in *Blackwood's Magazine* (20 [December 1826], 844-58). It is a strange fact that De Quincey, over-anxious not to offend Carlyle again, never acknowledged his undoubted authorship of this genial review-article, which was only reprinted in 2000.

Robert Pearse Gillies (1788-1858), 'Sage Kempferhausen, the grave and serene' of Christopher North's *Noctes Ambrosianae,* member of the Ballantyne circle and the Blackwood group,[1] and friend of Scott, Wordsworth and De Quincey, is known for his *Memoirs of a Literary Veteran* (3 vols, London: Richard Bentley, 1851).[2] He was taught German by Dr William Gardiner, 'formerly English pastor at Dantzig, and then a colleague of Mr Alison and Mr Morehead at St. John's Chapel', who had succeeded Johanna Schopenhauer's 'tutor, guide and counsellor' Richard Jameson[3] as British Chaplain in Danzig in 1790, and retired to Edinburgh in 1806, at which time, Gillies writes, 'all the booksellers' shops at Edinburgh could hardly have supplied more than a dozen volumes in [German].' Gillies, who is said to have been attracted to German literature by the way Scott talked to him about it,[4] first met De Quincey in Edinburgh in 1814, and came to know him well, saying that he lived in a world of his own and had studied 'all such books as are never read in that enlightened capital [Edinburgh]'. In De Quincey Gillies found 'the first friend who could profess to have a command over the German language and who was able *ex cathedra* to corroborate my notions of the great stores contained therein'.

In Edinburgh, De Quincey visited Gillies more frequently than he visited anyone else. Conversation apart, one attraction will eventually have been the 'valuable collection' of German fiction that Gillies had assembled, thanks in part to Joseph Charles Mellish of Blythe (1769-1823), whom Gillies met in Hamburg, where Mellish was British Consul, in May 1821. In 1796 Mellish, who was later said to combine 'alle Liebenswürdigkeiten eines Deutschen und eines Engländers' (all the most agreeable features of a German and an Englishman), had gone to Weimar,[5] where he met his future wife, Caroline Ernestine Frederica Sophia Freiin von Stein-Nordheim (1777-1824). Two years later, to enable the marriage, Herzog Carl August gave Mellish the title of a Prussian *Kammerherr*

---

1 See M. Batt, 'Gillies and *Blackwood's Magazine*', *Modern Language Notes*, 18/3 (March 1903), 65-9.

2 Most relevant in the present context is Vol. 2, 218-221 (memoirs of De Quincey).

3 See Patrick Bridgwater, *Arthur Schopenhauer's English Schooling* (London & New York: Routledge, 1988), 29-94.

4 See R. P. Gillies, *Recollections of Sir Walter Scott* (London: Fraser, 1837).

5 The best account of Mellish;'s life is that appended by Elke H. M. Ritt to her *Mary Stuart. A Tragedy (1801) von Joseph Charles Mellish* (München: tuduv, 1993).

(chamberlain). Mellish was on friendly terms with Goethe (who was godson to his son Richard), and with Schiller (who described him as 'ein sehr gebildeter, in alter und neuer Literatur vollkommen erfahrener Mann' [a very well educated person, equally at home in classical and modern literature]) and Wieland. The 'Schillerhaus' in Weimar was built for Mellish and sold by him to Schiller in 1802. Through Mellish, Gillies had a collection of recent works of German literature placed at his disposal, apparently in 1821, these books, which he could never have afforded, for he was as penurious as De Quincey, forming the basis for his subsequent work as a translator. It is reasonable to suppose that the collection included most of the volumes from which the tales in Gillies's *German Stories* were taken. In 1826, when Gillies's *German Stories* (3 vols, Edinburgh: Blackwood; London: Cadell) appeared, he and De Quincey were planning, at Scott's suggestion, to co-edit a journal on foreign literature. However, when Gillies founded the *Foreign Quarterly Review* in July 1827,[6] he did do without De Quincey, partly because he had realized that his opium-eating friend and Blackwood's colleague was not reliable enough, and partly because by then, ruined by the commercial crash of 1825, Gillies had removed to London, whereas De Quincey lived mostly in Edinburgh from 1822. Nor did Gillies himself assume the editorship of the new periodical, which, in the event, was taken up by J. G. Cochrane.[7]

German Stories is the best of the various anthologies of German tales of the time, and, more especially, the best of the handful of similar anthologies that appeared in 1826, some of which were vitiated by linguistic incompetence. In saying that, I am thinking, in particular, of *Popular Tales and Romances of the Northern Nations* (1823), co-published by Bohte, in which De Quincey's translation from Johann August Apel, 'The Fatal Marksman', first appeared. *Popular Tales and Romances of the Northern Nations* was described by the reviewer in *Blackwood's Magazine* (XIV, 1823, 293) as a disappointing publication likely to do more harm than good to the cause of German literature, there being no discrimination in the choice of pieces (from Veit Weber, Grimm, Laun, etc.), and little sign of competence in the [anonymous] translations,[8] which cannot have pleased De Quincey. Otherwise, *Popular Tales and Romances of the Northern Nations* confirms that by 1823 at the latest De Quincey knew about Veit Weber, some of whose work, most popular in England during the early Gothic period, he will surely (given his interest in secret societies) have read at Bohte's two years previously. Other contemporary anthologies include Richard Holcraft's *Tales from the German [Tales of Humour and Romance]* (London: Longman, 1826), Thomas Roscoe's *German Novelists* (4 vols, London: Colburn, 1826), and *Specimens of German Romance* (London: Whittaker, 1826) by George Soane, who was also a Gothic novelist. That De Quincey knew Holcraft's and Roscoe's anthologies is clear from his review of Gillies.

Holcraft, a competent but little-known translator, included in his collection, among other things, work by Jean Paul (De Quincey's favourite German writer and the one about whose work he had most to say), Hoffmann (of whom he had a mixed opinion), and August Friedrich Langbein and August Lafontaine (of both of whom he disapproved). Lafontaine,

6 See M. Batt, 'Gillies and the *Foreign Quarterly Review*', *Modern Language Notes*, 17/3 (March 1902), 165-70.

7 This was established by John Macray, see *Notes and Queries*, 2nd ser., VIII (1859), 127.

8 Alan Lang Strout's 'Writers on German Literature in *Blackwood's Magazine*' (*The Library*, 9 [1954], 35-44) does not list this review.

whose widely translated work was popular in England, was a Minerva Press author; under the title *Love and Gratitude* six of his 'novels' were translated by the Gothic novelist Eliza Parsons. Roscoe, for his part, included in his collection legends and tales from folk-books as well as tales from many writers of the time, some of them no longer known. More specifically, he included his translation (at the time, the third) of Schiller's *Der Geisterseher* (*The Apparitionist. A Fragment. Extracted from the Memoirs of the Count von O---*), and work by Grimm, Musäus, Tieck, and Langbein, among many others. De Quincey did not respond to Roscoe's version of *Der Geisterseher*, the first translation of which (*The Ghost-Seer,* translated by D. Boileau) he read in 1803; nor does he respond to Grimm, but then he seems – perhaps because the memory of his childhood reading with Elizabeth was too painful – to have had a blind spot for 'children's literature' as such. At the time no real distinction was made between the 'Gothic' tale (including ghost stories) and the 'fairy' tale, both of which were labelled popular tales or stories. As I have shown elsewhere,[9] Gothic and fairytale have much in common. In the present context Chamisso's *Peter Schlemihl* belongs to both genres, and De Quincey's *Klosterheim* includes more than a little of the fairytale.

The stories in Gillies's anthology are: Vol. I: Hoffmann, 'Mademoiselle de Scuderi'; Caroline Baroness de la Motte Fouqué, 'The Castle of Scharfenstein'; 'The Sisters' (anonymous here, it appeared in the *Gespensterbuch*, ed. Apel & Laun, the collection of ghost stories which inspired the Byron-Shelley circle to imitate them one evening in May 1816 at the Villa Diodati outside Geneva, and is by Laun; it is identical with 'The Fated Hour' in *Tales of the Dead*). Vol. II: Hoffmann, 'Rolandsitten'; Caroline Pichler, 'George Selding'; [Tromlitz,] 'The Siege of Antwerp'. Vol. III: 'The First of May, or Wallburga's Night' [sic]; Laurids Kruse, 'Oath and Conscience'; [Friedrich Laun,] 'The Spectre Bride' (printed without Laun's name, it too appeared in the Apel-Laun *Gespensterbuch*); Laurids Kruse, 'The Crystal Dagger'; and 'The Warning' (anonymous here, it appeared in a *Gespensterbuch* published at Rudolstadt in 1917, and appears to be by Laun, though I have as yet been unable to confirm this).

'Gillies's German Stories' is vintage De Quincey. It is true that, Uncle Toby-like as ever, he goes galloping off on one or other of his hobby-horses, starting off as he will go on, with 'an anecdote in Mungo Park's travels concerning „a Bilidulgerid lion“,' but he quickly reins in his hobby-horsical self to explain that '*we* are that same African lion, reposing under the ample umbrage of Blackwood's Magazine', while a passing reference to 'a male tiger from Hyrcania' reassures the reader that it is De Quincey who is in the saddle. Nor has this opening, seemingly far from the point, been wasted, for the reader learns that the 'Hyrcanian forest,' to which De Quincey is so attached, stands, in part, for 'the pathless forests of literature', a notion to which we shall have cause to return. As readers, we often need to pay less attention to his titles, which tend to be misleading markers, and more to his Shandean (or Jeanpaulian) digressions, which are often more apparent than real. Thus a reference, a couple of pages further on, to the effect that 'Von Hammer bores us with proofs that they [Joseph von Hammer's *Die Tausendundeine Nacht: Noch nicht übersetzte Märchen* (1823-4: *New Arabian Nights Entertainments*, tr. George Lamb, 1826), a selection of additional, newly translated stories belonging to the *Arabian Nights* canon] are genuine'

9 Patrick Bridgwater, *Kafka, Gothic and Fairytale* (Amsterdam & New York: Rodopi, 2003), 78-84.

is a reminder that Joseph von Hammer (Hammer-Purgstall from 1835) is also the author of a work entitled *Geschichte der Assassinen* (1818; *History of the Assassins*, tr. O. C. Wood, 1835), which De Quincey read in German at Bohte's, and with which he toys in 'On Murder Considered as One of the Fine Arts' (13: 62). When all is said and done, assassination, an aspect of the Fine Art of Murder, interests him more, and is in that sense more his subject, than the contents of Gillies's anthology.

Eventually he begins to circle round his immediate subject, contemporary German literature, first mentioned in the person of E. T. A. Hoffmann (see 3.3 below), but instead of addressing a work (*The Devil's Elixir*) on which he could have said much more than he chooses to say, and even that only obliquely, he goes off on another hobby-horsical digression about a work he knew from Bohte's, Bouterwek's (he misspells the name) *History of Literature* (*Geschichte der Poesie und Beredsamkeit*, 12 vols, 1801-1). If we recall that Bouterwek, whose lectures, Kantian in inspiration, Coleridge had attended in Göttingen in 1799, ended his old-fashioned literary history with the year 1800, it has to be said that De Quincey is here illustrating, at some length, his ignorance rather than his knowedge; the mostly German secondary literature on all manner of subjects, of which he seems to possess a bottomless bucket of knowledge, is often outdated. Given the way in which Coleridge, disappointed by Cambridge, revelled in Göttingen, it is tragic that De Quincey robbed himself of the chance of a similarly rewarding experience. Most of the Gothic *topoi,* he will have realized, are applicable to his life.

Before going off on a tangent again, he eventually comes, half way though his review, to another German work featured in Gillies's collection. Caroline Pichler's 'George Selding' he takes as an example (the only one in the anthology) of an unsuccessful novel of manners which 'tends to confirm what we have said of German domestic life'. Manners in general, and German manners in particular, are another hobby-horse. He concludes by writing 'we are happy to assure Mrs Pichler that she enjoys one distinction in Mr Gillies's collection, viz. that of having furnished by far the worst story'. The domestic tale is emphatically not to De Quincey's taste. He prefers tales of sentiment, provided they are written by Jean Paul, or, better, tales of action. The latter constitute 'a forest in which [the English selector] must beat about for game; and luckily it is inexhaustible', a variation of the forest of literature metaphor. It is with this reflection that he comes to the most interesting of his digressions, the story of the 'German circulating library' at which he took lodgings.

It seems that many of the 'three thousand tales, long and short' which he read on that occasion were 'spoiled for direct translation by machinery, not supernatural merely, but preternatural, resting upon no basis of popular tradition, and with which the whole course and habits of superstitious feeling, as it exists in Christendom, had unfitted us to sympathize', which confirms both that his religious feelings were a limiting factor in his literary taste, and that not a little of his reading at Bohte's consisted of 'Gothic' tales. The 'public voice', meaning Bohte, who was certainly the 'public voice [...] of Germany' among London booksellers, directed him to Fouqué, with whose *Kleine Romane*[10] De Quincey embarked on his read-in. This brings him to a digression on Fouqué's *Undine,* of which he says that it has been 'a good deal read, chiefly in connexion with the Outline

---

10 Which means not 'Little Romance' (WTDQ, 6: 333) but 'short novels'.

Illustrations of it, in the manner of those [by Retzsch] which accompanied the Faust of Goethe'. This means that he saw, at Bohte's, the outline illustrations of *Undine* by C. F. Schulze (1817) and Ludwig Schnorr (1817), both of which Bohte stocked. C. F. Schulze, who came from Dresden, may have been related to Friedrich August Schulze (Friedrich Laun). Whether this is confirmed or not, Bohte is likely to have drawn De Quincey's attention to Laun. I assume that Bohte's printer, G. Schulze of 13 Poland Street, is not related, for Schulze is a common enough name. One way or another, the explanation for Bohte's predilection for Laun's work may lie here. In writing that Fouqué was indebted to 'a story in the *Phantasus* of Tieck', De Quincey is confirming that he knew *Phantasus*, to which he alludes elsewhere, and more expecially the story of 'Die schöne Magelone'. He, who wrote that 'of [...] investigations of Shakspeare a very considerable library might be formed [...] in Germany' (4: 85), may be supposed to have known of Tieck as a Shakespeare scholar, enthusiast and translator; both men wrote about the supernatural in the work of the playwright whose name they both spelled Shakspeare. As to *Undine*, De Quincey has his reservations:

> As an Ariel, collateral to the main movement of the story, and connected by no tie with its human passions, such a being would do very well; but the Baron insists upon throwing the whole *human* interest upon these watery or aerial phantoms.

Sympathetic as he nonetheless is to Fouqué's creations, 'born apparently of Cobweb and Moonshine, in the Midsummer Night's Dream, less ponderous than an echo, less substantial than a dream', he is more engaged by Chamisso's *Schlemihl*, another tale he read at Bohte's, of which he writes at length in words that need quoting not least for the way in which they merge into the denunciation of another novel that is not named, but whose identity is not in doubt:

> there are worse monsters ranging about in the pages of German fiction – shadowless men, for example, thick as leaves in Vallombrosa – not the *Asci* of the geographer, who are so only in relation to a vertical sun; but unfortunate people who are absolutely disinherited of their own shadows under *any* position of the sun, having been swindled out of them on one pretence or another. What became of these shadows, or who pocketed them, was long a question with us, but at length we met with a novel which cleared this matter up. In that novel, one of the most interesting characters is the shadow of a pair of legs, which passes the window of a summer-house every evening, and is seen by reflection upon the opposite wall, at the very moment when the lady of the house is expecting her husband home to tea. She looks out of doors, and ascertains beyond a doubt that this shadow is wandering up and down without any owner: whence it appears that the shadowless bodies in this world of ours are compensated by the bodiless shadows. Pure logical entities, mere privations, absolute negations, have reality enough for German machinery: the ghost of an old parabola from the 16th century, or the apparition of a defunct cube-root, furnishes a sufficient *mormo* [a non-existent object of therefore baseless fear]. Physical or paraphysical; logical or paralogical; nay, even metaphysical or parametaphysical; nothing comes amiss to a German romancer.

He has thus far been writing of Chamisso's *Peter Schlemihls wundersame Geschichte* (1814, tr. 1824 by Sir John Bowring as *Peter Schlemihl, The Shadowless Man* [London: Whittaker], illustrated by George Cruikshank), which, although written for amusement, is a Gothic fairy tale in which the hero sells his shadow to the Devil in exchange for a bottomless purse that surely stands, in De Quincey's mind, for the bottomless depths of the unconscious mind, to which opium seemed to promise access, and therefore for the opium itself, which, while offering a false paradise, kept him excluded from the real paradise of real identity and real achievement. The purse proving a poor substitute for identity, Schlemihl becomes the accursed wanderer of the Bible (Cain), medieval legend (the Wandering Jew) and Gothic/fantasy; he gets rid of the purse, rejects the Devil and, with the aid of a pair of seven-league boots, dedicates himself to scientific research. De Quincey, while not missing an opportunity to mock German idealism, was attracted by the story, a reflection of which is seen in *Klosterheim,* in which The Mask appears to be just such a supernatural-seeming 'aerial phantom' until his reality/identity is revealed in a Radcliffean manner. De Quincey was probably attracted to *Schlemihl* because the man without a shadow was the natural other of himself, who sometimes felt himself to be a shadow without the man, and more specifically only a shadow of the writer he should have been. When he imagines himself seeing himself in a glass darkly in the early *Diary,* what he sees is 'a man in the dim and shadowy perspective and (as it were) in a dream. He passes along in silence, and the hues of sorrow appear on his countenance' (D 156). *Schlemihl* reversed, and thus as it were encrypted, that situation, so that it was only natural that he identified with Schlemihl, who in his mind will have represented his own Gothic self, his demonic or Satanic other. The 'mighty phantom [...] which strides after me' of *Confessions* (3: 232, 242) is that same other self, by which he is haunted.

And so we come, three quarters of the way through the review, to its ostensible subject, the writers and tales selected by Gillies, and very likely discussed with De Quincey as part of the selection process. The 'friend at our elbow' who said that the tale of the *Freyschütz* was not by Laun, but by Apel, is presumably Gillies. De Quincey had already translated the tale, probably at Bohte's bidding, to earn his keep, and at that time thought it was by Friedrich Laun. The mistake is understandable, for the tale first appeared in the *Gespensterbuch*, edited by Apel and Laun (6 vols, Leipzig: Göschen, 1811-17), to which I have already referred. It was Laun's contributions to the *Gespensterbuch* that caught the attention of the Byron-Shelley party at Coligny.

More to the point at this stage is De Quincey's exceptionally high opinion of two writers whose reputations are less high nowadays: Friedrich Laun and August von Tromlitz. Laun (pseudonym of Friedrich August Schulze, 1770-1849) he describes as a writer – unlike himself – of inexhaustible fertility and (allowing for his haste, for Laun was known for and admitted to *Vielschreiberei* [writing too much too quickly]) of great ability:

> it marks his great versatility of talent, that no German writer has managed the marvellous and the supernatural with so much skill [...] the devil is managed with great skill [...] in the tale of *The Dice.*The whole of that story, indeed, with the exception of one or two incidents at the [...] end, shows a writer capable of the very greatest effects; and Tromlitz [...] is not at all behind him.

In other words, he admires Laun as a writer possessing the fertility of imagination and facility of narrative technique that he knows himself to lack. Only such a personal reason would cause him to overrate a minor writer to this extent.

A. von Tromlitz, pseudonym of August von Witzleben (1773-1839), now virtually unkown, was in his day a best-selling writer of historical novels and tales, of which he published, in all, 108 (16mo) volumes. A distinguished army officer specializing in tales of the Thirty Years' War, he is, in literary-historical terms, one of the German imitators of

Scott, but in this capacity is less well known than Willibald Alexis, the author of *Walladmor* and *Schloß Avalon.* De Quincey's review ends in praise of Tromlitz's *The Siege of Antwerp* as 'the best story, the most effective, and in the noblest tone of feeling, which has yet been translated from the German'. In particular he admires the 'rapidity and concentration of the narrative'. *The Siege of Antwerp* is a dramatic fictionalization of the second half of Schiller's account of the Siege of Antwerp.[11] It is a vividly effective, psychologically persuasive tale of 'wild, insatiable ambition' and 'love even unto death'. When his *Sämmtliche Schriften* (46 vols, Dresden & Leipzig: Arnold, 1829-42) appeared, Tromlitz was rightly praised for his

> singular talent for combining romantic interest with almost unprecedentedly close adherence to history, a just development of historical characters, a bold conception and felicitous exemplification of the influence of the circumstances and opinions of different eras upon the human mind, a vigorous and often dramatic embodying of incidents, and a powerful imagination, one fruit of which is the happy use of a slight touch of superstition, and occasionally even of the supernatural.[12]

As we shall see, Tromlitz's *Die Pappenheimer* and *Vergeltung* parallel *Klosterheim* and *The Avenger* respectively in interesting ways, but there is no smoking gun of influence here, no question of De Quincey copying from either work.

Otherwise, he praises *Mademoiselle de Scudérie* [sic] and *Roland-sitten (Das Majorat)* as lacking the 'wildness and bizarrerie' in which Hoffmann usually indulged, in saying which he is quoting from Gillies's introduction. *Das Majorat*, unaccountably translated by Gillies as *Rolandsitten; or, The Deed of Entail*, has been called Hoffmann's 'most classically Gothic tale'.[13] It is a *Nachtstück* or literary nocturne, a black tale, the atmosphere and background of which are, to be sure, Gothic enough. As in so many Gothic tales, the hero of the piece is arguably the ruinous castle, here of R..sitten, that is, Rossitten (meaning, originally, the seat of a Russian family), a place in the middle of the Baltic coast of East Prussia. Hoffmann elaborates in artistic form a tale that was popularly told of a local family. A ghost-seer story[14] that would have been at home in the contemporary *Gespensterbuch* of Apel and Laun, it turns, as De Quincey noted, on the for him powerfully attractive idea of secret murder. De Quincey recognized the hand of the author of *The Devil's Elixir* in the way in which the murderer in question began to scratch at the walled-up former doorway (through which he has oprecipitated his victim to his death in the abyss below) 'as if under the infleunce of some deadly torment'. The 'same appalling interest of secret and mysterious murder' sustains three other tales, Laurids Kruse's *Oath and Conscience* and *The Crystal Dagger*, both of which appeared in different collections of stories published in 1823 by this 'German Professor',[15] whose *Kriminalgeschichten und romantische Erzählungen* were to appear in 1827 (6 volumes); the third murder story is the anonymous

---

11 Tromlitz naturally read Schiller's work in German; for an English translation, see *The Historical Works of Frederick Schiller*, tr. George Moir, 2 vols (Edinburgh: Constable, 1828), II, 333-360.

12 *Foreign Quarterly Review,* 12 (1833), 245.

13 Neil Cornwell, in *A Companion to the Gothic*, ed. David Punter (Oxford: Blackwell, 2000), 32.

14 See Kenneth Negus, 'The allusions to Schiller's „Der Geisterseher" in E. T. A. Hoffmann's „Das Majorat": meaning and background', *German Quarterly*, 32 (1959), 341-55.

15 Laurids Kruse, though born in Copenhagen and possessing a Danish forename, is a German writer: he wrote in German, and was one of the earliest translators of Hans Andersen's tales into German.

The Warning, a variation on the murderous incident in the forest outside Strasbourg in 'The History of Don Raymond' in Lewis's *The Monk* (Vol. I, ch. 3).

His praise of Laun and Tromlitz notwithstanding, it is a striking fact that De Quincey's real attention is held not by a writer (Laun) from whom he went on to translate a number of tales, or by another (Tromlitz) who had not a little to teach him, if he had been looking to be taught, but by five tales of secret murder. Of the five tales in Gillies's *German Stories*, it was Kruse's *Oath and Conscience* that meant most to De Quincey, who identified with the principal character, who is

> urged by conscience and gratitude to discover a murder which he had accidentally witnessed when a child, but is restrained by a superstitious reverence for an oath of secrecy which had been administered to him at that time, and by pious regard to the memory of his father, who had been a participator in the murder, but had since died repentant', of which he said that 'A situation of greater trial for a conscientious mind can hardly be imagined.

The combination of secret murder and a guilt going back to childhood gave the tale a secret, subjective appeal.

There remains 'the matter' of 'that principle of adaptation, *rifacimento* or *remaniement'* which Gillies advocated in his Introduction, and which is discussed in Chapter 7. For the present it is sufficient to say that De Quincey's ideas on the subject of *rifacimento* go much further than Gillies intended, and that what is unique about him in this respect is the fact that, with him, *rifacimento*, denotes not simply a form of ultra-free translation, but an almost inveterate literary method, which, whether there were literal translation involved or not, came to dominate and, arguably, to vitiate his work.

3.2. De Quincey's Translations

Discussed here are De Quincey's translations from his German contemporaries Schiller, Apel and Laun, who have been associated with 'Gothic Fantasy' on the grounds that the 'brooding atmosphere' of Gothic is also found in their work.[16] His better known and more important translations from Jean Paul, Lessing, and others, are not relevant in the present context, and the translation of 'Die Teufelsleiter' ('The Devil's Ladder') from Aloys Schreiber's *Gedichte und Erzählungen* (Heidelberg, 1812), recently attributed to him (WTDQ, 3: 411f.), cannot possibly be by De Quincey; the attribution has nothing to be said for it. Schreiber's *Handbuch für Reisende am Rhein* (1816: *Guide on a Voyage on the Rhine*) and *Sagen aus den Gegenden des Rheins und des Schwarzwaldes* (1829: *Traditions of the Countries of the Rhine*) were translated by Rev. Peter Will, best known as the translator of Grosse's *Horrid Mysteries*, but that is another story.

---

16 John Clute & John Grant, *The Encyclopedia of Fantasy* (London: Orbit, 1997), 424.

3.2.1. *The Sport of Fortune* (1821)

The Sport of Fortune is a translation of Schiller's 'Das Spiel des Schicksals'.[17] De Quincey will have found the original in Schiller's *Sämmtliche Werke* in 26 volumes (Vienna: A. Doll, 1810-11), which the *Quarterly Review* sent him for review in 1818. At Bohte's, in summer 1821, he will have seen it again in Schiller's *Kleine prosaische Schriften* in 4 volumes (Leipzig: Crusius, 1792-1802), but his translation had been made and published six months earlier. It first appeared in *Blackwood's Magazine* for January 1821, and was not reprinted until 2000, when it appeared in the third volume of the *Works of Thomas De Quincey*.

Based on historical fact, it is a revenge tale, as is *Der Verbrecher aus verlorener Ehre*, which De Quincey must also have known since it always appears in the same context. *Das Spiel des Glücks* is based on the 'awful destiny' of Schiller's godfather, General Philipp Friedrich von Rieger (1722-1782), the powerful, brutal first minister of Duke Karl Eugen of Württemberg from 1762 to 1767, who was subsequently incarcerated in the Gothic prison-fortress of Hohentwiel, for supposed high treason, as a result of a court intrigue on the part of Count Samuel Friedrich von Montmartin (Montinengo in the text). He was eventually restored to favour, in an equally arbitrary way, in 1775, and in 1776 became commandant of another Gothic prison-fortress, Hohenasperg.

In the present context this is the most important of De Quincey's literary translations, not because it is by Schiller rather than Laun, but because it is, while not a romance, based on Gothic reality. The tale has many Gothic features. Gothic are the arbitrary power exercised by the petty prince and his henchmen, and the loss of control and lack of security this engenders. The sudden change for the worse – 'that dreadful moment, at which, from being the object of universal homage, he was destined to sink down into that of the uttermost commiseration', the 'whole frightful revolution of fortune' – is as fundamental to Gothic as the incarceration in 'a hideous subterranean vault' on a trumped-up charge. The fact that such a fate could be said to serve him right in moral terms is beside the point; what counts is the arbitrariness of what befalls him: 'Wherefore was he brought hither? What offence had he committed? But no answer from above; the hands vanish, and the trap-door closes.' Ten years later he emerges, 'a ghastly and deathlike skeleton'. Gothic are the infamy and secret excesses, the 'Italian' dissimulation, and the ambiguity of the 'evidence', 'authentic or spurious' – 'a point upon which opinions are divided'. Gothic, too, are the way in which he is 'petrified [...] with death-like horror' and the way in which, in that dreadful dungeon, existence loses reality to the point where it becomes confused with nightmare. This is, then, a tale of multiple revenge. G*** himself rebuilt Hohentwiel 'under the impulse of ignoble revenge'; Martinengo has him incarcerated there out of vengeance; finally, G*** avenges himself on a nameless state prisoner, thereby forfeiting any sympathy the reader might otherwise have had with him.

---

17 An earlier translation, by William Tooke, 'The Sport of Destiny', appeared in his *Varieties of Literature* (1795).

3.2.2. *The Fatal Marksman* (1823)

De Quincey's translation of this tale by Johann Apel first appeared anonymously, without any indication of the identity of the author or translator, in *Popular Tales and Romances of the Northern Nations* (1823), and was probably commissioned by J. H. Bohte, the co-publisher of the three-volume set, either during or shortly after De Quincey's stay with him in 1821. When he was writing his review of Gillies's *German Stories*, De Quincey, was under the impression that the original, *Der Freyschütz,* was by Laun. Gillies put him right. It appeared originally as the first story in the first volume of the *Gespensterbuch*, ed Apel and Laun (Leipzig: Göschen, 1811-17), that eventually numbered six volumes; a recent selection, *Gespensterbuch*, ed. Johann August Apel & Friedrich Laun, sel. Robert Stockhammer (Frankfurt a. M. & Leipzig: Insel Verlag, 1992), includes the Apel text (a version of the folk legend of Wilhelm Tell) on which De Quincey's translation is based. The French translation of the first volume, *Fantasmagoriana*, tr. Jean Baptiste Benoît Eyries (Paris: Lenormant & Schoell, 1812) became famous as the 'German stories of ghosts' that fell into the hands of the Byron-Shelley party one cold and rainy evening at the Villa Diodati near Geneva, and which excited in them 'a playful desire of imitation'. As everyone knows, Mary Shelley's *Frankenstein* and John Polidori's *The Vampyre* were the outcome. *Fantasmagoriana,* and with it 'Der Freischütz', was translated by Sarah Elizabeth Brown Utterson as *Tales of the Dead* (London: White, Cochrane) in 1813.[18] De Quincey's was therefore not the first English translation of 'Der Freischütz' when it appeared in *Popular Tales and Romances of the Northern Nations* in 1823. It reappeared, anonymously, in the first volume of Hazlitt's *The Romancist, and Novelist's Library* (London: Clements, 1839), before being included in De Quincey's collected writings in 1859. Apel's original was reworked by another Dresden writer, Friedrich Kind, as the libretto of *Der Freischütz*, the work by Karl Maria von Weber (from 1816 Königlicher Kapellmeister [Court Director of Music] in Dresden) that established the German opera. De Quincey translates Apel's original, tragic ending and all.

The Fatal Marksman is not a Gothic tale as such, but a reworking of the folk legend that underlies Weber's opera, which has some 'Gothic' features. What makes it relevant in the present context are the central role played by the Devil and the sense of guilt leading to madness. The tale turns on a pact with the Devil, who is invoked by his Jewish name of Samiel (Samäel [alias Adam-Belial]): a weak young man, an apprentice forester who needs to prove himself as a huntsman-marksman, sells his soul to the Devil in exchange for some magic balls (bullets in modern terminology) that he hopes will enable him to overcome his sudden inability to shoot straight (itself the Devi's work) and thus qualify as a fully-fledged forester-huntsman. As usual in such cases, he is cheated by the Devil in sundry ways, notably in being robbed of his natural ability to shoot straight, in succumbing to temptation, and in being cheated of the hoped-for prize, in this case as a result of inadvertently shooting the girl he was to have married. Magic bullets, magic guns, and the idea that the Devil cannot be shot are well-known folklore motifs, but there is more to this tale than superstition, spells and 'superannuated prejudice' (13: 300). In folklore the Devil has only

---

18 See *Tales of the Dead,* ed. Terry Hale, 2nd edn (Chislehurst: The Gothic Society, 1994). It is odd that *The English Novel 1770-1829* states (II, 390) that 'No German original has been discovered', for the Insel selection includes, as its frontispiece, a copy of the front cover of the original.

one leg and is liable to appear in the guise of a huntsman. In Apel's tale he appears as (i) Kuno, (ii) the one-legged 'old soldier', (iii) the rider on a black horse (and other guises), and (iv) William, who destroys his wife-to-be and wrecks his own life. It is clear that De Quincey chose to translate this particular tale because he, who already saw himself as Satanic, could read himself into it. It belongs together with the *Confessions* that he had just completed at the time, for here, masquerading in quasi-folkloric disguise, are the idea of someone being seared by grief and hounded by 'diabolical' guilt to the point of self-destruction, and the idea of the wrecking of a life as a result of transgressive weakness. It is strange, given that the tale is not by him, that it touches De Quincey's future Gothic tales, notably *The Household Wreck,* at a number of points.

3.2.3. *Mr. Schnackenberger, The Dice, The King of Hayti* (1823); *The Incognito, The Defier of Ghosts* (1824)

These five pieces are by Friedrich Laun (pseudonym of Friedrich August Schulze [1770-1849], whose surname De Quincey invariably misspells). Three of them (*Mr. Schnackenberger, The Dice* and *The King of Hayti*) first appeared in the *London Magazine* for May and June, August, and November 1823 respectively. They, and the incomplete *The Defier of Ghosts*, are what De Quincey had in mind when he revealed to Richard Woodhouse that he was to 'translate and abridge some tales from the German' for the *London Magazine. The Incognito* first appeared in *Knight's Quarterly Magazine* (No. 5) in 1824. With the exception of *Mr. Schnackenberger* and *The Defier of Ghosts* all these tales appeared in the *Collected Writings*.

Friedrich Laun is known as a minor writer and a member of the Tieck circle in Dresden. When Tieck agreed to write a Foreword for Laun's *Gesammelte Schriften* (6 vols, Stuttgart: Scheible, Rieger & Sattler, 1843-), he will have amused and gratified his prolix friend by writing 'einige Mährchen, die halb ernst und halb launig sind, ersuche ich Sie [...] nicht zu vergessen' (I beg you not to forget [to include] some of those tales of yours that are half serious and half *jeux d'esprit*' ['launig' involves a pun, meaning both 'witty' and 'typical of Laun']), but it is noticeable that he writes mostly about himself and almost omits to praise Laun, whom he is known to have advised to devote less paper and more time to his work. It seems, in fact, as though De Quincey has a higher opinion of Laun than Tieck has, and indeed a higher opinion of Laun (whose work he knew well) than he has of Tieck (of whose vast output he may only have known *Phantasus*). In the review of Gillies, he described Laun as 'a writer of inexhaustible fertility', adding that 'no German writer has managed the marvellous and the supernatural with so much skill [...] the devil is managed with great skill [...] in [...] *The Dice*'. In a note prefixed to *The Incognito*, which is described as 'possessing considerable intrinsic merit in the lighter department of comic tales', he praised Laun again:

> The tales of Dr. Schulz [sic] have exactly that merit, and pretend to that merit, neither more nor less, which we look for in a clever one-act dramatic after-piece: viz. the very slightest basis of incident; a few grotesque or laughable situations; a playful style; and an airy, *sketchy* mode of catching such fugitive revelations, in manners or in character, as are best suited to a comic treatment. The unelaborate narratives of Laun are mines of what is called *Fun*; which, [...] even when German fun, is no bad thing. (12: 417f.)

The fact that De Quincey writes thus, without so much as mentioning Tieck, I take as evidence that he knew little of Tieck, with whom he has much in common, including a similar attitude to the teenage Gothic reading which 'held a certain fascination for him during the whole of his life',[19] although he never derided that early reading in the way in which Tieck did. De Quincey's daughter said he never outgrew the Gothic novelists he read in such numbers in his teens, and the truth of this is borne out by the nature of his own fictional writings; but he does not mention them in later life, presumably in order to avoid ridicule. It is a point that has to be borne in mind when we are trying to weigh up his knowledge of German literature. Tieck vilified Schiller, whom he idolized. Did De Quincey do the same in regard to Hoffmann? Laun is in many ways a poor man's Tieck, a fluent and versatile writer of 'popular tales', which may as well be fairy tales, or fantastic or comic tales, as Gothic ones. The marvellous and the supernatural are, of course, the province of the fairy tale and the Gothic tale, but what De Quincey most appreciates is Laun's lightness of touch, in other words, the absence in his work of what was generally thought of as German stodginess. Laun is an entertainer. To praise the amiable but only moderately gifted like this, while saying nothing about Tieck (a remark which I will attempt to justify presently) and little that is not downright critical about Hoffmann, who are the real masters of the field that Laun ploughs, tells us more about De Quincey and his preconceptions than about his subject.

Mr. Schnackenberger, which De Quincey identified as being by Laun, is a translation of 'Zwei Herren für einen Hund' from the first volume of Laun's *Erzählungen und Schwänke* (2 vols, Berlin, 1818-19). It includes some potentially Gothic motifs (transgression, lawlessness, incarceration, confusion of identity, masquerade), but by no stretch of the critical imagination could it be considered other than a comic adventure.

The Dice De Quincey identified as 'undoubtedly by Laun' in the review of 'Gillies's German Stories', in which his use of the word *Kleinstädtigkeit* (he omits the *Umlaut*) suggests that he may have known Laun's *Kleinstädtereien* (2 vols, 1818). That said, *The Dice* is a translation of 'Die Glückswürfel' from Laun's *Die Traumdeutung, Herr Blitz, Die Glückswürfel* (1814), which De Quincey will have read at Bohte's in 1821; Laun returned to his theme (a common one at the time) in *Glitt's gesellige Abende – Die dritte Sechs* (1819). It is easy to see why De Quincey was drawn to this tale, a Gothic tale of the compact-with-the-Devil type and, in that sense, of the supernatural. Schroll, who, like De Quincey, assumes the *Adelsprädikat* (title of nobility [de, von, van, etc.]) to which he is not entitled, is, like De Quincey, though in a different sense, a 'coiner' (another of Laun's tales is entitled 'Der Dukatenmacher'), and becomes a multiple murderer: he causes his father to die of a broken heart, is responsible for the judicial murder of Weber,[20] and murders his own first wife. This is a tale of guilty conscience, which the Evil One personates. From the fateful discovery of the father burning the old document in which his son's fate is foretold, to his own death, the tale illustrates the inexorable series of turns for the worse that is typical of Gothic. That De Quincey, in translating it, will have identified with Schroll alias von Schrollhausen is not to be doubted.

---

19 Trainer, 34. The novelists in question include Spieß, Weber, Grosse, Rambach, Walpole, and M. G. Lewis.

20 In a firing-squad scene like that famously depicted by Goya.

The King of Hayti is a translation of 'Der Mohrenkönig' from the second volume of Laun's *Erzählungen und Schwänke* (Berlin, 1819), which probably represented his (Laun's) reaction to an anonymous piece, 'Über Hayti und den König Henri' that appeared in a volume entitled *Miscellen aus der neuesten ausländischen Literatur,* Heft 11 (Jena: Bran, 1817, 137-62). The motif of one masked guest too many, revealed when the guests are counted, was used again by De Quincey in *Klosterheim*. The tale reflects De Quincey's preoccupation with identity, real and assumed, and with masquerading.

The Incognito, which De Quincey identified as another piece by Laun, is a translation of 'Das Inkognito', which was itself a retake on Friedrich Kind's *Prinz Incognito* of 1802. On the face of it, *The Incognito* is a comic tale pure and simple, a comic masquerade involving the impersonation of a petty prince. Count Fitz-Hum is well named, but Baron von Hoax is contrived; Baron von Pranck or von Jux would have been better. In terms of its subject matter this tale of a hoax belongs together with *Walladmor*. One has only to peruse the front page of the *Morning Chronicle* to realize how very popular masquerades (*bals masqués*) were at this time.

The Defier of Ghosts, left unfinished by De Quincey, is a translation of 'Der Geisterläugner', which appeared in Apel and Laun's famous *Gespensterbuch*. It is another comic tale, with 'Gothic' touches (murder, 'boggarts').

3.2.4. *The Love-Charm* (1825)

The translation of Tieck's *Liebeszauber* printed in Masson first appeared (together with an appended note on the author) in *Knight's Quarterly Magazine* in 1825, and was for long something of a mystery. De Quincey did not include it in his *Writings* because he did not remember writing it, which should have been conclusive. It was only printed by James Hogg in *The Uncollected Writings of Thomas De Quincey* (1890) after he had been told, about 1852, by Charles Knight that De Quincey 'wrote a translation of *The Love-Charm* of Tieck, with a notice of the Author'. It was subsequently included in Hogg and then in Masson, but there are good reasons for thinking that De Quincey wrote neither the translation nor the note on Tieck. Hans Galinsky pointed out in 1937 that an 'almost identical' translation appeared in *The Old Man of the Mountain; The Love Charm; and Pietro of Abano* (London: Moxon, 1831) by Julius Charles Hare.[21] There are three reasons for doubting De Quincey's authorship of *The Love-Charm* as printed by Masson: (i) that De Quincey did not remember it as his, (ii) that it is almost identical with the version in (Hare's) *The Old Man of the Mountain,* the main difference being the fact that the 1831 version follows Hare's idiosyncratic spelling rules (which Charles Knight would not have allowed him to indulge in) and (iii) the fact, not commented on before now, that the Note appended to the translation is neither in De Quincey's style nor in line with his knowledge of and preconceptions regarding German literature, whereas Galinsky showed it to be plausibly attributable to Hare. For this last reason the attribution to De Quincey of this translation and the appended note must be considered unsafe and unsound. Given that the

[21] Hans K. Galinsky, 'Is Thomas De Quincey the author of *The Love-Charm?*', *Modern Language Notes,* 52 (1937), 389-394. The 1831 collection was widely reviewed (see *German Literature in British Magazines 1750-1860*, ed. Morgan & Hohlfeld (Madison, Wisconsin: University of Wisconsin Press, 1949), 218-220.

Note begins by referring to the fact that Tieck has 'lately' been introduced to the English reader by translations of two other stories [in (Colburn's) *New Monthly Magazine and Literary Journal,* 15 (1825), 268-71], the translation and note must be by the same person, viz. Julius Hare. It is a curious coincidence that a pseudonym used by De Quincey in January-May 1825 is Lepus (Hare), but it is probably taken from the name of a murderer (see 4: 60f.).

Leaving aside the likelihood that it is the work of Hare, the attribution of the note to De Quincey was always intrinsically unlikely. Why should it be in an essay on Tieck, in the context of the literary revival in Germany of which he has repeatedly written elsewhere, and always in the same terms, that he should have written, for the first time, the names of Hegel, Steffens, Schleiermacher, Novalis and Tieck? Would he have been likely to write of Germany being 'rendered illustrious by Fichte'? Would he have been capable of writing of that early part of his own life without listing Kant and Schiller? Or would he who was so rapidly disillusioned by German metaphysics in the person of Kant, have put so much emphasis on Kant's lesser successors, not even mentioning Schopenhauer? I think not. Besides, he has so much in common with Tieck, who shared the young Thomas De Quincey's boundless enthusiasm for what has been called 'the below-stairs area of the literary edifice, popular fiction in the mode of the Gothic novel',[22] which retained its place in his affections too, that he would hardly have written of him in this way. The style is not De Quincey's, and what Eaton calls the 'sentimental langour' of *The Love-Charm* is not his style either.

22 Roger Paulin, *Ludwig Tieck. A Literary Biography* (Oxford: Clarendon Press, 1985), 14.

4. De Quincey and Gothic

4.1. Gothic

By the end of the eighteenth century, England was not only awash with Gothic novels and tales; according to Johann Wilhelm von Archenholz, a distinguished, once-sympathetic German traveller, who knew the country well, it had itself, in the aftermath of the French Revolution, which was feared to be part of a more general conspiracy against society, turned into a monstrous Gothic prison 'at whose portals brutal and fearful inquisitors are stationed'.[1] In other words, fantasy had been displaced into reality, and vice versa. We have already seen that the same thing happened with regard to De Quincey's inner life.

'Gothic', a term that is currently subject to slippage, has many meanings and many connotations. Literary Gothic started as a cluster of motifs, borrowed from fairytale, that quickly turned into a formula as rigid as that of fairytale itself, and has now spread to the point where it threatens to engulf all, its indeterminacy increasing exponentially as it does so. It is, of course, only partly the matter of Gothic imagery, machinery and motifs that was originally thought to constitute the genre, although the key component is arguably still the edifice, whether this comprises aerial architecture à la Piranesi, a crumbling Gothic pile, some kind of unstable 'subterraneous chamber' or system of passages, or their metaphorical/textual equivalents. Marked by inherent instability and the role of the dream or subconscious in the generation of text, it is both historically and formally subversive. Gothic are above all the sudden turn for the worse, the loss of control that this involves, and the uncertainty, destabilization and fear that ensue. Gothic are the uncanny, the monstrous, the threatening, the unsettling, and the grotesque or macabre, especially in combination. Gothic is a sense of blocked entrances and exits, of broken connexions and lost or eroded meaning(s), a lost past and the threat of a lost future. It involves a sense, and the reality, of disempowerment, privation, helplessness, abandonment, and alienation, and therefore the sense of a 'malign agency' (De Quincey's term, applicable to his work, helps to define its gothicity). In other words, it involves a sense that the whims, whams and vagaries of the life-force are indifferent to the individual, and with this a sense of claustrophobically contracting space and of being caught in a labyrinth without an exit. Basic to Gothic are abjection (the Cain-figure, the outcast or pariah) and of power abused by one person leading to another's (or others') disempowerment, although the adversary may in fact be that person's other, as is the case with De Quincey. A feature of Gothic is the idea of 'primordial dissolution [that favourite Gothic word]',[2] 'decomposition' in both the psychological and the physical sense. The underlying preoccupation of Gothic is the naked human condition of mortality: the ultimate Gothic locus is the grave. In terms of Coleridge's 'The Rime of the Ancient Mariner', the 'frightful fiend' that treads close

---

1 J. W. von Archenholz, *Annalen der Brittischen Geschichte,* Vol. 19 (Tübingen: Cotta, 1799), 445. In *Walladmor,* De Quincey would write of the country being 'sealed against foreigners' (WTDQ, 4: 316).

2 Hogle, 11.

behind us is the dead self we all carry within us: 'la précarité, l'abîme et le manque, cette réalité gothique[, c']est la vie'.[3]

A variety of 'fantasy', owing much to the fairy tale from which Ann Radcliffe derived her Gothic, and to the related oriental tale from which De Quincey progressed to the Gothic, and to dream and nightmare, Gothic is a highly conventionalized literary form that spawned the modern thriller, but also, because of the way in which its 'machinery' came to be internalized, the psychological novel (Hoffmann's *Die Elixiere des Teufels*, say, and Kafka's three novels). Often black in humour (hence *le genre noir* and *schwarze Romantik)*, it revolves around the idea of transgression (against the law of the father, even when this is displaced and personalized in the wicked stepmother or abbess) and the ensuing incarceration that is literal in the early Gothic novel, but soon became metaphorical in the wake of Kant's description of the 'internal tribunal' of conscience. In the 'striking incident in a modern novel' retold in *Suspira de profundis*, the Abbess holds the key in the figurative sense as well as the literal, not only because the nun's sufferings are also hers, but because they both represent De Quincey's largely self-inflicted agony. His internal world, as we shall see, is a pervasively Gothic one, dominated by loss, guilt and anxiety.

A revolutionary form of the novel, the Gothic novel or, better, romance, embodies the radical uncertainty generated by the collapse of the *ancien régime* and its attendant certainties (including the Augustan novel), which it subverts. Cixous has defined the Gothic text as 'a territory of overdetermined incertitude', an overstated way of making an important point, for Gothic texts not only, like the graveyard poetry that was another of their starting-points, emphasize the instability and impermanence of things, but tend to generate often extreme uncertainty in the reader's mind as to their meaning that mirrors the uncertainty in the protagonist's mind as to the meaning of a life so subject to violent, arbitrary change. Subversion is basic to the Gothic novel, as it is to fantasy and the fantastic generally. The Gothic novel thus comes to be marked, above all, by a multiform instability that may be authorial/narratorial (problem of identity), textual (problem of meaning), generic (problem of genre: the novel becomes a mixed form, no longer predictable, no longer distinguishable from autobiography, fairy tale and myth, poetry), or moral (Sade). Reality and fantasy become notably unstable concepts, as in Hoffmann, De Quincey and Kafka. Kafka's novels, like De Quincey's *Confessions*, question whether what they describe is real, or fictitious and therefore spurious. In each of them Kafka hides away a metaphor implying that the whole thing is a tall story, a construct, a lie. By the same token De Quincey rightly implies that he is less a creative writer as such than a 'coiner' who 'forges' a text. The blurring of the distinction between fact and fiction that is associated with the name of E. T. A. Hoffmann comes about, in the case of the typical *Blackwood's* contributor of De Quincey's day, as a result of copying the realism of the true-crime narrative. The typical author of a *Blackwood's* tale of terror eschews the often rather vague suggestiveness of the early Gothic novel in favour of a more precise and ultimately clinical (Poe-like) description, so that 'there are, in the early volumes of *Blackwood's* scarcely any short stories that one could plausibly describe as Gothic'[4].

---

3 Maurice Lévy, *Le roman ‹gothique› anglais 1764-1824* (Paris: Albin Michel, 1995), back cover.

4 Robert Morrison and Chris Baldick, in the Introduction to their *Tales of Terror from Blackwood's Magazine* (Oxford: Oxford University Press, 1995), xviif.

As a 'border epistemology',[5] gothicism challenges rationalism and rational perceptions and valuations in much the same way that mid-twentieth-century chaos theory[6] was to challenge and in part subvert Newtonian perceptions about the world, but the fact that the Gothic novel explores the irrational (subconscious) does not mean that it should be credited with the invention of a systematic discourse of the irrational (subconscious), credit for which belongs to the fairytale, from which Gothic, as I have argued elsewhere,[7] in large measure derives. Thus Musäus's *Volksmärchen der Deutschen* came into the domain of the Gothic novel when it was translated into English, supposedly by William Beckford,[8] as *Popular Tales of the Germans* (2 vols) in 1791. What makes this excellent, little known translation so interesting is the fact that it was greeted by a reviewer in the *European Magazine* (19 [1791], 350-2) as 'a very singular display of the most risible absurdities of the Gothic Romance'. In other words, even informed readers of the time found it impossible to tell the fairytale from the Gothic tale. Anthologies such as *Popular Tales of the Northern Nation*s (3 vols, 1823) made no distinction between them, and even as late as 1849 a collection entitled *Tales of Fairy-Land: or, Legends of the Olden Time* contains, as the echo of Veit Weber's *Sagen der Vorzeit* would lead readers to expect, a mixture of fairytales and Gothic tales. 'Fairy' ('faery') could be tantamount to 'fancy' or 'fantasy'.

The Gothic romance represented a challenge to the *ancien régime* of the novel at a time when contemporary notions of art were being undermined by men like Friedrich (who, as we shall see, can be said to have painted De Quincey's Hercynian forest), Runge and Turner. Gothicism is a *schwarze Romantik*, a Dark Romanticism, Romanticism's collective Other. It provides the shadow-text for Romanticism: 'Dark Romanticism is the drama of the mind engaged in the quest for metaphysical and moral absolutes in a world that offers shadowy semblances of an occult order but withholds final revelation and illumination'.[9] If it is true that Gothic 'texts within texts' can 'act as mirrors, emitting a reflective light that comments upon even as it confuses the image of the originating text',[10] then De Quincey's technique, which is absolutely fundamental to his work, as well as being typical of 'translation' in the age of Gothic, is prototypically Gothic.

Gothic is the shocked discovery of the meanglessness and lack of security at the heart of a world hitherto believed to be meaningful and secure. The world of Gothic is therefore a world in which sequence is replaced by consequence, and logic, which is continuous, is replaced by the discontinuous episode. In a forced confrontation with self, the protagonist appears as pariah and prisoner (ostensibly of the super-ego, but ultimately of the self, as a result of the paradoxical combination of the flight from, and search for, the self). Protagonists, finding themselves trapped, are outraged, racked by insecurity. Fiedler speaks of 'the tremulous *anima* [...] seeking to evade the shadow cast by itself'[11] (the opposite of the Schlemihl situation), which applies to *Suspira de Profundis,* and the reader too is liable

5 Daneen Wardrop, *Emily Dickinson's Gothic* (Iowa City: University of Iowa Press, 1996), xiii.

6 See James Gleick, *Chaos* (New York: Penguin, 1988).

7 Bridgwater, *Kafka, Gothic and Fairytale*, 76-84.

8 Recent research has shown that the translator was not Beckford but, as Walter Scott knew all along, Thomas Beddoes (1760-1808), 'a man of real genius' (4: 343) and father of the Gothic poet.

9 G. R. Thompson (ed.), *The Gothic Imagination: Essays in Dark Romanticism* (Pullman: Washington State University Press, 1974), 6.

10 Wardrop, 162. Cf. De Quincey's reference to 'that camera obscura, the sleeping mind' (13: 335).

11 Leslie A. Fiedler, *Love and Death in the American Novel* (Normal, IL: Dalkey Archive, 1997), 109.

to be destabilized as a result of empathy. In the gothic text, reality and unreality are deliberately confused, and the reader is confronted, and liable to be thrown, by that confusion The reading experience, unnerving when the reader is faced with a text whose meaning is elusive, is part and parcel of the gothicism of the text. By the time of late Romanticism the Gothic text is liable to challenge not only its own meaning, but meaning as such, including the meaning of existence.

Gothic involving 'the fear of a secret hidden at the core of something',[12] a secret within which the protagonist is effectively immured, De Quincey is very much a Gothic writer, forever trapped within the persona of the 'English Opium-Eater', which was itself more fiction than fact, for he did not even eat opium. His basic, Gothic experience is that of entrapment within a guilty habit, a spider caught in its own web, and the flawed text that is spun out from it. If Gothic is a dark or shadow Romanticism, the night-side of Romanticism, then De Quincey epitomizes it: he is a Romantic not only guilty – in his own eyes, for it was he who unwisely chose the persona behind which he has been trapped ever since, like a fly in amber – of self-indulgence and the damage to himself and others that flowed from it. To make matters worse, he is so aware of being overshadowed by Wordsworth and Coleridge as to have profound misgivings about his own adequacy and identity. Notwithstanding all that has been written about Wordsworth in this context, De Quincey probably felt more overshadowed by Coleridge, for Wordsworth, though a more successful writer than De Quincey, was 'only' a poet, which de Quincey was not, whereas Coleridge was a direct rival, more successful than De Quincey in precisely the fields that De Quincey thought of as his own, notably German metaphysics, but also several others, including translation. Is De Quincey ever himself? Is he himself when he writes those remarkable passages of impassioned prose, or is he putting on an act, waxing lyrical? Clearly he is not being himself when, in *Walladmor*, he hides within another writer's work like a ghost crab in some convenient shell, unless, of course, it is argued that he is being himself precisely when he is skating on the edge of plagiarism. Is he being himself when, in writing about another writer, he chooses to say what applies to himself? Pater was to go much further and be far more systematic in this respect, but there is no doubt that De Quincey, in seeming to write about another, is in reality not infrequently writing about himself. It is another aspect of his literary masquerade, of the way in which, in the words of the 1803 diary, he 'wraps himself up in the dark recesses of his own soul'.

4.2. De Quincey's Gothic

Spurned by conservative writers, but hugely popular with the reading public, in the air in the decisive preparatory part of De Quincey's career as a writer was the English Gothic novel and tale and its German equivalent, for which I use the term 'Gothic' because there is, at the time, no German term for the Gothic novel as such and its subdivisions (*Schauerroman*, *Räuberroman*, *Bundesroman* or *Geheimbundroman*) (the novel of terror, the *bandito* novel, the secret society novel) are mostly unimportant in the present context.

---

12 Wardrop, xi.

De Quincey is a Gothic writer in both yesterday's and today's terms, for he wrote, in addition to a novel, a free translation, and a number of tales that use the conventions of early Gothic, and are therefore Gothic in an historically backward-looking sense, and a body of work centred on the *Confessions,* which appeared in book-form in 1822, the year that is generally taken to mark the end of the early Gothic novel, but was also the year that saw the completion of the *Black Paintings* by Goya that illustrate Gothic in all its horrid particularity. *Confessions* and *Suspira* are 'imbued with the underlying structures and traits of Gothic fiction'.[13] In the *Confessions*, which can be read, as Joel Porte has shown, as a Gothic narrative of sin and retribution or divine vengeance,[14] Gothic is internalized and used in a more modern way, with the emphasis on uncanny dream-experience and the instability of the inner world and its constructs. Indeed, De Quincey was 'drawn to the Gothic mode [because] he was keenly sensitive to the labyrinthine complexity of experience and the delicate balance between illusion and reality'.[15] Lindop has described the 'essays and prose-poems' as 'Gothic both in their weird emotional intensity and their digressive complexity of structure',[16] but the complexity of the work is transgressive as well as digressive, and its 'enigmatic symbols of psychological [...] power' are, in truth, symbols of the loss of power. So far as his most creative work is concerned, Gothic was not merely nearest to hand; *le genre noir* was the only form adequate to the needs of De Quincey and his Dark Interpreter alter ego.

The third letter to Wordsworth, already cited in connexion with the supposedly character-building effect of German drama, is even more interesting as a Gothic narrative:

> I gradually came under the dominion of my passions, & from frequent meditation on some characters of our own, & some of ancient story, & afterwards on some of the German drama, I began to model my conduct & my aims on theirs: by degrees, being dazzled by the glory thrown on such objects by the voice of the people, & miserably deluding myself with the thought that I was led on by high aims, & such as were most worthy of my nature[,] I daily intoxicated myself more & more with that delirious & lawless pleasure which I drew from the hope of elevating my name in authority and kingly splendour above every name that is named upon earth. For I felt myself unable to live in the pursuit of common objects, & unfettered by any ties of common restraint – & I felt, too, or imagined myself able to compass any plans capable of gratifying that stimulating class of desires which I then thought ebullitions of the highest state of moral improvement, but which I now consider as only a less degrading species of sensualism. (J 37)

This is an extraordinarily Toadish piece of work, hubristic to a degree, the would-be Emperor's clothes borrowed in part from Schiller's *The Robbers*, and maybe from Beckford's *Vathek*; but it is also 'a gothic fable that exploits a consciousness of its own genre: a gothic about the perils of gothic', for 'the allusion to his literary influences places De Quincey's letter squarely within the gothic tradition.'[17] His Gothicism is thus far from being an incidental, more or less harmless leftover from his youthful reading, and, as such, marking an immaturity of taste and judgment that his daughter Emily will not have been

---

13 R. L. Snyder, '*Klosterheim:* De Quincey's Gothic Masque', *Research Studies*, 49 (1981), 129.

14 Joel Porte, 'In the hands of an Angry God: Religious Terror in Gothic Fiction', in *The Gothic Imagination*, ed. Thompson, 47-50.

15 Snyder, *Research Studies*, 49 (1981), 130.

16 Grevel Lindop, in the Introduction to his edition of Thomas De Quincey, *Confessions of an English Opium-Eater* (Oxford: Oxford University Press, 1998), vii.

17 Margaret Russett, *De Quincey's Romanticism* (Cambridge: Cambridge University Press, 1997), 17.

alone in deploring. He is not merely a 'Gothic hero', although he is the ultimate hero of all his Gothic fictions; he has also been described as a 'Gothic parasite', as 'Wordsworth's gothic interpreter', and so on, but 'Gothic', in his case, is more than an epithet. If Gothic is a code for the exploration of the fragmented subject, the deep structures of the self and its anxieties,[18] then the core of De Quincey's work is Gothic *par excellence*, by which I mean Gothic, seen from today's perspective, in a more complete sense than Monk Lewis or Ann Radcliffe, although De Quincey's affinity with Ann Radcliffe needs to be stressed. Like her work, which he much admired, his is about haunted consciousness and, more generally, about, interiority, interior space. Terry Castle's analysis of the 'uncanny Radcliffean metaphor of haunted consciousness',[19] and with it the spectral nature of Gothic, is strikingly applicable to De Quincey's work, in which the dead haunt the minds of the living, who become thus become living spectres. Elizabeth, who is dead, is no less real, and arguably more real, than Thomas, who is alive as his own zombie or other. Those whom he had lost to death were ever-present on the screen of De Quincey's consciousness. The Gothic text thus becomes a 'textual event in which boundaries between inside and outside, life and death, the spectral and the real, the illusory and the rational, disarmingly fade'.[20]

If one excludes *Walladmor*, the further gothified remake of an already Gothic novel, as being not exactly his own work, the only fictional work published in book form in his lifetime was *Klosterheim,* a Gothic tale salvaged from the *New Canterbury Tales* project on which he claimed, hyperbolically, to be working in 1830. All his tales are, however, either Gothic or Gothic-related, and the same goes for many of his translations. The autobiographical sketches, of which so much of his work consists, are Gothic above all in terms of their psychological instability, but also of their metafictionality and generic instability, and 'supplementarity' is as much a feature of Gothic as *rifacimento*. Most Gothic works feed off their kind, so that Gothic itself became 'parasitical'; the only remarkable thing about De Quincey in this respect is that he is an incomparably more serious writer than most of those who copied one another *ad nauseam*. However, while he may seem to afford the spectacle of a reputable, high-brow writer using the disreputable methods of the typical low-brow writer of the time, to make a distinction between high- and low-brow work, or to argue that De Quincey dwells 'in that limbo between literature as mass-produced good and literature as the product of imaginative genius',[21] is hardly helpful, for the former begs too many questions, including that of the kind of Gothic that is involved, and the degree of prejudice we bring to the discussion, while the latter is contradicted by the facts. The historical phenomenon of a tension between literature as consumer product and literature as the product of imaginative genius does not tell us much, if anything, about De Quincey's fascination with the Gothic and the partly cross-generic works that reflect it.

---

18 Robert Miles, *Gothic Writing 1750-1820. A Genealogy,* 2nd edn (Manchester & New York: Manchester University Press, 2002), 3, 21.

19 Terry Castle, 'The Spectralization of the Other in *The Mysteries of Udolpho*', in *The New Eighteenth Century: Theory, Politics, English Literature*, ed. Laura Brown and Felicity Nussbaum (London & New York: Methuen, 1987), 250.

20 Miles, 119.

21 E. Michael Thron, in *Bicentenary Studies*, 5f.

Klosterheim, though written to enable De Quincey to claim a fee he had been promised, and which he could not afford to forego, is the only completed part of the *New Canterbury Tales* project, which was planned not in a mercenary spirit but as a tribute to a writer the young De Quincey had idolized. He allowed himself to be hustled into writing *Walladmor*, hustle led to hastle, and the game proved – from his point of view – scarcely worth the candle. The Gothic tales and translations of other 'Gothic' writers are no different from his other magazine contributions, and the *Confessions* complex, in which I include both its sequel *Suspira de Profundis* and the Gothic dream-fantasia *The English Mail-Coach*, was purportedly written, for therapeutic reasons and as a 'record', to 'display the faculty [of dreaming]', a statement that is demonstrably not wholly true and therefore untrue. That the *Confessions* became a bestseller, was an incidental spin-off.

Republished in book form in 1822, The *Confessions of an English Opium-Eate*r is a kind of Gothic novel; indeed, Eve Kosofsky Sedgwick, in an important book on Gothic conventions, argued that

> As an essayist and autobiographer, Thomas De Quincey was a great Gothic novelist. The subjects he approached with the most characteristic sympathy were certain heightened versions of privation and immobilization: dreams and trances, submergence under a massive space, the unspeakable. If we add to these themes those of the pariah and of the loss of the past, and [...] the sense of helplessness washing over everything else, we have a sketch of the most powerful part of De Quincey's fourteen volumes and more of prose.[22]

That the body is paralyzed while the brain is dreaming adds additional weight to her analysis, which is discussed in 5.1 below; the further the mind descends into the Gothic depths of its dream or nightmare, the more massive the space (incubus) beneath which it is submerged.

There are many recipes for a Gothic novel, many mostly satirical lists of the parts that originally went to make up a Gothic whole. Sedgwick's recent list, which introduces a book in which De Quincey's Gothic looms large, is both serious and pretty inclusive:

> the Gothic novel [is] pervasively conventional [...] its *mise-en-scène:* an oppressive ruin, a wild landscape, a [...] feudal society [...] the novel's form [...] is likely to be discontinuous and involuted, perhaps incorporating tales within tales, changes of narrators, and such framing devices as found manuscripts or interpolated histories [...] characteristic preoccupations [...] include [...] sleeplike and deathlike states; subterranean spaces and live burial; doubles; the discovery of obscured family ties; [...] unnatural echoes or silences, unintelligible writings, and the unspeakable; [...] the poisonous effects of guilt and shame; nocturnal landscapes and dreams; apparitions from the past; Faust- and Wandering-Jew-like figures; [...] the charnel house and the madhouse.[23]

She concludes that the self is 'massively blocked off from something to which it ought normally to have access', and adds that 'Of all the Gothic conventions dealing with the sudden, mysterious, seemingly arbitrary, but massive inaccessibility of those things that should normally be accessible, the difficulty the story has in getting itself told is of the most obvious structural significance.'[24] Because he lacks the fiction-writer's imagination, his 'story' has particular difficulty in getting itself told (see 8). In relation to De Quincey language is

---

[22] Eve Kosofsky Sedgwick, *The Coherence of Gothic Conventions* (New York: Methuen, 1986), 37.

[23] Sedgwick, 9f.

[24] Sedgwick, 12, 13.

shown to be tantamount to live burial. He is blocked off from the past, which has been lost, and from the future, because he is blocked off from what should have been a better life and literary career. Gothic, because of its formulaic nature, represents a place where he belongs, a place where his guilt and the ruin of his life can be seen as part of a wider pattern, thus countering his pariah self-image and making some sort of sense of the Gothic ruin of his life. Because in his case Gothic gives meaning to a life that is otherwise meaningless, he could not have afforded to move away from it, even if he had wanted to; as it is, Gothic is, like the rock at the end of Goethe's *Tasso* and its flip side, the barrel at the beginning of *Walladmor*, something to cling to.

With him the 'oppressive ruin' of Gothic has less an historical than a personal connotation: the ruin stands for the ruin of his life, by which he is saddened and perplexed. He is his own double, for there are, in a range of senses, two De Quinceys: the young Thomas Quincey and the autoscopic older Thomas De Quincey, the bourgeois and the (Gothic) hero, the High Churchman and the recusant, Faust and his Mephistophelean Other, the opium-eater (a heroized, mythologized version of the drug-addict) and the man who secretly identified with Satan. The tension between his 'intense faith' and his 'perverse logical recusancy' (7: 177) is part of a larger pattern.

His interest in the 'colossal exhibition of fiendish grandeur' afforded by Harriet Lee's *Kruitzner* is as much Gothic and Shakespearian as Schillerian, but his interest in the 'noble criminal' was fired by *Die Räuber*. Schiller, following the example of Milton, speaks of the 'majesty' of his Robber, that 'honourable malefactor, the majestic monster' (*Ungeheuer mit Majestät*). The scene (Act 5, Scene 2) in which Amalie throws her arms around Karl Moor's neck exclaiming 'Murderer! Fiend! Whate'er thou art, Angel to me, I will not let thee go!' deeply impressed the young De Quincey, any lingering doubts being swept aside by the thought that no less a poet than Milton had shown the 'majesty' of the Devil. Schiller, in his *Selbstrecension der Räuber,* had likened Karl Moor to Milton's Satan.

The prototype of the 'heroic villain' of the Gothic novel is Milton's Satan, celebrated by Edmund Burke for his sublimity and heroized by the Gothics for his resistance to patriarchal power:

> the hero of *Paradise Lost* (1667-1674) is none other than Satan [...] The ridiculous Devil of our [medieval] ancestors has become in Milton's hands a giant and a hero [...] an epic, majestic figure, a Promethean character [...] During the period of the Romantic revolt in all European countries Satan was considered [...] a Prometheus of Christian mythology. He was hailed as the vindicator of reason, of freedom of thought, and of unfettered humanity.[25]

Though Satan is in reality not the hero but the God-sized villain of *Paradise Lost*, the personification of the sublime of evil, he is the ultimate hero of many Gothic novels in which diabolical possession is an important motif. This extraordinary anachronistic vogue was started, so far as late eighteenth-century England is concerned, by a romance by Veit Weber (ps. of [Georg Philipp Ludwig] Leonhard Wächter), *Die Teufelsbeschwörung* (1790), translated by Robert Huish as *The Sorcerer* (1795), to which Lewis was indebted for the dramatic ending of *The Monk* (1796).

---

[25] Maximilian Rudwin, *The Devil in Legend and Literature* (Chicago & London: The Open Court Company, 1931), 10, 15.

Now in a useful article marred only by the customary inaccuracy as regards De Quincey's German links (it is not true that 'the German Romantics [...] were [...] imitated by De Quincey'; nor is it true that he 'translated [...] many romantic tales from the German'; he merely translated one from Schiller and a handful from a *Pseudoromantiker*, Laun) Karen M. Lever has argued that '[Milton's] Satan is a significant, though unacknowledged, model for De Quincey'. She quotes Mario Praz to the effect that

> Milton conferred upon the figure of Satan all the charm of an untamed rebel [...] Towards the end of the eighteenth century Milton's Satan transfused with his own sinister charm the traditional type of generous outlaw or sublime criminal [...] Rebels in the grand manner, grandsons of Milton's Satan and brothers of Schiller's Robber, began to inhabit the picturesque, Gothicized backgrounds of the English 'tales of terror'.[26]

De Quincey does indeed bear an uncanny personal resemblance to *Homo Satanicus* as described by Praz ('mysterious [but conjectured to be exalted] origin, traces of burnt-out passions, suspicion of a ghastly guilt, melancholy habits, pale face, unforgettable eyes'), but more telling is what Lever writes about his unconscious (unadmitted) identification with Satan and the fact that his repeated descent into depth after depth parallels Satan's nine-day fall into the 'bottomless pit', which the Piranesi-image encapsulates, for while it shows a figure ascending towards the transcendent or absolute sublime, the transcendent is merely 'an abyss in which [the imagination] fears to lose itself',[27] so that it is in reality a Fall-image.

The pit (abyss, chasm, ravine, etc., but also the ocean and the dizzying height that, as so notably in the Piranesi image discussed in Chapter 9, involves the idea of falling) is one of two Gothic images that are recurrent in De Quincey's work, the ascent and descent imagery of which recalls that of Beckford's *Vathek.* The Gothic tradition, it has been well said, 'replays with almost infinite variations the myths both of the temptation and fall in Eden and of the perilous experience of the post-lapsarian wilderness'.[28] In terms of the dream-work that applies to *Confessions*, the chasm stands for the archaic, anarchic underworld of the self, the subconscious and its unplumbed, unfathomable depths. In either case the idea of live burial is involved, for 'I seemed every night to descend [...] into chasms and sunless abysses, depths below depths, from which it seeemed hopeless that I could ever re-ascend. Nor did I, by waking, feel that I had re-ascended' (3: 435). Every abyss represents the 'maelstrom' (13: 337) or maws of death, for that extraordinary image in the *Confessions* of the 'sea [...] paved with innumerable faces' is a variation on the image of the abyss and the emptiness of Piranesian architecture. It is ultimately the 'abyss of death' (13: 347), in brief, 'the abyss'. De Quincey himself makes the obvious connexion:

> To my architecture succeeded dreams of lakes and silvery expanses of water; these haunted me so much that I feared lest some dropsical state [...] of the brain might thus be making itself [...] objective [...] The waters gradually changed their character – from translucent lakes, shining like mirrors, they became seas and oceans. And [...] upon the rocking waters of the ocean the human face began to reveal itself; the sea appeared paved with innumerable faces, upturned to the heavens; faces, imploring, wrathful, despairing; faces that surged up-

---

26 Mario Praz, *The Romantic Agony* (London: Oxford University Press, 1933), 57-60.

27 Kant, *Critique of Judgment*, tr. J. H. Bernard (New York: Hafner Press, 1951), 97.

28 Stephen C. Behrendt in his Introduction to Percy Bysshe Shelley, *Zastrozzi and St Irvyne* (Oxford & New York: Oxford University Press, 1986), xiv.

wards by thousands, by myriads, by generations: infinite was my agitation; my mind tossed, as it seemed, upon the billowy ocean, and weltered upon the weltering waves. (3: 440f.)

In his dream the water he was afraid of having on the brain ('hydrocephalus' was thought to have played a part in Elizabeth's death) has become the waters of death, transformed by the dream-work into that remarkable image in which the ocean replaces the usual chasm or abyss, into which the drowned sink.

The sky, as well as the sea, having its 'blue depths', when he took leave of his dead sister Elizabeth he had a vision of 'A vault [that]seemed to open in the zenith of the far blue sky, a shaft which ran up for ever' (1: 42), and in the unrevised *Suspira* he wrote that the 'terrific grief' that he experienced following the death of his sister Elizabeth 'drove a shaft for me into the worlds of death and darkness which never again closed, and through which it might be said I ascended and descended at will, according to the temper of my spirits'.[29] A variation on this is the passage in *Suspira* where he writes 'That faculty [for dreaming], in alliance with the mystery of darkness, is the one great tube through which man communicates with the shadowy' (13: 335). The 'shaft' to heaven and the 'rapture of life' is the opposite of the shaft to hell and the 'horror of life' (13: 350). All these images go back to the violent disrupture of his childhood, when he fell victim to 'rapacious grief' (1: 46).

These images of descent show that he sees life in Gothic terms: the imagery of space predominates, perhaps because his sense of space is enhanced by laudanum, but also because we are in the realm of dream, where time is expressed by space, and because his imagination is in any case visual. In *Suspira* he writes of '[life's] vast corridors, and [...] the recesses opening upon them from either hand [,] halls of tragedy or chambers of retribution' (13: 352). Those vast corridors, life's 'long suites of corridors' (13: 352), so closely echoed in Kafka's images of the lawcourts of life, and the recesses acting as a reminder of Sophia Lee's *The Recess*, by which he was so deeply moved, are part of the Gothic spatialities of life as seen by De Quincey from such a traumatically early age. The idea of 'immurement in subterraneous chambers' (1: 129) in the tale of Aladdin never left his imagination. The implication of all this is that he lived much of the time in a state of metaphorical live burial. Subterraneous chambers, chambers of retribution, chambers of the brain (its layers of images implying the idea of descent, for they are steps), chambers of the text, its reservoirs of meaning, but also its lacunae: positive or negative, all is space. At the same time, these are all images of interior space, the imagery of the mind itself.

The other, related recurrent master-image is that of the (vast Hercynian) forest, standing for the danger of getting (or being) lost in life and in the text; in *Confessions* he writes of 'the mazes of a boundless forest' (3: 416). The two images come together in a passage in Shelley's *Zastrozzi:*

On the right, the thick umbrage of the forest trees rendered undistinguishable any one who might lurk there; on the left, a frightful precipice yawned, at whose base a deafening cataract dashed with tumultuous violence

[29] Quoted from De Quincey, *Confessions of an English Opium-Eater and Other Writings,* ed. Aileen Ward (New York: New American Library, 1966), 118.

around missapen and enormous masses of rock; and beyond, a gigantic and blackened mountain reared its craggy summit to the skies.[30]

In De Quincey, the 'Hercynian forest' is a metaphor for the hermeneutic sublime in the sense of 'an encounter with a darkness encrypted within a text'.[31] De Quincey regularly gets lost in the text, losing sight of his object (or appearing to do so, for his real object is not always clear from the title or even from the context); but the forest also stands for the idea of getting lost existentially as the drug-habit, which is the engine of his Gothic, saps his will and sense of purpose. The forest, cathedral and long gallery are all related symbols of his own train of thoughts. The darkness of life is within. At this point a De Quinceyan digression is called for.

Klosterheim stands within an apparently endless forest that points to the 'vast Hercynian forest'[32] of the 1856 revision of the *Confessions*, and therefore to the idea that

> every intricate and untried path in life, where it was from the first a matter of arbitrary choice to enter upon it or avoid it, is effectively a path through a vast Hercynian forest, unexplored and unmapped, where each several turn in your advance leaves you open to new anticipations of what is next to be expected, and consequently open to altered valuations of all that has been already traversed. (*Confessions,* ed. Hayter, 182)

This passage fully justifies Baxter's remark that *Klosterheim* is 'informed by considerations of autobiography',[33] for it is above all to autobiography that the 'altered valuations of all that has already been traversed' (sc. in life's journey) refers. But the forest equally certainly carries other meanings as well. In terms of the Gothic fantasy that is *Klosterheim* it denotes the threat (both to the Klosterheimers and to the incoming travellers) that obtains at such a time of lawlessness and uncertainty, for the forest is a Gothic trope and the romance of the forest a sub-category of Gothic. That this historical meaning applies to nineteenth-century Europe is shown by De Quincey's comment in an article entitled 'Political Anticipations' (in *Blackwood's Magazine*, 28 [Nov. 1830], 720): 'Now, in 1830 [...] Europe is overshadowed, as by some great Hercynian forest, with a rank growth of anti-social desires and disorganizing principles.' The historical parallel explains, in part, why De Quincey set *Klosterheim* in the seventeenth century.

Behind this, however, lies a further meaning, for the forest also has metaphysical implications, as can be seen via a parallel with Caspar David Friedrich's *Early Snow*, painted about two years before *Klosterheim* was written. It is an archetypal Romantic 'forest picture', the viewer of which in effect stands on a snow-covered path that disappears into a forest. No human figure is present, although the artist is present as an invisible *Rückenfigur* (figure seen from behind) on the path, outside the frame, for we see the scene from eye-height. The patch of blue sky above the forest affords the viewer/wanderer a tantalizing glimpse of what may lie beyond it, that is, of the 'beyond' with all its

---

30 Shelley, *Zastrozzi and St Irvyne*, ed. Behrendt, 69.

31 Clej, 233f.

32 De Quincey's 'Hercynian forest' (the primal forests of central Germany) and the 'Hyrcanean forest' of Frederick Chamberlain's *Lucretia, or: The Robbers of the Hyrcanean Forest* (chapbook romance, London, n.d.). both refer to the forests of Germany; Chamberlain, a Gothic hack, has confused Hercynia with Hyrcanea (on the south-eastern coast of the Caspian Sea

33 Baxter, 116.

imponderable connotations and implications, but the question, as with Friedrich's *Wanderer above a Sea of Mist,* is whether it is accessible. One is put in mind of Kafka's aphorism 26: 'Es gibt ein Ziel, aber keinen Weg' (There is a goal, but no way [of reaching it]). At this point the work takes on the aspect of *Märchen* and nightmare. The fact that the snow on the path leading into the forest bears no footprints suggests that this entrance into the forest, like the comparable entrance to the Law in the talmudic *exemplum* of the Doorkeeper in Kafka's *Der Proceß,* is intended for the viewer (reader) alone. We have to follow the path to its symbolical conclusion or conclusions, for it is our path, it is there for us alone. There is – again, as later in Kafka – some doubt as to whether the path is the right path, for it is a 'Holzweg', and 'auf dem Holzweg sein' means to be on the wrong path. Viewers will find in the forest whatever they expect or fear to find there, for they are themselves the subject of the picture: the forest is our unconscious, a mirror in which we find ourselves, our hopes and fears. At the same time we need to be aware that Friedrich 'gives the observer the chance to see in his pictures something quite different from what he had himself intended, thus diverting superficial curiosity from his real intentions,'[34] in doing which he once more anticipates Kafka. *Early Snow,* then, needs the viewer's reading of it in order to be complete, as does the work of De Quincey and Kafka. The path leads round to the right, but we cannot see where it leads, if indeed it leads anywhere. Like Kafka's K., we can only go on in unjustified hope or turn back, renouncing any hidden certainty, or just wait there, nonplussed by this baffling image, like the Man from the Country in the Parable of the Doorkeeper in *Der Proceß.* The heart of the forest is dark, giving it the connotation of menace and hostility it was to have for Max Ernst. Is what is to be found there a womb-like security or a tomb-like final resting place? That the question arises is shown, graphically, by the companion piece, *Chasseur in the Forest* (1813/14), which depicts a lost French *chasseur* entering a forest in which he is to find his death (in this earlier work the symbolism is unambiguous). *Early Snow* thus acts as a model for, and a key to, the forest pictures that spanned much of Max Ernst's creative life. These typically show an impenetrable forest with a large enigmatic sun partly in view behind the forest. The ambiguity of these pictures is explained by Ernst's childhood feelings vis-à-vis forests as such, and by the more accessible symbolism of Friedrich's *Early Snow,* a marvellously ambiguous, thought-provoking work. De Quincey's subject is the subject of autobiography in much the same way that Caspar David Friedrich's is the subject of landscape.[35] Able only to write 'confessions', 'autobiographic sketches', stabs at autobiography, he is not writing autobiography; he is writing about autobiography, writing around it.

With De Quincey the forest overlaps with another important Gothic motif, that of darkness, which represents privation, loss, a sense of being cut off from meaning and, with it, the 'salvation' in which De Quincey must have believed, even if his recusant Gothic alter ego did not. He badly needs Aladdin's 'enchanted lamp' as he struggles, alone, in the 'subterraneous chamber' of his guilt and shame; but, having lost his boyhood innocence, it is not for him. The sorcerer whose murderous intent it was to leave Aladdin to die immured in that same chamber accordingly stands for De Quincey's Gothic (Satanic) self or id. Here too we are left with the image of live burial.

---

34 H. Börsch-Supan, *Caspar David Friedrich*, tr. Sarah Twohig (Munich: Prestel, 1974), 10.

35 There is much in Joseph Leo Koerner's brilliant *Caspar David Friedrich and the subject of landscape* (London: Reaktion Books, 1990, repr. 1995) to interest the theorist of Gothic.

Lever has shown that the final specimen of an opium-dream in *Confessions*, the one beginning 'The dream commenced with a music', is based on a series of echoes from *Paradise Lost,* with De Quincey dreaming from Satan's point of view. This hidden identification with Satan, convincing in the detail Lever adduces,[36] is highly revealing, for it takes account, alike, of De Quincey's view of himself, in the *Confessions* and *Suspira de profundis,* as a philosopher with an intuitive eye for the mysteries of human nature, standing nearer to the 'type of the original nature in man', and – therefore – dwelling in clouds of gloomy grandeur, seared by grief that is made all the more terrible by his inability to experience it fully, and hounded by inexpiable guilt. He thus mythologizes himself and his life, creating for himself a Gothic persona that combines the twin souls of a Faust (attracted by secret societies and forbidden knowledge) and a Mephistopheles (who led Faust to seduce a young woman named Margaret). It is at this point that his failure to write what he, more than anyone, had it in him to write about Goethe, makes sense: he cannot write about *Faust* without revealing more of himself than he is prepared to reveal. It is the same reason that made Hoffmann's *Die Elixiere des Teufels* too painful to dwell on, after he had been drawn to the novel by its title pointing to the devil's elixir to which he had all too frequent recourse.He is prepared, through a Dark Interpreter or shadow self, to shed an always deniable oblique light on his inner nature, and to be honest to that extent; but to be totally honest, to reveal all, is completely out of the question: the process would be unbearable, for he would lose his self-belief and, with it, the ability to carry on. He is, in this respect, as in so many others, in much the same situation as Kafka, who also identified with the devil, except that he lacks Kafka's humility, for what makes De Quincey tick is the pride that makes him repress his 'secret' identification with the Gothic hero, Satan.

Many critics have seen De Quincey as the author of 'a Gothic tale or two',[37] these being so many aesthetic indiscretions or potboilers. The latter word, which crops up repeatedly, makes little sense, for strictly speaking virtually all his work was written, in the appropriately Gothic metaphor, to keep the wolf from the door. It could be argued, for a variety of reasons, that all his Gothic writings (novels, tales, translations, *rifacimenti,* autobiographical dream-narratives, romances, fantasias, and even a couple of essays) were written to enable his opium-eating and to prevent starvation, but the argument is specious, for the same applies to his non-Gothic published essays and reviews. It is the self-evident fact that he could, in theory, have chosen to write potboilers of a different kind, that makes his choice of the Gothic 'masque' significant. Gothic is a 'blatantly fictional style'[38] that goes out of its way to draw attention to its (meta)fictionality and thus to its unreliability, and therefore involves the idea of the counterfeit or fake, the writer as coiner, and there is also the gothicism of 'phantom-self autobiography' and the dream-narrative. While all of this was highly attractive to De Quincey, he was probably drawn to the Gothic mode above all because he was so keenly sensitive to the labyrinthine complexity of experience and the delicate balance between illusion and reality.[39]

Not only *Klosterheim*, but all his Gothic writings are 'masques', a point demonstrated by the fact that a figure (and autobiographical persona) named Max (Maximilian) is found

---

36 Lever, 336ff.
37 Thron, in *Bicentenary Studies*, 7.
38 Hogle, 5.
39 See Snyder , *Research Studies*, 49 (1981), 130.

not only in *Klosterheim* but in *The Avenger* as well. The protagonist of each of his fictional works is an autobiographical self-projection. De Quincey invariably wears a mask of one kind or another, one of them being that of the 'scholar', but, as we have seen, the scholar-emperor's clothes wear thin when it becomes apparent that he is parading greater knowledge than he possesses or is wearing a borrowed garment.[40] His wearing of a mask, which closely parallels that of Walter Pater and George Moore (among many others), may or may not owe something to Jean Paul's use of fanciful *Einkleidungen* (*einkleiden* means both to 'clothe' and to 'couch' [in a particular form of words]); more certainly it is rooted in the psychological need to compensate for both real and imaginary shortcomings. His use of the mask is at its most elaborate in *Walladmor*, a novel written by a German writer called Wilhelm Häring, who is hiding behind the visible (dis)guise of the 'translator' and the invisible pseudonym of Willibald Alexis (*alexis* is Latin for herring), and, in that double (dis)guise, impersonating Scott. De Quincey then elaborates the whole masquerade further by hiding behind the fiction of being the 'translator' of a supposedly 'translated' work which he claims to have 'corrected', making it a double forgery in the process; he has not corrected it, just altered or further falsified it. At that distance from the text a writer can get away with murder, as De Quincey often does.

John C. Whale has noted that in De Quincey's fiction 'the Gothic mode frequently engenders a comfortable combination of sentimentality, politenesss and horror':

> In his purely scholarly writings the accurate presentation of knowledge is assumed to predominate; no obvious disjunction between the point of view of the scholar and his authoritative information can be detected. But in De Quincey's various autobiographical writings – particularly *Confessions, The English Mail-Coach,* and *Suspira de Profundis* – and in his papers on murder the combination is more complex because it is less constrained.[41]

The combination is linked to the fact that what De Quincey knew best, and what most influenced him, was female Gothic with its threatened inner space. The very fact that his autobiographical writings combine the scholarly (or, rather, what we assume to be the scholarly, for there may in fact be a 'disjunction' in the form of the reliability or otherwise of the supposedly authoritative information purveyed by the would-be creative writer, or journalist, hiding behind the mask of the scholar) and the 'Gothic', means that in this respect too the 'Gothic' is central to De Quincey's *oeuvre.* His Gothic masquerade goes way beyond 'a youthful infatuation with the Gothic'[42] which he never outgrew, for the more he seemed to outgrow surface early Gothic, the more deeply late Gothic his work became.

In the final analysis the attraction of Gothic was more psychological than literary. In clinging to what was, in historical terms, an outmoded form, he was clinging to his own past. Gothic amounted to a description of himself and his work, offering the pariah-writer a possible way forward, though it was in the nature of things a flawed enterprise from the outset. Its formulaic nature gave him the narrative certainty he needed, while the emphasis on the loss of control and lack of security that marked every day of his postlapsarian existence made it more personal than any other form of writing could ever have been. It had

---

40 Cf. the Clothes Philosophy of Carlyle, which, *qua* philosophy, owes much to Goethe.

41 In *Bicentenary Studies*, 35.

42 Clej, 24.

the advantage of enabling him to write about himself, expressing his deepest concerns, while wearing a mask: the writer as the man in the iron mask. One thinks of what Oscar Wilde was to say in 'The Critic as Artist', the very title of which points back to De Quincey: 'Man is least himself when he talks in his own person. Give him a mask and he will tell you the truth'. Or, as Dorian Gray puts it, 'To become the spectator of one's own life [...] is to escape the sufferings of life'. Gothic, as I see it, goes to the very heart of De Quincey's life and life's work. Much, and that the most interesting part, of his work is essentially Gothic. Before addressing what is arguably his most deeply Gothic work, the *Confessions*, there remains the question of his attitude towards Hoffmann's *Die Elixiere des Teufels*.

4.3. De Quincey and *The Devil's Elixir*

The main literary exponents of Gothic in Germany are Schiller (in *Der Geisterseher*), the Schiller-imitator Grosse (of *Horrid Mysteries* fame; De Quincey read his *The Dagger* without commenting on it, and it is inconceivable that he did not also read the overrated *Horrid Mysteries*),[43] Hoffmann (above all, in *Die Elixiere des Teufels*), Veit Weber, and the early Tieck. De Quincey has nothing to say of *Der Geisterseher* or of Grosse and Weber, and whether or not he knew Tieck's work at all, he seems not to have known that part of it that is closest to his own interests. Given that the editor of the volume of Bentley's Standard Novels in which the first half of *The Ghost-Seer* appeared together with Mary Shelley's *Frankenstein* noted that 'there is no work in the circle of [German] romance, in which the reader is so irresistibly impelled through the pages; or wherein his longing is more acutely excited for a solution of the mystery of the plot', it is strange that De Quincey seems to have had no thought for Schiller's narrative means, from which he could have learned so much. The fact that 'The agency, supernatural as it seems, is [...] all the effect of imposture and extensive confederacy' will have ensured his attention, makes it all the more remarkable that his only recorded comment on the novel, in the 1803 diary, was to the effect that he imagined 'a banquet or carousal of feodal magnificence – such [...] as in Schiller's Ghost Seer, in the middle of which a mysterious stranger should enter, on whose approach hangs fate and the dark roll of many woes, etc.' This is a non-comment. We have seen that he had the opportunity, while staying at Bohte's, to read other German 'Gothic' novels by Grosse, Naubert, Spieß (in particular), Vulpius, Weber, Zschokke, and others, but there is no conclusive evidence that he read any of them. Earlier he had read Grosse, *The Dagger*, Zschokke/Lewis, *The Bravo of Venice*, and Hoffmann's *Die Elixiere des Teufels*, which is a particularly interesting case. Given that what he read at Bohte's was probably historical criticism rather than Gothic fiction, his knowledge of German Gothic fiction was almost certainly far less extensive than has been supposed.

The reference in 'Gillies's German Stories' to 'Hoffmann, that should have been persecuted by kings' refers, of course, to E. T. A. Hoffmann, whose 'infernal stories we [= the De Quinceyan royal 'we', as in the opening 'We remember'] will not [read]'. The

[43] The image of 'the sea [...] paved with innumerable faces' in *Confessions* (3: 441) invites comparison with the 'grand ocean of images' in Grosse's famous novel (*Horrid Mysteries*, tr. P. Will, 2 vols [repr. London: Robert Holden, 1927], I, 142).

following references to 'a crazy German novelist' with his 'monstrous crudities' also refer to Hoffmann, whose *Die Elixiere des Teufels* (*The Devil's Elixir* [sic]),[44] translated by Gillies and published in two volumes, in Edinburgh by Blackwood and London by Cadell in 1824, barely two years earlier, prompted George Borrow to comment, in a review of the novel, that 'the rage for German horrors is again on the ascendant after an obscuration of a quarter of a century'.[45] De Quincey was evidently unable to stomach it, which is a pity, for it is not only the most Gothic work of one of the most gifted German writers of the time, but one which, if De Quincey had given it a chance, might have been expected to leave its mark on his work. As it is, it left an indelible mark on his mind. The very idea of a 'Devil's elixir' (of opium) will have made him shudder, for it was because his addiction was tantamount to a compact with the Devil, that he identified with Milton's Satan. Presumably he found too near the knuckle of his personal identity problem this Gothic early 'psychological novel' of one who is and yet is not. A reference later in his review, to Richard Holcraft's successful translation of Hoffmann's 'Das Fräulein von Scudéry' in his *Tales from the German,* shows that De Quincey was not opposed to Hoffmann, just to *Die Elixiere des Teufels*.

He must have known Gillies's translation of *Die Elixiere des Teufels, The Devil's Elixir*, although he does not mention it (or indeed the German title) as such. This is all the more remarkable in that *Blackwood's Magazine* (16 [1824], 55-67) carried a review of *The Devil's Elixir* that is said to have profoundly impressed Poe. De Quincey must have known the review, always assuming he did not have a hand in it. It was the work of J. G. Lockhart,[46] or was written by Lockhart with someone else, maybe De Quincey,[47] it may be thought, who misspells *Doppelgänger* in the same way (doppel-ganger), and whose review of *Walladmor* follows much the same pattern as that of *The Devil's Elixir.* There is, however, no reason to suppose that De Quincey was much involved, for the view of Hoffmann in the review is that of Lockhart and Scott, not De Quincey, whose view exactly corresponded to that of the reviewer in the *Literary Gazette* (August 1824, 504), who in one-paragraph disapproval commended Gillies's translation 'to those who like this class of tale', adding 'we do not'. Unless I am much mistaken, De Quincey will have found Hoffmann's Gothic masterpiece too disturbing for him to be willing to devote close attention to it. The evidence suggests, on the contrary, that he backed away from it in horror.

Much of the review consists of chunks of Gillies's translation. The main critical-descriptive part reads as follows:

> THE DEVIL'S ELIXIR is [...] our [...] favourite among the numerous works of a man of rare and singular genius [...] there is one particular idea on which this author, when in his horrible vein, is chiefly delighted to expatiate. This is the idea of [...] a *doppel-ganger;* that is to say, of a man's being haunted by the visitations of *another self – a double* of his own personal appearance [...] The superior excellence of the Devil's Elixir lies in the skill with which its author has contrived to mix up the horrible notion of the double-goer with ordinary

44 *Elixiere* is plural.

45 Quoted from Oppel, II, 8.

46 See M. C. Hildyard, *Lockhart's Literary Criticism* (Oxford: Blackwell, 1931, 154), and the letter (in Mrs Oliphant, *William Blackwood and His Sons* (2 vols, London: William Blackwood, 1897, I, 208) in which Lockhart writes to Blackwood: 'Do try to get the 'Devil's Elixir' out of Gillies's hands'.

47 Cf. Strout, 39: 'I am not sure that Miss Hildyard is right in ascribing the piece to Lockhart alone.'

> human feelings of all kinds [...] the admirable art with which the author has married dreams to realities [...] the horrors of the Monk Medardus affect our sympathies [...] because this victim of everything that is fearful in the caprices of an insane imagination is depicted [...] as living among men, women, and scenes, in all of which we cannot help recognizing a certain aspect of life and nature, and occasionally even of homeliness.

In brief, Lockhart rightly sees the work as turning on the tension between *das Heimliche* and *das Unheimliche*, the homely and the uncanny. Freud was to add that 'there is [in *The Devil's Elixir*] a doubling, dividing and interchanging of the self', and, to confound the reader further, 'the constant recurrence of the same thing'.[48]

Now in his review of *Gillies's German Stories* De Quincey went on, immediately after discussing Chamisso's *Peter Schlemihl*, to write of another case of double identity, which is in fact that of the Monk Medardus:

> Of this latter species of agency, we have an example in the *Doppelgänger*, or cases of double identity – where a man runs in a curricle, as it were, with a repetition or duplicate of himself: all the world is duped by the swindling facsimile; and even the poor injured man is not always able to distinguish between his true and spurious identity, but is hoaxed, like other people, by his own rascally counterfeit. At this point of German phantasmagoria, we begin to find ourselves no longer under any laws of creation, but amidst the anarchy of chaos: the dreams of dyspeptic lunacy can go no further [...]

When he said that the English would not read the infernal stories of Hoffmann, meaning that he himself would not, he was referring in the first instance to *Die Elixiere des Teufels*, and now, in the passage just quoted, he first sympathizes with Medardus ('the poor injured man is not able to distinguish between his true and spurious identity') to the point of identifying with him, only to make it clear that he finds this tale of radically confused identity distasteful because disturbing. Now Walter Scott, who in a letter dated 6 March 1823 asked his son Walter to send him 'Der Teüfels Elixire' (sic), was in 1827 invited by Gillies, founder of the newly-established *Foreign Quarterly Review*, to review Hoffmann. In the guise of a review article entitled 'On the Supernatural in Fictitious Composition; and particularly on the Works of Ernest Theodore William Hoffmann', which barely mentions *Die Elixiere des Teufels*, Scott wrote a lay sermon denouncing the introduction of the supernatural into fiction: 'They are not the visions of a poetical mind, they have scarcely even the seeming authenticity which the hallucinations of lunacy convey to the patient.'[49] In short, Scott regarded Hoffmann's imagination as operating 'nearly on the verge of [...] insanity'. De Quincey shared this rather 'old-fashioned' view of a writer whose 'wildness' and over-heated fancy they both deplore. In his review of Gillies, De Quincey in effect follows Scott's thesis: that German (Romantic) fantasy goes too far. Scott's view of Hoffmann corresponds to Goethe's view of Romanticism as unhealthy. De Quincey, ever conservative, follows suit, but beneath the mask of Scottian moral disapproval there lurks profound apprehension. For the man in doubt about his own identity *The Devil's Elixir* made profoundly uncomfortable reading.

He probably first read *Die Elixiere des Teufels* shortly after its publication in 1815-16, or, more likely, in 1821, when Bohte will have spoken of it as a remarkable novel of a kind

---

48 Freud, *Art and Literature*, 356.

49 See *Sir Walter Scott on Novelists and Fiction*, ed. Ioan Williams (New York: Barnes & Noble, 1968), 352. In his diary for 5 May 1827 Scott noted that he was 'working away on those wild affairs of Hoffmann'.

likely to appeal to his English lodger, who was busy writing the *Confessions*. The two works are Gothic in some similar ways. *Confessions* is not merely a Gothic novel in fancy dress, but precisely the mix of *Bildungsroman* and *Schauerroman* that is so characteristic of Jean Paul and Hoffmann, and especially of *Die Elixiere des Teufels*, in which 'the process of self-formation is organized around stations of personal terror'.[50] De Quincey is preoccupied with the occasions when his life was serially wrecked to the accompaniment of terror. Hoffmann's novel can, of course, be read in various ways, 'each of which is legitimate and none of which completely excludes the other',[51] but it involves, among other things, the 'confessions' of the self-confessed monk-murderer Medardus, who, it turns out, is not a murderer at all, written as a form of penance. *Confessions,* the writing of which must have proved a form of penance, for De Quincey was too proud to enjoy the kind of self-exposure the work involved, shows the man who, like Medardus, believed himself a murderer, in the grip of the 'Devil's elixir' of opium. Both *The Devil's Elixir* and *Confessions* (and its sister dream-texts) are studies of 'the surfacing of the subconscious'.[52]

De Quincey could not have failed to read with subjective reference a novel involving 'a profoundly traumatic, distorted version of a family romance'.[53] The novel, as a whole, was too near the knuckle for one whose experience of family was essentially traumatic, and who will have recognized that in *Die Elixiere des Teufels*, as in his own life, the 'process of self-formation is organized around stations of personal terror' involving confrontations with his phantom self or Other. It was the death of his sister Elizabeth that marked what Jean Paul calls the birth of self-consciousness, which in De Quincey's case meant not only the recognition that 'immer zwei Ich in der Stube sind' (there are always two of you present in the room at any given time) – the awareness of self as both subject and object – but the awareness of a threat to the existence of that 'Ich' (self). Phantoms there were many, but the 'crowned phantom' was Death, the 'trial' that is 'moving subterraneously in [...] all men's natures' (13: 304).

The word *Doppeltgänger* was first used by Jean Paul in *Siebenkäs*,[54] the novel from which De Quincey borrowed the pseudonym X.Y.Z (cf. *Siebenkäs*, I, ii: 'XYZ'),[55] to denote autoscopic individuals ('Leute, die sich selber sehen') of the type found throughout Romanticism, but especially in the work of two of the German writers who most impressed De Quincey, Jean Paul himself and Hoffmann. Although De Quincey has much to say of Jean Paul and little of Hoffmann, it does not by any means follow that he is reacting to them in different ways, for what he describes at some length is Jean Paul's style. Of Jean Paul's ideas and images, which in some respects overlap with those of Hoffmann, he has nothing to say. In particular, he has nothing to say of Jean Paul's play with the *Doppelgänger* or the way in which his work, like Hoffmann's *Die Elixiere des Teufels*, combines the

---

50 Andrew J. Webber, *The Doppelgänger. Double Visions in German Literature* (Oxford: Clarendon Press, 1996), 184.

51 Blackall, 230.

52 Blackall, 235.

53 Webber, 186.

54 The word was first used by Jean Paul in 1796-7 and, in anglicized form, by Lockhart and De Quincey in 1824. The *Shorter Oxford Dictionary* is therefore wrong to date the first appearance of the word to 1895.

55 X.Y.Z. was also used as a pseudonym by Emanuel Friedrich Wilhelm Ernst Follenius, who wrote the best-known continuation of Schiller's unfinished *Der Geisterseher,* which De Quincey could also have known since it appeared in 1796.

Bildungsroman and the *Schauerroman*. Nor does he have anything to say of Jean Paul's first novel and most 'Gothic' work, *Die unsichtbare Loge* (1793), with its underground secret society, the 'invisible lodge' in question.

This is all the more remarkable in that De Quincey was, from an early age, aware of a phantom self, a second identity projected from his consciousness, to say nothing of the individual's 'two selves', meaning the infant and the adult self, of which he writes in *Suspira*. This double or other was, in part, his might-have-been self, for he was haunted by ghostly might-have-beens: the person he might have been if his father and sister Elizabeth had not died early, if he had not run away from school, if he had not become addicted, if he had not run away from his viva at Oxford, if he had not run away from the philosophy of Kant and Fichte, if he had been able to deliver what he so richly promised, and so on. The 'deadly pale visage' of his second self that Medardus beholds at the end of *The Devil's Elixir* cannot but have reminded De Quincey of his own guilty (Gothic, Satanic) Other. This is the 'phantom of himself' that he encountered sitting beneath 'the gloomy archway' of some past crisis and barring any further advance as he sought to retrace the past (PW, 1: 25). This phantom self he described as 'a sham, that was either nobody at all, or oneself repeated once too often' (11: 460f.). 'Oneself repeated once too often' must have been, in a nutshell, his reaction to *The Devil's Elixir*. Elsewhere he wrote that 'Any of us would be jealous of his own duplicate; and if I had a doppel-ganger who went about personating me, copying me, and pirating me, I might [...] attempt the crime of murder upon his carcase' (11: 460f.). The Spectre of the Brocken turned out to be 'a dilated reflection of himself' (1: 52).

It is in relation to dreams that he writes of the double at most length, for it is there that the *Doppelgänger* comes into his own:

> The dreamer finds housed within himself – occupying,as it were, some separate chamber in his brain – holding, perhaps, from that station a secret and detestable commerce with his own heart – some horrid alien nature. What if it were his own nature repeated, – still, if the duality were distinctly perceptible, even that – even this mere numerical double of his own consciousness – might be a curse too mighty to be sustained. But how if the alien nature contradicts his own, fights with it, perplexes and confounds it? How, again, if not one alien nature, but two, but three, but four, but five, are introduced within what once he thought the inviolable sanctuary of himself? (13: 292)

From this it is but a small step to (or from) Medardus's traumatic experience: 'Mein eigenes Ich [...] in fremdartige Gestalten zerfließend [...] Ich konnte mich selbst nicht wiederfinden') (My very self [...] dissolving into alien shapes [...] I could not find myself again) (H 2 59). Here, surely, is the reason for De Quincey's reticence on the subject of *The Devil's Elixir*. As Webber has said, the prior (in Hoffmann's novel) 'foresees how this fantasm [...] will lure Medardus to the abyss, casting identity into nonentity'.[56] The abyss by which De Quincey was haunted is this very abyss of nonentity: 'the abyss represents the threat of identity being ungrounded, cast into a void [...] the abyss of nonentity'.[57] Nothing filled De Quincey with greater terror than the idea of his identity, problematical at the best of times, becoming permanently unstuck, like Schlemihl's shadow, which for this reason

---

[56] Webber, 186.
[57] Webber, 189.

held his attention.[58] Hoffmann's brilliant novel, which shows all too clearly what Webber calls 'the damage, the psychosomatic mutilation done to those who fall into the abyss of nonentity',[59] must have filled with horror the man whose *horror vacui* reflects his fear of being discovered – as by Charles Lloyd – to be a 'non-ens'.

Die Elixiere des Teufels, as a classic example of the *mise en abyme* in which structures or figures are reflected within one another, parallels De Quincey's whole Gothic masquerade with its endless encapsulations (Russian dolls of the mind) and reflections. The *mise en abyme*, 'token [...] at once of identity and projection into nonentity'[60] is central to De Quincey's work, the 'abyme' concretized in the 'abîme' imagery which ultimately stands for the nonentity to which all revert in death, but also for the nonentity in life of which De Quincey had a greater horror. The depth after depth of the unconscious, of which he is so aware, also involves the *mise en abyme*, as does Jean Paul's idea of the endless image as in mirrors reflecting one another. The *Doppelgänger* and its concomitant *mise en abyme*, envisioned in Piranesi's famous image of the aerial abyss,[61] typify the work of both Jean Paul and Hoffmann and of De Quincey.

58 *The Devil's Elixir* and *Peter Schlemihl* came together in a Gothic melodrama or 'musical romance' by Edward Fitzball produced in April 1829, *The Devil's Elixir; or, The Shadowless Man* (See *The Hour of One. Six Gothic Melodramas*, ed. Stephen Wischhusen [London: Gordon Fraser, 1975]).

59 Webber, 189.

60 Webber, 24.

61 For the classicist 'abyss' denotes a world of endless depth or height.

5. Dream-Texts

The three linked texts discussed in this chapter are re-worked fragments of autobiography, with emphasis on the (Gothic) dream element, of which Margaret Drabble, taking a magisterial view, has written that De Quincey's great, though never completed, achievement was

> his psychological study of the faculty of dreaming in 'Suspira de Profundis', and 'The English Mail Coach', in which he traced – twenty-five years before Freud was born – how childhood experiences and sufferings are crystallized in dreams into symbols which can form and educate the dreamer's personality, and can also give birth to [...] poetry [and] 'impassioned prose'.[1]

In the general preface to the Masson edition of his works, De Quincey writes of 'the perilous difficulty besieging all attempts to clothe in words the visionary scenes derived from the world of dreams' (1: 14), the 'phantasmagoria' of which well up out of the 'great deeps of life' (13: 315, cf. 'the noiseless deeps of the Infinite', 13: 344), a 'horrid chasm, a ravine, a shaft' (8: 20f.) in the mind and are caught by 'that mysterious *camera obscura*, the sleeping mind' (13: 335).

Gothic, as I have written elsewhere,[2] is essentially a dream literature, its hallmark the realized nightmare. The Inquisition, which features in many Gothic nightmares, was so concerned about the heresies expressed in dreams, that it sought to control them, and the literary Gothic Revival was preceded and accompanied by a preoccupation with dreams in general and the nightmare in particular. J. Bond published *An Essay on the Incubus, or Nightmare* in 1753 (the year of Smollett's in some respects proto-Gothic *The Adventures of Ferdinand Count Fathom*), and Adam Friedrich Wilhelm Saalfeld's *A Philosophical Discourse on the Nature of Dreams* (1764) came out, appropriately, in the same year as *The Castle of Otranto*, which was said to be based on 'the very imperfect recollection of a dream'. De Quincey shows no awareness of either study. Saalfeld's work prepared the way for Fuseli's 'The Nightmare' (1781, parodied in 1794 in Richard Newton's 'A Night Mare'), which in turn opened up the way for further dreams in art, including Fuseli's own 'An Incubus Leaving Two Sleeping Girls' (*c.* 1793), in which the iconography of the dream is tinged with eroticism. Shelley wrote a related horror tale, 'The Nightmare', unfortunately lost, which he had wanted Fuseli to illustrate.

Writing of the 'modern novel' in 1800, Sade argued that it was necessary to 'call hell to the rescue [...] and to find in the world of nightmare images adequate to the history of man in this Iron Age of ours'.[3] More than adequate nightmare images were subsequently found by Goya, who did indeed 'call hell to the rescue' when he produced his terrible *Black*

---

1 *The Oxford Companion to English Literature*, ed. Margaret Drabble, 5th edn (Oxford: Oxford University Press, 1985), 268.

2 Bridgwater, *Kafka, Gothic and Fairytale*, 58-61.

3 I quote the paraphrase by Leslie A. Fiedler (*Love and Death in the American Novel*, 136) as being more to my point than a literal translation.

Paintings at the end of the Gothic period proper, in the early 1820s. If anything is 'enhorrored' (Shelley's word), it is those paintings. Fiedler, quoting Sade, commented that 'The key words are „nightmare“ and „hell“, revealing how consciously [...] some gothic writers turned to the night side of life, the irrational world of sleep, for themes and symbols appropriate to the terrors bred by the Age of Reason,'[4] and there is a further point, also admirably made by Fiedler:

> Implicit in the gothic novel from the beginning is a final way of redeeming it that is precisely opposite in its implications to the device of the explained supernatural, a way of proving not that its terror is less true than it seems but more true. There *is* a place in men's lives where pictures [...] bleed, ghosts gibber and shriek, maidens run forever through mysterious landscapes from nameless foes; that place is, of course, the world of dreams and [...] the repressed guilts and fears that motivate them. This world the dogmatic optimism and shallow psychology of the Age of Reason had denied; and yet this world it is the final, perhaps the essential, purpose of the gothic romance to assert.[5]

Fiedler rightly saw symbolic fiction, in which character, setting and incident are true 'not in their own right, but as they symbolize in outward terms an inward reality'[6] as coming to a climax in Kafka, who is compared with De Quincey in my final chapter.

Such fiction originated in the period of literary High Gothic, which saw the appearance, in 1814, of an important work, Gotthilf Heinrich von Schubert's *Die Symbolik des Traumes*, in which it was argued that the dreamer is confronted by certain qualities or actions in the guise of persons and of ideas in the form of pictorial images; that dreams take metaphors literally, work by means of association of ideas, and tend to invert their meaning; and that in 'Halbschlummer' (Freud's 'hypnagogic state', the state with which both De Quincey and Kafka were so familiar), the two different, alternative languages of waking and sleep are liable to intermingle. For good measure, there is much talk of the 'shadow-side of the self', thus anticipating one of Jung's most important ideas as well as a number of Freud's. Schubert regarded the symbolic language of dreams as superior in expressivity to the language of waking.[7] It is surprising, given his scholarly pose, remarkably wide knowledge of German historical criticism, and interest in his own interior life, to say nothing of the fact that Coleridge had, back in 1809, suggested that he should undertake a survey of scientific publications on psychology, that De Quincey does not refer to Schubert's *Die Symbolik des Traumes*, which he very likely read at Bohte's in 1821, and that he seems unaware of the series of works bearing the title *De Incubo* published in Germany in the second quarter of the nineteenth century (S. Simpson, 1825; H. J. Wolter, 1827; J. C. F. Adler, 1827; F. Dony (1829); C. D. F. Hainlin, 1830; J. Kutsche, 1842).[8] His ignorance or silence is remarkable, given the depth of his interest in his own dreams and the fact that J. H. Bohte thought

---

4 Fiedler, 136. The concept of the 'night-side' of life entered the English language in 1848 with Catherine Crowe's *The Night-Side of Nature*, which was inspired by Gotthilf Heinrich von Schubert's *Ansichten von der Nachtseite der Naturwissenschaft* of 1808. De Quincey appeared between the same covers as Mrs Crowe in *Glasgow Athenœum Album* (1848).

5 Fiedler, 140.

6 Fiedler, 141.

7 See Eric A. Blackall, *The Novels of the German Romantics* (Ithaca & London: Cornell University Press, 1983), 148ff. That is why Hoffmann regarded artistic activity as a superior form of dream.

8 For details of these and earlier works on the same subject, see Ernest Jones, *Nightmare, Witches and Devils* (New York: Norton, n.d.), 14.

highly enough of Schubert's book to stock it; one can only wonder whether De Quincey was 'afraid' of psychology. Be this as it may, there is a limit to the extent to which it is possible to interpret a writer's silences.

Nor, so far as one can tell, was he aware of Arthur Schopenhauer's astutely provocative romantic/gothic question in 1818: 'We have dreams, [but] may not our whole life be a dream? Or, more exactly: is there any sure way of distinguishing between dreams and reality, between phantasms and real objects?'[9] Schopenhauer (1788-1860), most genial and literary of philosophers, is the philosopher of Gothic as Goya (1746-1828) is its illustrator. The alternative, virtual reality of the dream is basic to Gothic. Fiedler's statement that 'The flight of the gothic heroine into a dark region of make-believe [...] along the shadowy corridors of the haunted castle, which is to say, through a world of ancestral and infantile fears projected in dreams'[10] puts the reader in mind of Kafka's *Der Proceß* and *Das Schloß,* but also of his *Der Verschollene*, in which Karl Rossmann plays the reverse-gender part of Gothic heroine against the theatrical backdrop of an extraordinary Gothic mansion. There is, of course, much more to Gothic than a psychological reading, however brilliant, but Fiedler's analysis cannot be dismissed as an outdated flight of fancy.

The somewhat literary picture of the nightmare painted by R. Macnish in his *The Philosophy of Sleep* (1834) was clearly influenced by nightmare experiences as described in the Gothic novel with which he grew up, and to which he refers:

> If [...] we have been engaged in the perusal of such works as 'The Monk', 'The Mysteries of Udolpho', or 'Satan's Invisible World Discovered', and if an attack of night-mare should supervene, it will be exaggerated into sevenfold horror by the spectral phantoms with which our minds have been thereby filled.[11]

What makes this doubly interesting is the fact that De Quincey, whose mind was stocked with nightmare scenes from Gothic novels and tales, must have known Robert Macnish (1802-1837), who contributed what has been called his one masterpiece in fiction ('a seminal tale of the fantastic') 'The Metempsychosis', to *Blackwood's Magazine* in 1826. Indeed, Macnish even appears, fleetingly, as one of *Blackwood's* 'German' authors, when his 'The Barber of Göttingen' (signed A Modern Pythagorean) appeared in *Blackwood's Magazine* (20 [Oct. 1826], 604-610); in Blackwood's Contributors' Book, 'The Barber of Göttingen, Robert Macnish' is followed by 'Gillies's German Stories, Thomas De Quincey'. Macnish's most significant work, *The Philosophy of Sleep*, dates from 1830. His use of the terms 'nightmare' and 'daymare' may well reflect his reading of *Confessions* (which first appeared in the *London Magazine* in 1821), in which De Quincey wrote of 'day-dreams or night-dreams'. Macnish quotes the 'English Opium-Eater' on how the sense of space and time is affected in dreams:

> The sense of space and, in the end, the *sense of time* were both powerfully affected. Buildings, landscapes, &c., were exhibited in proportions so vast as the bodily eye is not fitted to receive. Space swelled, and was amplified to an extent of unutterable infinity. This, however, did not disturb me so much as the expansion of

9 Schopenhauer, *The World as Will and Idea*, tr. R. B. Haldane & J. Kemp (London: Kegan Paul, Trench, Trübner, n.d.), I, 20.

10 Fiedler, 128.

11 Macnish, 137.

> time. I sometimes seemed to have lived for seventy or a hundred years in one night; nay, sometimes had feelings representative of a millenium passed in that time, or [...] of a duration far beyond the limits of any human experience.[12]

Referring to De Quincey, together with Hoffmann and 'Polydori' (sic),[13] he uses the term 'daymare' to describe the waking nightmare that was to form the basis of Kafka's work, which represents the most consistent attempt to make literary texts speak the language of the dream. He must have been known to De Quincey.

The 'natural and mighty palimpsest' of the brain (cf. the Jungian collective unconscious) holds 'everlasting layers of ideas, images, feelings' corresponding to the endless strata of leaves shed by 'aboriginal forests' (13: 346, 348), and, more generally, to the detritus of millenia that builds up on the surface of the earth and the floor of the ocean: 'Everlasting layers of ideas, images, feelings, have fallen upon your brain softly as light. Each succession has seemed to bury all that went before. And yet, in reality, not one has been extinguished.' Fundamental is the spatial geometry of Gothic in which Piranesi's aerial trap and the 'horrid' chasm (deep as oblivion [13: 348], deep as death), seemingly reverse images one of the other, their equivalent on the vertical level endless corridors, are in truth both images of falling, and therefore of De Quincey's own 'aboriginal fall'. Caverns are associated with the cavern-dwelling chthonic architect-god Trophonios (3: 394), but also with the 'dreadful mouth of Acheron' (3: 347) and its watery equivalent, the maelstrom; they lead into the interior darkness, to the unconscious underworld of hidden fears, to personal hells ('the caves of hell', 3: 446). The marine and submarine imagery is remarkable. De Quincey writes in *Suspira* that 'A dark ocean would seem the total expanse of life from the first; but far darker and more appalling would seem that inferior and second chamber of the ocean which called him away for ever' (3: 351), and the Gothic wreck/shipwreck imagery of the German *Walladmor*, which De Quincey proceeds to develop, is part of a recurrent pattern of ruination; he even writes of 'wrecks of forgotten delirium' (3: 366).

To his own 'unpardonable folly' he traces 'many ruins' (3: 231), so that 'ruin' has a similar connotation to 'wreck; he writes, with subjective reference, of the wreck of a life and the wreck of a person (3: 356). Savannah-la-Mar is a submarine Pompeii, a complete, negative version of life lost in the 'noiseless deeps of the Infinite'. Typically, he imagines 'incoherent libraries [of shipwrecked books] on the floors of the hungry sea', and even writes of 'that vast submarine Bodleian, which stands in far less risk from fire than the insolent Bodleian of the upper world' (3: 341). To the classicist, the world of the ocean floor is the lower world of hell, as, too, is 'the boundless ocean of London' (3: 338). Most memorable is the image of a sea 'paved with innumerable faces' (3:441). The faces of the fluctuating crowds on the streets of London among which he sought in vain for Ann's face were transformed by the dream-work or the day-dreaming mind into this extraordinary image, generated by the sense of loss that Gothic embodies. He writes of the 'tyranny of the human face' (3: 441), for in later years the human face tyrannized over his dreams (3: 394).

Central is the image of the cave, cavern and abyss, a fact that serves as a reminder that Gothic goes back not just to the sixteenth century, but to the ancient world. Edith Birkhead

---

12 Macnish, 60.

13 Macnish, 94, 95, 155.

wrote of the novel *Babylonica* by the Greek second-century neoplatonist Iamblikhos as anticipating the Gothic novel, and rightly added that a Latin novel of the same time, Apuleius's *The Golden Ass*, included incidents as 'horrid' as any of those devised by the writers of Gothic romance. De Quincey's cave or cavern image has models in the ancient Greek literature to which he was so attached, in the shape of Plato's cave, Empedocles' grotto, Trophonios' cave, and so on. Plato pictures humans dwelling in a sort of subterranean cave or cavern (cf. the 'subterraneous chamber' of the Tale of Aladdin), his cave-metaphor serving to illustrate the limits of human knowledge; here is Holberg's starting-point for his *Journey to the World Under-Ground.* Juan's cave in De Quincey's *The Peasant of Portugal* is based on the cave of Trophonios, which, situated in the depths of the woods, and approached from above by a ladder, opened into a cold, black, yawning chasm. Trophonios is a Cain-figure with whom De Quincey identifies. In Greek and Latin 'abyss' indicates a world of endless depth or height, thus underlining the fact that the aerial space of Piranesi's prison-images can be read as an upside-down cavern, just as the cavern itself is equivalent to what German calls a *Satansburg*, meaning an inverted (underground) castle, with the symbolism inverted, so that it is a Devil's Castle. More generally the abyss represents sleep, death (the abyss of death and [...] its secrets, 3: 347), the infernal, and the unfathomable.

The works discussed in this chapter belong to Gothic in the sense that it 'opened up to fiction the realm of the irrational and of the perverse impulses and nightmarish terrors that lie beneath the surface of the civilized mind'.[14] In symbolical terms, all De Quincey's major symbols – the cavern, chasm/abyss, forest, ocean – represent the unconscious, so that the hidden terrors of the forest represent fear of what the unconscious may reveal. Caverns, which are (via's Plato's cave-metaphor) prison-images, have also been said to symbolize 'the locale of identity formation'.[15] The very ubiquity of the cavern-image suggests that De Quincey was continually probing the involutions of his mind, continually searching for his real identity, which he identified with his lost past self, continually trying to make sense of his life and its hidden depths.

In his work, recesses, nooks, cells and crypts (13: 357) are everywhere in evidence, as are their metaphorical counterparts of hidden, encrypted meanings, and of chasms in the sense of 'disfigurations of my little work' (3: 226). Since his most vivid and harrowing dreams are associated with a profound sense of guilt (at surviving Elizabeth, at surviving Ann, at surviving the wife he neglected), the 'chancery of dreams' (3: 395) can be compared to Kant's tribunal of conscience, Kafka's experience showing that opium is not needed to reveal the working of this inner chancery or tribunal. It is when he is describing the sleep (dreams) of the guilty that Robert Macnish writes of the 'abyss of slumber' and the sleeper 'visiting the depths of his spirit', in either case using a metaphor that fits into the pattern of De Quincey's Gothic oneiric imagery:

> The power of imagination is perhaps never so vividly displayed, as in those dreams which haunt the guilty mind. When any crime of an infamous character has been perpetrated, and when the person is not so utterly hardened as to be insensible of his iniquity, the wide storehouse of retributive vengeance is opened up, and its appalling horrors poured upon him [...] from the abyss of slumber they start forth, as the vampyres from their

---

14 M. H. Abrams, *A Glossary of Literary Terms,* 7th edn (Orlando, FL: Harcourt Brace, 1999), 111.

15 *The Penguin Dictionary of Symbols*, ed. Jean Chevalier & Alain Gheerbrant (London: Penguin, 1996), 171.

sepulchres, and hover around him like the furies that pursued the footsteps of Orestes [...] in the silence of the night, the 'still small voice' is heard like an echo from the tomb; then a crowd of doleful remembrances rush in upon the criminal, no longer to be debarred from visiting the depths of his spirit; and when dreams succeed to such broken and miserable repose, it is only to aggravate his previous horrors, and present them in a character of still more overwhelming dread.'[16]

The truth of this is illustrated by the passages of vivid hypnagogic imagery in De Quincey's work, but what makes Macnish's passage even more interesting is the fact that when he goes on to quote a passage from another writer in support of his view, what he quotes (without naming him) is De Quincey's picture of Caligula as drawn by Suetonius (6: 313, first in *Blackwood's*, 33 [1833], 59). It is because his own dreams are not so very different that De Quincey quotes Suetonius with such approval: his own inner life, the world of his imagination and dreams, is like Caligula's palace, 'radiant with purple and gold, but murder everywhere lurking beneath flowers.' The difference is that the 'murders' on De Quincey's mind are imaginary ones.

Alina Clej is right to emphasize, in a particularly interesting chapter,[17] that De Quincey is concerned to re-enact, rather than 'interpret', his dreams. Writing these dream-texts is a matter of 'back-translation' *(Rückübersetzung)*, of substituting words for the pictorial images ('symbols' he calls them) used by the dream-work to express the latent dream-thoughts. His dream-life is in essence a *recherche du temps perdu*. He takes over from Jean Paul the definition of sleep as 'the ante-chamber of the grave' (11: 288).

5.1. *Confessions of an English Opium-Eater* (1822)

The *Confessions of an English Opium-Eate*r, republished in book form in 1822, is, as the title indicates, a text of many kinds. Generally taken to echo Rousseau's *Confessions*, a retrospective exercise in self-analysis and self-justification, De Quincey's title also recalls the *Confessions of William Henry Ireland* (1805) in which Ireland – no mean Gothic novelist – confessed to having fabricated works purporting to be by Shakespeare. It is also a typical Gothic title, recalling Charlotte Dacre's *Confessions of the Nun of St Omer* (1805) and the eight other novels with titles beginning with *Confessions* listed in Montague Summers' *Gothic Bibliography*; nearer to home there is R. P. Gillies's *The Confessions of Sir Henry Longueville* (1814). These are all highly appropriate associations. The original Preface speaks of 'spontaneous and extra-judicial confessions', but the spontaneity of the *Urtext* was lost in the rewriting. De Quincey's dislike of the notion of textual closure, of the idea of a text, coffin-like, being 'closed and sealed inexorably' (3: 221), which he regarded as a form of premature death or live burial, led him to spoil *Confessions* and *Suspira* in the rewriting, which left the dreams, the imaginative high-points, awash in a sea of relatively mundane autobiography. *The Daughter of Lebanon,* evidently intended as a visionary transfiguration or apotheosis of Ann the Outcast, who figures in it as the Magdalen of Lebanon, makes one wonder whether it is not what he accused Coleridge of producing, 'a fabrication of his own dreams' (3: 228), those 'secret inscriptions on the mind' (3: 432), the

---

16 Robert Macnish, *The Philosophy of Sleep*, 2nd edn (Glasgow: W. R. M' Phun, 1834), 103, 104.

17 Clej, ch. 5.

'immediate and proximate cause of shadowy terrors that settled and brooded over his whole waking life' (3: 433), on which this chapter focuses. Every night he 'seemed [...] to descend into chasms' (3: 435); he writes of the 'monstrous scenery' (3: 443) of his Oriental dreams, in which the murderous subterraneous chamber of the Tale of Aladdin was activated. Space, in particular, was 'amplified to an extent of unutterable self-repeating infinity' (3: 345), the inescapable effect of which, like that of 'Piranesi's dreams', was gothically claustrophobic. Ultimately it produces the vision of past life, seen before imminent death as a pattern of simultaneous (spatial) images (see 13: 347f.), but also, by implication, as a pattern of reiterated self-betrayal.

The opening of *Confessions* is far from spontaneous and far from transparent. Implicitly identifying with 'demireps, adventurers, [and] swindlers' (3: 210), he says 'my self-accusation does not amount to a confession of guilt', only to add '[but] if it did'. He says 'Guilt I do not acknowledge', only to add 'and, if I did' (3: 210f.). These caveats make it impossible to avoid the conclusion that *Confessions of an English Opium-Eater* is, in the first instance, precisely what it claims not to be, a confession of guilt, which the word confession inescapably implies. He may speak of 'opium-eating' as involving a 'fascinating enthralment' (3: 211), but the enthralment is more in evidence than the fascination. There is no such ambiguity when it comes to confessing 'this fatal error in my life' at the age of sixteen (3: 271) in the form of running away from school, 'that ruin [...] which threw me out a homeless vagrant upon the earth before I had accomplished my seventeenth year' (3: 272). Over the text, like some mighty avenger-god peering into the very recesses of his dreams, where even a Pariah might look for rest (3: 242), stands 'that mighty phantom [of] a life-long repentence' (3: 232). It is his self-perception as the victim of divine retribution that makes him dwell on the idea of revenge.

Beneath its pseudo-autobiographical and proto-Freudian masks *Confessions* is a kind of Gothic novel. Karen M. Lever has demonstrated the fictionality of the narrator, relating him to the Gothic (Byronic, Satanic) hero, and more recently Jan B. Gordon has related De Quincey's imagery, technique, and characterization in *Confessions* to the Gothic novel.[18] Margaret Russett has written of the motifs of Gothic fiction in *Confessions* as including 'the flight from oppression [,] the pursuit „into the central darkness"[and] the tenancy of a „large unoccupied house," with its „Blue-beard room" (3: 357f.) full of law parchments [which Ann believed to be permanently haunted]',[19] and there are many more Gothic images in that same section of the text ('the brink of a precipice', 'horror recoiling from that unfathomed abyss in London', 'wild it was beyond all description, and dark as „the inside of a wolf's throat",' 'fatally tortuous paths', and so forth. London is seen as a hell swallowing alive those who approach its dreadful maws. Here, borrowed from the classical world,[20] is the maelstrom that Poe was to take from De Quincey, which persists to this day in the form of the Bermuda Triangle.

---

18 Karen M. Lever, 'De Quincey as Gothic Hero: A Perspective on *Confessions of an English Opium-Eater* and *Suspira de Profundis', Texas Studies in Literature and Language*, 21 (1979), 332-46 ; Jan B. Gordon in *Bicentenary Studies*, 239-262.

19 Russett, 101.

20 Cf. the monster whale in Lucian, the prototype of that in Melville's *Moby Dick*, that roams the ocean swallowing ships whole.

The imaginary journey (most often a voyage, as in Lucian, the *Arabian Nights,* Swift, Holberg, and Munchausen), by which De Quincey was fascinated, provided him with a model which he proceeded to conceptualize and internalize in his imaginative work. Frank, summarizing Lever, has rightly argued that 'Visions of self-destruction and recreation induced during the opium trance link De Quincey's interior voyagers to the deep questions of Gothic literature'.[21] In particular, the late Gothic imagery of descent (into the subconscious) and ascent (into convoluted hyper-consciousness) represents an internalization of the early Gothic motif of incarceration and liberation. In short, *Confessions of an English Opium-Eater* is important for its elaborate use of Gothic convention on several different levels and definitions, for its profound influence on the development of the autobiographical novel, and for its place, alongside G. H. Schubert's *Die Symbolik des Traumes* (1814), Coleridge's note on the 'Language of Dreams',[22] and Robert Macnish's *The Philosophy of Sleep* (in which the *Confessions* is cited), in the history of dream theory. If language as such involves a form of live burial, the formal language of the dream represents the raising of the dead, who are then buried anew as the dream's pictorial images ('symbols' in De Quincey's terminology) are verbalized.

Like much Gothic fiction, *Confessions* 'strives to speak the unspeakable language of the dream',[23] the unspeakable, with the uncanny, marking the threshold of the Gothic and with it the idea of a forbidden liminality:

> The *Confessions* demands attention because of its thematic and formal affinities with the gothic and autobiographical novel [...] the giving of the dream account is not only a part of the recovery from an illness but also a literal act of authorship – the production of a text. Beneath the manifest plot of these novels, then, is another plot – a plot of 'recovery' or 'reconstruction' that determines the narrative structure of the texts and reveals the attitudes that the narrators take toward the materials they dream and write about [...] of central concern [...] is the attempt to discover an appropriate language with which to represent and master the unsettling experience of their dreams.[24]

There is a fundamental connexion between the Gothic imagination and dreams, both of which produce, from the unconscious, visual material that needs to be translated from images into words before it can become part of a text. De Quincey, like Kafka after him, was much concerned with this process of verbalization. Ronald R. Thomas has argued that, as Freud said of Wilhelm Jensen's *Gradiva,* Gothic novels were 'working over the same material' that he would theorize; they were simply using a 'different method' to express it. De Quincey's work is dreamlike not least in that in it significance is displaced, so that the most significant passages appear to be digressions.

If Gothic 'opened up to fiction the realm of the irrational and of the perverse impulses and nightmarish terrors that lie beneath the orderly surface of the civilized mind',[25] revealing what Fiedler calls the 'world of ancestral and infantile fears projected in

---

21 I quote F. S. Frank's summary, from his *Guide to the Gothic* (Metuchen N. J. & London: The Scarecrow Press, 1984), 329f.

22 Coleridge, *Notebooks,* III, 4409.

23 Ronald R. Thomas, *Dreams of Authority: Freud and the Fictions of the Unconscious* (Ithaca & London: Cornell University Press, 1990), 99.

24 Thomas, 81.

25 Abrams, 111.

dreams',[26] there could not be a better example of Gothic than the nightmare visions of De Quincey's *Confessions*. What is Gothic there is not merely the use of archetypal imagery, situations and locations, but the inherent instability of the text that is thus generated, its meaning indeterminate, in other words, the way in which reconstruction and deconstruction go hand in hand. The crucial difference between *Confessions* and the autobiographic sketches that shadow and link some of the material, is the fact that the fictionalization of the original material in *Confessions* involves a simultaneous gothification.

De Quincey's subject is the operation of the subconscious and its obsessive 'involutes', but these 'involutes' are part of a pattern of convulutes, for 'gothic', which also means 'baroque', involves the disjointed, serpentine language that Worringer associates with Gothic form.[27] Even his language is, in these dream-narratives (*Confesssions, Suspira, Mail-Coach*), gothically disjointed, writhing like the *forma serpentinata* of the early 16th century (the original Gothic period in the modern sense) as his sentences stretch along the edge of meaning, almost beyond meaning, thereby generating almost as much darkness and uncertainty as light and certainty. This stretching towards surreality is transgressive in that its aim is to reveal what nature chooses to conceal in order not to overburden consciousness. *Confessions,* as I read it, is not primarily about laudanum and its effects, but about the state, described in so many Gothic novels, to which the human mind is reduced under pressure. The chronic passion of anxiety ('deep-seated anxiety and gloomy melancholy') and perpetual sense of abandonment, betrayal and 'blank treachery' are quintessentially Gothic, as is De Quincey's obsession with mystery, riddles, secret societies, orders of assassins, 'household hieroglyphics', and 'dreadful symbolic meanings', that reflects the fact that he grew up, in a period of great historical change, with the 'romantic terrror' of the idea of a universal conspiracy against society.

What we have in De Quincey's 'Gothic' texts, and especially in the quasi-autobiographical dream-texts, is a typical late-Romantic internalization of Gothic, what Poe called 'terror of the soul'.[28] 'The subjects he approached with the most characteristic sympathy', Sedgwick wrote, 'were certain versions of a privation and immobilization: dreams and trances, submergence under a massive space, the unspeakable'.[29] This is true, of course, but the space is internalized, so that what is in question is submergence, while paralysed, under a massive burden of guilt. As he explores 'the topography of depth and interiority',[30] the 'chasms and sunless abysses, depths below depths, from which it seemed hopeless that he could ever reascend' of the *Confessions* threaten him, via claustrophobia and fear, with extinction, the spectre of literal non-entity, for at the bottom of the abyss, its literal bottom line, is death. Gothic convention thus allows him to 'simulate a Romantic interiority through a process of metonymic displacement. The intricate plot line and labyrinthine architecture of the Gothic novel are used to construct an image of psychological complexity'.[31]

---

26 Fiedler, *Love and Death in the American Novel*, 128.

27 See Wilhelm Worringer, *Form in Gothic*, tr. & ed. Herbert Read (London: Putnam's, 1927).

28 E. A. Poe, *The Collected Works of Edgar Allan Poe*, ed. Thomas Ollive Mabbott, 3 vols Cambridge, Mass.: Harvard University Press, 1969), II, 473.

29 Sedgwick, 17.

30 Sedgwick, 38.

31 Clej, 234.

Though not exactly a Gothic novel, *Confessions* is haunted by the Gothic even as the narrator is haunted by the phantasmagoric figure of Ann; the loss first of Elizabeth, and then Ann, the central event of *Confessions*, behind which stretch all the other deaths he felt guilty for surviving, is there 'split into a thousand fantastic variations' (3: 444). It is, however, the city of London as mirrored in the structure of the text that is most Gothic:

> the city of London, with its dark passages and labyrinthine streets, is constructed by De Quincey in a knowingly Gothic fashion; the convolutions of which, in turn, inform the often equally labyrinthine structure of the *Confessions*' narrative, with its constant deferrrals and displacements of information, its promises of narrative revelations which never arrive, and its passages which, all too often, lead frustratingly nowhere.[32]

To find a similar construction of city and text one would have to turn to the Old City of Prague as embodied in Kafka's *Der Proceß*. The *Confessions* were to have had a third and fourth part, entitled 'The Pariah Worlds' and 'The Kingdom of Darkness' respectively, that would have underlined the Gothic nature of this dream realm.

5.2. *Suspira de Profundis* (1845-)

The vast corridors, halls of tragedy and chambers of retribution, of which De Quincey writes in *Suspira de Profundis,* constitute the house of his Gothic self; they are all 'chambers of a human brain' (13: 335), of the Gothic interior space in which he has his being:

> Great is the mystery of Space, greater is the mystery of Time. Either mystery grows upon man as man himself grows; and either seems to be a function of the godlike which is in man. In reality, the depths and the heights which are in man, the depths by which he searches, the heights by which he aspires, are but projected and made objective externally in the three dimensions of space which are outside of him. He trembles at the abyss into which his bodily eyes look down, or look up; not knowing that abyss to be, not always consciously suspecting it to be, but by an instinct written in his prophetic heart feeling it to be, boding it to be, fearing it to be, and sometimes hoping it to be, the mirror to a mightier abyss that will one day be expanded in himself. (8: 15)

In his work space looms larger than time, what counts being space in its fourth, interior dimension.

It is typical of him that a 'striking incident in a modern novel' going back to his early Gothic reading is hidden away in *Suspira de Profundis*, as an illustration of the 'situation of one escaping by some refluent current from the maelstrom roaring for him in the distance, who suddenly finds that this current is but an eddy wheeling round upon the same maelstrom':

> A lady-abbess of a convent, herself suspected of Protestant leanings, and in that way already disarmed of all effectual power, finds one of her own nuns (whom she knows to be innocent) accused of an offence leading to the most terrific of punishments. The nun will be immured alive if she is found guilty; and there is no chance that she will not, – for the evidence against her is strong, unless something were made known that cannot be made known, and the judges are hostile. All follows in the order of the reader's fears. The witnesses depose; the evidence is without effectual contradiction; the conviction is declared; the judgment is delivered; nothing

[32] Julian Wolfreys, in *Victorian Gothic*, ed. Robbins & Wolfreys, xii.

remains but to see the execution done. At this crisis, the abbess, alarmed too late for effectual interposition, considers with herself that, according to the regular forms, there will be one single night open, during which the prisoner cannot be withdrawn from her own separate jurisdiction. This one night, therefore, she will use, at any hazard to herself, for the salvation of her friend. At midnight, when all is hushed in the convent, the lady traverses the passages which lead to the cells of prisoners. She bears a master-key under her professional habit. As this will open every door in every corridor, already, by anticipation, she feels the luxury of holding her emancipated friend within her arms. Suddenly she has reached the door; she descries a dusky object; she raises her lamp; and, ranged within the recess of the entrance, she beholds the funeral banner of the holy office, and the black robes of its inexorable officials. (3: 337f.)

Nothing shows more clearly than this story just how deeply De Quincey's inner life is rooted in the Gothic, for this quintessentially Gothic tale illustrating the idea that all is lost refers to the death of Elizabeth and thus to the 'horror of life' experienced in childhood.

The dream-city of Savannah-la-Mar (a Jamaican port submerged by a tidal wave in 1780, but the fact is less important than the symbolism) is a submarine Pompeii and as such a city of the dead seen in another 'vision of sudden death'; it prefigures the Mighty Minster of *The English Mail-Coach,* as do the 'towering gates of ingress' (13: 337).

In the final section of *Suspira de Profundis*, 'Levana and Our Ladies of Sorrow', De Quincey returns to the 'dream' in the sense of the visionary experience he had experienced in 1804, under the influence of opium. It is a repressed memory activated and released by the drug as he descends to depth below depth of his unconscious:

> Once again the elder nurse, but now dilated to colossal proportions, stood as upon some Grecian stage with her oplifted hand, and [...] smote me senseless to the ground. Again I am in the chamber with my sister's corpse [...] Dream forms itself mysteriously within dream (1: 49f.)

This terrible woman, the very embodiment the 'ancestral and infantile fears' of Gothic, whose colossal proportions indicate the degree of terror she inspired in the young Thomas, who banished the memory of her action until opium prised it from the unconscious, achieves an undeserved mythical status in 'Levana and Our Ladies of Sorrow'. The dream represents a literalization of the way in which the nursery maid in question smote him as with a thunderbolt with the news that Elizabeth was dying, which shattered his whole childhood illusion as to the nature of life. In the dream his feeling of guilt for having kissed 'the lips that I should kiss no more' has lent the elder nurse those 'colossal proportions' of Gothic nightmare.

In *Suspira* the nurse is transmogrified into Levana, the goddesss who 'controls the education of the nursery' (13: 362), whom De Quincey knew from *Levana oder Erziehungslehre* (1807),[33] in which Jean Paul pays tribute to Rousseau's *Emile*: 'Oftentimes at Oxford I saw Levana in my dreams.' At that time De Quincey was reading Jean Paul's *Levana*, which he probably borrowed from Schwartzburg shortly after publication. In it the 'motherly goddess who was formerly entreated to give a father's heart to fathers', appears in her classical role. By 1844, when he began exploring, in *Suspira de Profundis*, the 'metamorphoses whereby experiences of the outer life became transformed into the matter of dream' (L 353), Levana had become a 'macabre parody'[34] of Jean Paul's motherly

---

33 English translation *Levana; or, The Doctrine of Education* (London: Bell, 1901), 75 (for quotations).

34 See Black, 49f.

goddess. De Quincey cannot have failed to be struck, in his final year at Oxford, by Jean Paul's words a few lines later to the effect that 'The demands of the state or of learning [...] rob the child of half its father'; death, he will have reflected, had already robbed him of the other half. In 'Levana and Our Ladies of Sorrows' the 'elder nurse' appears as Levana, her *terribilità* being displaced onto the three Furies (for such they are). It was his sister Elizabeth on her childhood deathbed who became, in Lindop's words, 'the archetype, around whom crystallized the images of suffering female innocence which haunted his nightmares and reveries throughout his adult life' (L 10) and fed into his Gothic fictions, which, inspired as they are by his early reading of female Gothic, reproduce images that are central to it.

In *Suspira de Profundis,* the 'The Dark Ladie', familiar to De Quincey from Bannerman and Coleridge, has led, via the high church liturgy to which he was emotionally attached, to 'Our Lady of Darkness', of whom he says that

> Her kingdom is not large, or else no flesh should live; but within that kingdom all power is hers [...] She is the defier of God. She is also the mother of lunacies, and the suggestress of suicides [...] she can approach only those in whom a profound nature has been upheaved by central convulsions; in whom the heart trembles and the brain rocks under conspiracies of tempest from without and tempest from within. (13: 368)

The whole tone here shows that Our Lady of Darkness, like Our Lady of Tears and Our Lady of Sighs, has deep personal significance. All three of these 'awful sisters' or Ladies of Sorrows represent the effects upon De Quincey of tragic experience. Our Lady of Tears is the *mater lachrymarum,* the feminine sensitivity or anima that reduces the grown man to tears. Our Lady of Sighs is the spirit of submission. Our Lady of Darkness, by contrast, is the spirit of despair, of 'suicidal despondency', of endless torment, the Devil in his female guise ('the terrifying embodiment of a female Other'),[35] the Queen of Hell. The name for the figure is taken from Anne Bannerman's 'Dark Ladie', but in his imagination De Quincey, who will later have known Coleridge's 'The Ballad of the Dark Ladie' (in his *Sibylline Leaves*), has transcended and mythologized a figure in a minor poem, thereby taking her back to her source in Mallory and the darkness of Celtic myth and legend. She is the Urdar of Norse mythology, hence one of the Anglo-Saxon Wyrdes or Three Weird Sisters. She is the Spectre of the Brocken of German legend, in the sense not of anything as vaporous as a mere optical illusion, but as the queen of the witches who are supposed to foregather in revelry there on Walpurgis Night. By naming her 'Our Lady', thereby making her a figure of prayer and supplication, he has given her an Anglo-Catholic (Marian) cloak of respectability, analogous to the Madonna of the Sorrowful Mysteries; but beneath that cloak she is an avenger figure straight out of classical and non-classical mythology alike, where such 'awful sisters' come in threes. She is one of Sophocles' Daughters of Darkness, that is, one of the avenging Erinyes or Furies, supposedly ghosts of murdered people, tasked to torment those who had murdered a near relative. In the first instance this must refer to Ann of Oxford Street, a 'lady of the night' whom De Quincey bitterly blamed himself for abandoning (for all he knew, to her death), and who haunted him for the rest of his life; but by a kind of symbolical syncretism, Ann shades into his sister Elizabeth and into Kate

---

35 See also Joseph Andriano, *Our Ladies of Darkness, Feminine Daemonology in Male Gothic Fiction* (Pennsylvania: The Pennsylvania State University Press,1993), 91-98.

Wordsworth, who complete a triad of the beloved for whose sake he had become enamoured of death, while his neglect of his wife is hyped by conscience into murder. She is therefore one of the Harpies who carried off the daughters of Pandareos (cf. both Ann and Elizabeth) and gave them to the Erinyes as servants. More generally, she is a Medusa figure, and as such a symbolical relative of the Prince of Darkness, by whom De Quincey evidently felt he had allowed himself to be systematically tempted, and who had demanded constant payment involving the blighting of all De Quincey's hopes and the undermining of his whole literary-scholastic enterprise. His inner world is what Scott, in *Guy Mannering* (ch. 33), calls a mental phantasmagoria prepared by conscience, for, as we shall see presently, De Quincey was as much a victim of conscience as Kafka.

5.3. *The English Mail-Coach* (1849)

The last dream-vision is the 'Dream-Fugue' that brings the Gothic fantasia *The English Mail-Coach* (*Blackwood's*, 1849) to a close. It is based on the preceding 'Vision of Sudden Death', which tells of a fatal coaching accident narrowly avoided. Closely related to the Piranesi passage in *Confessions,* and to *Suspira de Profundis*, it is a prose poem or exercise in 'impassioned prose', Gothic in the ambivalence, complementarity and precarious balance of its sweep. The 'monstrous coachman' and 'storm-flight of [...] maniacal [supernatural] horses', and especially the headlong, hell-bent pace of the 'chariot' in the final apocalyptic vision

> Two hours after midnight we approached a mighty Minster. Its gates, which rose to the clouds, were closed. But, when the dreadful word that rode before us reached them with its golden light, silently they moved back upon their hinges; and at a flying gallop our equipage entered the grand aisle of the Cathedral. Headlong was our pace. (13: 322)

point back to the 'ghastly huntsman' of Bürger's 'Der Wilde Jäger' ('The Chase' in Scott's translation, st. xv: 'Still forward, forward! On they go') and to 'Lenore' (st. xliv: 'As headlong on they speed'), and forwards to Stoker's *Dracula*, in which 'Lenore' is invoked, for in the imaginative terms that count here, it is only the dead who ride as fast as that ('Die Toten reiten schnell', swiftly ride the dead), or rather only the dead and the impassioned carried away on the wings of fancy, for the whole point of this vision is its ambiguity. The 'mighty Minster' with its gates as high as the clouds and its phantasmagorically (gothically) shifting aisle (said, in the 'Author's Postscript', to derive from the 'arrow-like section of the road, six hundred yards long', to which its length of 'seventy leagues' [some twenty miles] by no means corresponds) is the 'heavenly cathedral' of *The Spanish Military Nun*, but also, in what is at the same time a *Vision of Sudden Death,* a vast Gothic necropolis inhabited by the countless dead, and as such a precursor of Pater's House of the Dead in *Marius the Epicurean:* we have aleady seen that images of ascent evoke those of descent. And of course it is also, in a characteristic pairing, the House of Meaning of language.

The fugal motif here, repeating in different keys 'the drama of a mysteriously threatened and miraculously saved female',[36] is more than an echo of De Quincey's Marian Christianity, although this comes into it:

> there is more here than ingenious displacement and curious psychological economy which puts every detail to multiple use, There is at bottom a joyous glorification of being intermeshed with a titillating fear of not-being, a combination which is reflected structurally in the fugal process of repetition ironically modified by tantalizing incompletion like Piranesi's vision. Each pattern is constructed, deconstructed, and reconstructed in a version of what Schlegel called '*Selbstschöpfung und Selbstvernichtung*' [...] the artistic satisfaction comes chiefly in the balancing interplay of being and not-being.[37]

The motif envisions De Quincey's life. He is himself the mail-coach:[38] the mail-coach is his mind (see 3: 162), in which fears of nonentity in life alternate with fears of not-being in death, for the mail-coach combines the chariot of life and the Juggernaut of death. The crucial vision in the fourth section ('Immediately, in trance, I was carried over land and sea to some distant kingdom, and placed upon a triumphal car') goes back to Macnish's description of the victim of nightmare in *The Philosophy of Sleep:*

> Imagination cannot conceive the horrors [nightmare] frequently gives rise to, or language describe them in adequate terms. They are a thousand times more frightful than the visions conjured up by necromancy or *diablerie;* and far transcend everything in history or romance [...] the wretched victim feels as if pent alive in his coffin[...] he is prostrated by inevitable destiny beneath the approaching wheels of the Car of Juggernaut.[39]

The Car of Juggernaut is one of De Quincey's central symbols; it recurs in *The Household Wreck.* The 'dreadful word [...] with its golden light' is Death, which means both succumbing to the Dark Ladie and being joined in apotheosis with the three White Ladies of his love (his wife Margaret lends her name to the heroines of his Gothic tales, but is exluded from this final beatitude). The 'Dream-Fugue' ends in what, despite its largely Christian symbolism, can best be termed a re-entry into Paradise, a Paradise regained that prefigures and in imaginative/psychological terms explains his apparent reclaiming of his lost childhood paradise in death ten years later. Since the laurel stands for immortality, and especially intellectual glory, the 'laurelled heads' may be taken to represent the ranks of the literary immortals De Quincey was hoping to join.

---

36 John E. Jordan, in *Bicentenary Studies*, 202. De Quincey had no time for Friedrich Schlegel (see 10: 42ff.).

37 Jordan, ibid.

38 'As the mail-coaches go down daily to London to the inspector of mails, so we rolled out of the nursery at a signal given, and were minutely reviewed in successsion. Were the lamps of our equipage clean and bright? Were the springs properly braced? Were the linch-pins secured?' (E 19).

39 Macnish, 17ff.

6. Essays

6.1. *Historico-Critical Inquiry into the Origin of the Rosicrucians* (1824) and *Secret Societies* (1847)

The first of these is a series of papers that amounts to no more than a *rifacimento* of an obscure German work, *Ueber den Ursprung und die vornehmsten Schicksale der Orden der Rosenkreutzer und Freymaurer. Eine historisch-kritische Untersuchung*, (Göttingen: Roewer, 1804) by Johann Gottlieb Buhle (1763-1821). De Quincey's condensed and revised version is linked to his Gothic work in three ways: (i) insofar as Rosicrucianism generated a sub-genre of Gothic, the Rosicrucian novel (Godwin's *St. Leon*; Maturin's *Melmoth the Wanderer*; Bulwer-Lytton's *Zanoni*; P. B. Shelley's *St. Irvyn*) and the related German *Bundesroman* or *Geheimbundroman* (secret society novel)[1] and *Rosenkreuzerroman* (Rosicrucian novel) which range from Schiller's epoch-making *Der Geisterseher* via a string of once renowned Schiller-imitations to the pits of the sub-Gothic); (ii) in that De Quincey shares the late eighteenth-century preoccupation with secret societies (Order of Asssassins, Order of the Rosy Cross, Order of Illuminati, etc), and (iii) through its status as a 'translation' of much the same kind as *Walladmor* and *The Spanish Military Nun*. De Quincey states that he has 'abstracted, rearranged, and in some respects [...] improved' on Buhle's work: 'It was a paper in this sense mine, that from me it had received form and arrangement; but the materials belonged to the learned German' (7: 201f.). Most of the supporting materials were in fact omitted by De Quincey, who paraphrases each paragraph in turn, translating the key sentences literally;[2] even his conclusion comes from Buhle. His scholarly pose here, as elsewhere, is a charade, part of the tools of the 'coiner'; his real interest, as so often, is in mystery for mystery's sake. What Pascal Niklas has written of Shelley

> The Gothic imagination, as in P. B. Shelley's *St. Irvyne, or: The Rosicrucian*, is stimulated less by the reforming intentions of the Illuminati and other secret societies than by their subversive and mysterious character.[3]

applies to De Quincey, except that in his case the interest in mystery comes before that in subversion.

The 'mysterious character' of the 1803 diary (page 192) is De Quincey's own nascent Gothic self. The idea of retiring, possibly for generations, behind thick curtains of secrecy

---

1 See, especially, Rosemarie Nicolai-Haas, 'Die Anfänge des deutschen Geheimbundromans', in *Geheime Gesellschaften*, ed. Peter Christian Ludz (Heidelberg: Lambert Schneider, 1979), and two books by Marie Roberts, *British Poets and Secret Societies* (London: Croom Helm, 1986) and *Gothic Immortals. The Fiction of the Brotherhood of the Rosy Cross* (London & New York: Routledge, 1990).

2 See Erhart H. Essig, *Thomas De Quincey and Robert Pearse Gillies as Champions of German Literature and Thought* (Diss. Northwestern University, 1951), 159f.

3 In *The Handbook to Gothic Literature*, ed. Marie Mulvey-Roberts, 275.

so evidently has his approval that when he writes 'To be hidden amidst crowds is sublime; to come down hidden amongst crowds from distant generations is doubly sublime', we may assume this to be the context in which his whole Gothic masquerade belongs. The essay *Secret Societies*, for its part, is important less for its ostensible subject, characteristic and Gothic though that may be, than for its digressions, especially one in which de Quincey writes of the secret heart of the labyrinth, likening himself to the 'coiner'. Only in this digressive, transgressive manner do we come at the heart of the matter:

> Was the honourable reader ever in a real labyrinth, like that described by Herodotus? We have all been in labyrinths of debt, labyrinths of error, labyrinths of metaphysical nonsense. But I speak of literal labyrinths. Now at Bath, in my labyrinthine childhood, there was such a mystery [...] the Sydney [Gardens] Labyrinth [...] I mention this simply to teach the stranger how secure, how impregnable, is the central cell or heart of a labyrinth [...] You may sit in that deep grave-like recesss; you may hear the steps of the Avenger approaching, but laugh at them. If you are coining, and have all the implements of coining round about you, never trouble yourself to hide them. Nobody will in this life ever reach you. (7: 203f.)

This is an extraordinary passage and an extraordinarily revealing one. Here are the sources of the labyrinth that dominates De Quincey's work, as it does Kafka's. Here is De Quincey in the deep grave-like recess – for all the world like Kafka's Burrower in the burrow that represents the construct in which he has trapped himself – that represents the underground world by which he is fasincated, of which the secret society is at once a metaphor and a dimension. And here, in the most revealing metaphor of all, is De Quincey as 'coiner', in other words, as counterfeiter, passing as his works what are at best only partly so; but this is also an image of De Quincey as Gothic writer knowingly dealing in 'blatantly counterfeit fictionality'.[4] There he is, a one-man secret society, apparently unaware that he too is trapped. He knew the *Confessions of William Henry Ireland* (1805), in which Ireland, who was, of course, no mean Gothic novelist, confessed to being a literary counterfeiter or 'coiner' (of Shakespeare manuscripts). It could, I think, be argued that what is really original about De Quincey is that he forges his own work, and may therefore have regarded W. H. Ireland as an 'ironic double, a fictive alter ego'.[5] Indeed, it could even be argued that – as in the matter of the 'German ciculating library' – he seems to 'coin' his own life.

It is not in *Secret Societies*, but hidden away in the autobiography, under the heading of the First Irish Rebellion, that we find a reference to two of the most elaborate and successful of all secret societies recorded in history, one of which is German and Gothic-related:

> the Fehm-Gericht, or court of ban and extermination, which, having taken its rise in Westphalia, is usually called the Secret Tribunal of Westphalia, and which reached its full development in the fourteenth century. [...] The German Society disowned the legal authorities as too weak for the ends of justice, and succeeded in bringing the cognisance of crimes within its own secret yet consecrated usurpation. (1: 230)

4 Hogle, in *Cambridge Companion*, 16.

5 The phrase is used by A. S. Plumtree' (in *Bicentenery Studies,* 150f.), who argues that the murderer John Williams was De Guincey's ironic double, a fictive alter ego through whom he could exact a vicarious, imaginary revenge on all those who had tormented him.

The *Vehmgericht* (Secret Tribunal) or *heimliches Amt* (Secret Office) was an open-air court or tribunal, held in Germany, and especially in Westphalia, from the fourteenth to sixteenth centuries, for the suppression of crime, notably heresy and witchcraft, at which the death-sentence, the only sentence available to the court, was carried out immediately after an admission of guilt. It featured notably in Goethe's *Götz von Berlichingen* [1773], Benedikte Naubert's *Hermann von Unna* (1788, one of the first of the German Gothified histories to be translated into English [*Herman of Unna: A Series of Adventures of the Fifteenth Century [...]*, London: Robinson, 3 vols, 1794], the text being preceded by a prefatory 'Essay on the Secret Tribunal and its Judges, formerly existing in Westphalia', said to be by one Baron Bock), Naubert's *Alf von Deulmen* (tr. A. E. Booth, London: Bell, 1794, preceded by a similar essay), Veit Weber's *Wolf; or, The Tribunal of Blood* (tr. James Powell, London: Hughes, 1802), and in Chapter 20 of Scott's *Anne of Geierstein* (1829), and is as much a Gothic institution and feature of Gothic as the Spanish Inquisition itself.[6] This is shown by the way in which it also features in other, untranslated German Gothic novels such as J. B. Durach's *Die Adelritter, ein Gräuelgemälde aus den Zeiten der Vehmgerichte* (1793), Veit Weber's *Die Heilige Vehme* (Vol. 6 of his *Sagen der Vorzeit,* 1796), and a novel, *Die gerechten Vehmrichter oder der unglückliche Holger von Daneburg* (1810), that De Quincey may have read at Bohte's. *The German Museum* included, in 1801, an 'Essay on the Secret Tribunals' adapted from the third volume of Veit Weber's *Sagen der Vorzeit* by Rev. Peter Will, which Bohte very likely showed De Quincey, and there is also an early Gothic anonymous chapbook, *The Secret Tribunal: or, The Court of Winceslaus. A Mysterious Tale,* published in London in 1803.[7] The prisoner who appears before this Secret Tribunal is told, in Scott's novel, that 'you would be safer if you were suspended by the hair over the abyss of Schaffhausen, or if you lay below an axe which a thread of silk alone kept back from the fall'. Kant's account of the workings of conscience, and Schopenhauer's analysis of it, provided Kafka with an elaborate model for the 'court' in *Der Proceß*[8] which links with Gothic in that Kant refers to this internal tribunal or 'supernatural assize', as Schopenhauer calls it, as a 'disguised *Vehmgericht* that takes place in the mysterious darkness inside us'. The way in which the *Vehmgericht* in effect becomes a metaphor for conscience is an excellent example of the internalization of Gothic forms, in which Kafka naturally goes much further than De Quincey.

If De Quincey had been to Germany, and had been in the right place, he would have been profoundly impressed, if not overwhelmed, by the sight of 'subterraneous chambers' where the *heilige Vehme* held its meetings. Washington Irving wrote to his sister from Baden-Baden in 1822:

> Underneath the [grim old] castle we were shown subterraneous apartments that equalled the fabrications of novelists. There were chambers where the secret tribunal held its meetings, and where its victims were confined, and, if convicted, tortured and executed. This was a mysterious association that, some centuries since, held all Germany in awe. It was a kind of Inquisition that took cognizance of all kinds of offences. Its sittings were held in secret; all its movements were wrapped in mystery. Its members consisted of all ranks, from the highest to the lowest; all sworn to secrecy; all forbidden to make known their being members; and all sworn

6 The Star Chamber and the Chambre Ardente were similar institutions.

7 Andrew Block, *The English Novel, 1740-1850. A Catalogue* (London: Dawsons, 1967), 211.

8 It is discussed at greater length in Patrick Bridgwater, *Kafka and Nietzsche,* 2nd edn (Bonn: Bouvier, 1987), 67-78.

> by the most imposing oaths to inflict the punishment decreed by the tribunal, without regard to any tie of kindred or affection. A man, therefore, once condemned by the tribunal had no chance of escape. He knew not where to fly, or in whom to confide; his bosom friend, his very brother might be a member of the terrible tribunal, and, of course, obliged to be his executioner. The subterraneous apartments of the old castle of Baden was one of the places where the secret tribunal was held. The place was worthy of the institution. You can imagine nothing more dismal than the cells and dungeons of which it was composed. There was one vaulted room, black with the smoke of tapers, in which the judges of the tribunal had held their sittings. Narrow winding passages through walls of prodigious thickness led to the dungeons of the prisoners and the places of torture. All these were completely shut [off] from the light of day, and the doors were formed of immense blocks of stone that turned heavily on their pivots, groaning as they moved. There was one great pitfall, down which, we were told, prisoners were precipitated after execution[9]

Whence came De Quincey's knowledge of the *Vehmgericht* is not clear, although it hardly came from Naubert, whose novel was known to Ann Radcliffe,[10] the prefatory essay of which would, had he known it, have provided him with much additional material that he would surely have used, probably in his own essay on *Secret Societies* As it is, he shows the limits of his knowledge of the *Vehmgericht* and of the German Gothic in which it plays an important role, by his cursory reference to it. What is so striking is not how much he knows about the *Heilige Vehme*, but how little he seems to know about it. He appears to have known hardly any of the material that, for all sorts of reasons, he might reasonably be expected to have known. It is the same with other subjects.

De Quincey's fascination with secret societies went way beyond the appeal of the *heilige Vehme* or the Illuminati to the Gothic imagination (cf. 3: 25, 4: 211). It has its roots in the 'sense of belonging to a secret order of outcast initiates, chosen by powers outside the confines of normal human experience' (L 357) that helped him to overcome the guilt that defined his life and the adverse conditions that shaped it. The importance, for the outcast, of a sense of being one of the elect or enlightened, who included men like Goethe and Herder in their ranks, cannot be overstated. De Quincey shared in the anti-Enlightenment penchant for mystery and mystification that, in his case, was probably first triggered by the secrets and injunctions to secrecy of the *Arabian Nights*. His more specific interest in 'the mystery that surrounds Secret Societies' also began at an early age, when he came across the *Vehmgericht,* the 'Turmgesellschaft', the Freemasons, and the Illuminati in the work of Goethe and Schiller; but even before that he had read Barruel's *Mémoires pour servir à l'Histoire du Jacobinisme* (4 vols, London, 1797-8; *Memoirs Illustrating the History of Jacobinism*, tr. Robert Clifford (London: Burton, 1798), which Shelley also used.[11] John Robison's *Proofs of a Conspiracy against all the Religions and Governments of Europe* (Edinburgh, 1797), which he also mentions, he did not read, although he frequently heard it discussed.

He was introduced to Barruel's work by Lady Carberry, who gave full credence to the grand conspiracy theory,[12] and was fascinated by what he read there about 'a regular

---

9 P. M. Irving, *The Life and Letters of Washington Irving* (New York: Putnam, 1863), II, 111f.

10 Tompkins, 376.

11 M. H. Dodds, 'Shelley's Use of Abbé Barruel's Work on Secret Societies', *Notes and Queries*, CXIII (March 1917), 196.

12 See Montague Summers, *The Gothic Quest* (New York: Russell & Russell, 1964), 131, and two books by Nesta Webster, *World Revolution: The Plot against Civilization* (London: Constable, 1921) and *Secret Societies and Subversive Movements*, 5th edn (London: Boswell, 1936).

conspiracy throughout Europe for exterminating Christianity', a plot which 'stretched its horrid fangs, and threw out its forerunning feelers and tentacles, into many nations, and more than one century' (7:173f.). It was the intellectual grandeur of the thing that fascinated him. Unlike Shelley, who reacted idealistically to Barruel, De Quincey was left in two minds, writing of his anxiety to

> reconcile my own secret belief in the Abbé with the strong arguments for not believing [in the idea of an anti-Christian conspiracy] [...] my earnest desire to see *how* the learned gentleman could be right whom my intense faith certified beyond all doubt to *be* so, and whom, equally, my perverse logical recusancy whispered to be continually in the wrong. I wished to see my own rebellious arguments, which I really sorrowed over and bemoaned, knocked down like ninepins[,] shown to be utterly worthless in the eye of reason. (7: 177)

Shelley, for his part, according to his friend Hogg, swallowed 'with eager credulity the fictions and exaggerations of that readily believing, or readily inventing author'.[13] Taking a romantic view of the Assassins (see his incomplete [Gothic] romance, 'The Asssassins'), and objecting to Barruel's vilification of the Illuminati, Shelley declared the book to be 'half filled with the vilest and most unsupported falsehood'.[14]

Both Barruel and Robison linked German literature with atheism and Jacobinism, and they were not alone in doing so: a correspondent of *Der Genius der Zeit* (17 [1799], 498) described the German writers and philosophers of the time as being, to a man, Freemasons, Illuminati and 'leidenschaftliche Beförderer der königs-mörderischen französischen Freiheit' (passionate supporters of the regicidal French notion of Liberty). *The Anti-Jacobin* and its successor, *The Anti-Jacobin Review,* took a similar view. It may well be, given his conservatism, that De Quincey was put off some of the more advanced aspects of German literature by such reports, and that this constitutes another, secret reason for his failure to come to terms with German Romanticism as such. Coleridge, reviewing Lewis's *The Monk* back in February 1797, had argued that any attempt to import German horrors [into] Britain would precipitate a decline of its literature',[15] and the following year (4 and 11 June 1798) the *The Anti-Jacobin* implicitly defined German drama as 'morally promiscuous and bent on overthrowing all government'.[16] It was because of *The Anti-Jacobin's* attitude that Scott decided to put off publication of his 'Germanized brat',[17] *The House of Aspen* (1830). After being greeted in the earlier 1790s with the excessive enthusiasm that De Quincey belatedly echoes, German literature was then 'demonized by being associated with French revolutionary excess';[18] wartime xenophobia did the rest.

At the silent centre of the essay on *Secret Societies*, a typical rigmarole in which De Quincey continually sidetracks himself, is a concern with secrecy for its own sake, and more especially with the idea of a secret truth that is likened to Aladdin's lamp. The passage in question is marked by an obsessive over-use of the word 'sublime' that implies an extraordinary fascination:

---

13 T. J. Hogg, *The Life of Shelley*, 2 vols (London: Moxon, 18588), I, 376.

14 *The Letters* of Percy Bysshe Shelley, ed. Frederick L. Jones, 2 vols (Oxford: Clarendon Press, 1964), I, 264 (letter to Elizabeth Hitchener of 27 February 1812).

15 Michael Gamer, *Romanticism and the Gothic* (Cambridge: Cambridge University Press, 2000), 77.

16 Quoted from Gamer, 129.

17 *The Letters of Sir Walter Scott*, ed. H. J. C. Grierson (London: Constable, 1932), I, 124.

18 Gamer, 222.

in Barruel I had heard only of Secret Societies that were [...] formed for mischievous ends [...] Soon I read of other societies, even more secret, that watched over *truth* dangerous to publish or even to whisper, like the sleepless dragons that oriental fable associated with the subterraneous guardianship of regal treasures. The secrecy, and the reasons for the secrecy, were alike sublime. The very image, unveiling itself by unsteady glimpses, of men linked by brotherly love and perfect confidence, meeting in secret chambers, at the noontide of night, to shelter, by muffling with their own persons interposed, and at their own risk, some solitary lamp of truth – sheltering it from the carelessness of the world and its stormy ignorance; *that* would soon have blown it out – sheltering it from the hatred of the world; *that* would soon have made war upon its life: all this was superhumanly sublime. The fear of those men was sublime; the courage was sublime; the stealthy, thief-like means were sublime; the audacious end – viz. to change the kingdoms of earth – was sublime. If they acted and moved like cowards, those men were sublime; if they planned with the audacity of martyrs, those men were sublime. (7: 181f.)

The logic of dreams links these 'secret chambers' with the secret chamber of the mind, so that these 'superhuman' guardians of the lamp stand for the super-ego of the pariah who would be king of his own sublime realm, as he was of his imaginary childhood realm of Gombroon, the name of which (a town on the Persian Gulf) points to the *Arabian Nights*.

6.2. *On Murder Considered as one of the Fine Arts* (1827)

At first sight De Quincey's morbid, obsessive interest in murder is of a piece with the fascination with violence of that other scholar-poet, Walter Pater. De Quincey was fascinated by gangs of murderers such as the Jewish Sicarii (7: 150, 13: 64), the Islamic Order of Assassins (13: 21, 62), and the Thugs of India (7: 151, 8: 428f.), which he will have put together in his mind with the murderous secret societies rampant in English and German Gothic, for instance in Grosse's *The Genius,* which he, who read Grosse's less well known *The Dagger* in 1802, must also have known, to say nothing of the work of which *The Genius* was said to be a 'wretched imitation', Benedikte Naubert's *Herman of Unna.* It was from this that Grosse lifted his account of the secret tribunal. As the paper *On Murder* shows, De Quincey's knowledge of the Assassins came from a forgotten early work of Joseph von Hammer (1774-1856, from 1835 Hammer-Purgstall), *Geschichte der Assassinen* (1818), a work that in its day inspired a number of fictional works, including one written five years after De Quincey's paper, Franziska von Stengel's *Die Assassinen, oder die Eroberung der Königsperle durch den Bund der Blutigen. Eine historisch-romantische Geschichte* (Mannheim: Tobias Löffler, 1832, repr. 1835). In his history Hammer compared the Shi'ite Assassins to the Templars, the Jesuits and the regicides of the French Revolution.[19] P. B. Shelley's unfinished novella *The Assassins: A Fragment of a Romance* (1814), which was begun during the Shelley party's peregrinations in post-revolutionary Europe in August/September 1814, has no connexion with von Hammer. In her Preface to her late husband's *Essays &c.,* Mary Shelley wrote that

The Assassins were known in the eleventh century as a horde of Mahometans living among the recesses of Lebanon, – ruled over by the Old Man of the Mountain [the collective title of a series of heads of the order]; under whose direction various murders were committed on the Crusaders, which caused the name of the peo-

19 Robert Irwin, *The Arabian Nights A Companion* (London: Allen Lane, 1994), 20.

ple who perpetrated them to be adopted in all European languages, to designate the crime which gave them notoriety.

On Murder considered as one of the Fine Arts, which includes an elaboration of a point from the world of murder that was included four years earlier in that classical study of the mind of a murderer, *On Knocking at the Gate in Macbeth,* involves a deliberate echo and deconstruction of Coleridge's *Essay on the Fine Arts* (1815), in which the poet followed Jean Paul in making a subsequently famous distinction between Fancy and Imagination, is gothified by being presented as the text of a lecture which has fallen into the Author's hands, and masked by being modelled on Aristotles' *Poetics*. For good measure, following Joel Black's argument that the paper was 'a sustained satiric critique of a philosophical tradition epitomized by Kant',[20] Frederick Burwick has read it in the context of Kant's *Kritik der Urteilskraft,* satisfying himself that it involves a 'spoof on Kantian aesthetics'.[21] Neither of these arguments is wholy convincing. The fact that the paper can be read as a 'spoof on Kantian aesthetics' does not mean that it was conceived as such, nor does it of itself prove that De Quincey had sufficient knowledge of the *Kritik der Urteilskraft* – a subject on which he is surprisingly silent – to justify such a reading of what is more obviously a neo-Swiftian satire.

What is more certain, then, is that in De Quincey's paper murder is aestheticized by being presented as a 'fine art':

> Everything in this world has two handles. Murder, for instance, may be laid hold of by its moral handle (as it generally is in the pulpit and at the Old Bailey), and *that*, I confess, is its weak side; or it may also be treated *aesthetically*, as the Germans call it – that is, in relation to good taste. (13: 13)

De Quincey's approach to his subject is unambiguously aesthetic: it is only possible to speak of 'the perfect revenge' or murders 'the sublimest and most entire in their excellence that ever were committed', or to speak of the murderer being 'transfigured', if one is adopting an amoral point of view, although this does not mean that the lecture, or murder itself, is to be regarded as 'art for art's sake',[22] for in the end it was the moral factor that both killed the London murderer of 1811, John Williams, and made his name. Nor does it mean that De Quincey is being serious – or that he is not.

One might have expected that De Quincey's aesthetic interest in murder would lead him to quote examples of murder from the pages of the novel of terror, but it did not, for his interest was in real murder. In November 1821, while staying at Bohte's, he dined at Charles Lamb's in the company of other literary men, one of whom, the aesthete Thomas Griffiths Wainewright, later proved to be a murderer. De Quincey shared the interest in criminality of men like Schiller and Tieck; he was interested in outcasts and criminals, murderers and their victims, but particularly in the murderer-as-artist and the artist-as-murderer, and in the related figures of the coiner (counterfeiter), forger and plagiarist. The 'Postscript' to *On Murder Considered as One of the Fine Arts,* a real-life tale of murder

---

20 Joel Black, *The Aesthetics of Murder* (Baltimore: The John Hopkins University Press, 1991).

21 See Frederick Burwick, 'De Quincey and the Aesthetics of Violence', *The Wordsworth Circle,* 27/2 (Spring 1996), 78-86.

22 On this, see John C. Whale, in *Bicentenary Studies*, 49.

based on the notorious Williams murders committed in London in 1811, serves to link his work with Poe and with other (Gothic) writers who take an interest in and collect material on real-life criminals (murderers and robbers). In Germany a case in point is Schiller's *Der Verbrecher aus verlorener Ehre* (1786), which is a retelling, in literary form, of the story of a real-life criminal (Johann Friedrich Schwan, executed 1760), with emphasis on the evolution of a criminal character. Schiller, fascinated by criminality and the moral ambiguity surrounding some criminal acts, edited *Merkwürdige Rechtsfälle als ein Beitrag zur Geschichte der Menschheit* (4 vols, Jena, 1792-95), a selection of cases from François Gayot de Pitaval's *Causes célèbres et intéressantes* (26 vols, 1734-71), which was continued by Julius Eduard Hitzig and Wilhelm Häring (Willibald Alexis) as *Der neue Pitaval* (67 vols, Leipzig: Brockhaus, 1842-87). Ann Radcliffe knew Pitaval, which she used in *The Romance of the Forest*, while Charlotte Smith, in her *The Romance of Real Life* [A collection of tales based on Pitaval] (3 vols, London: T. Cadell, 1787; German translation, *Gemälde menschlicher Schwächen und Leidenschaften*, Leipzig, 1789), argued that 'real-life' romance and fable are as attractive as romantic fiction'.[23] In Germany there was, in the 1790s, a vogue for accounts of the careers of criminals and other outcasts. C. H. Spieß's *Biographien der Wahnsinnigen* (4 vols, Leipzig: Voss, 1795-96, repr. Darmstadt: Luchterhand, 1976) was followed by the volume of *Biographien berühmter Schwärmer, Gauner, Mörder, Mordbrenner und Strassenräuber* that Ludwig Tieck, then in his Gothic phase, published in Hanover in 1797 in collaboration with his former teacher and literary mentor, the Gothic novelist[24] Friedrich Eberhard Rambach. Like Charlotte Smith, Schiller,Tieck and Alexis, and later Gothic writers such as William Ainsworth and G. P. R. James, De Quincey is interested in the mentality of criminals and 'crypto-criminals' ('The class who have left secrets, riddles, behind them': PW [Japp] 1: 82), and in the history of crime; in old age he is said to have evinced a morbid interest in criminal trials.

Because two of the murders he describes took place in Mannheim and Cologne, Frederick Burwick has argued that De Quincey may have found the relevant material during a visit or visits to Germany. This does not follow: De Quincey need not have travelled to Germany to read about the murders in question. He could, for instance, have heard about them from Bohte, or, more likely, read about them in Bohte's German Reading Room, and might well have come across the *Conversations-Lexikon* in question (Leipzig: Brockhaus, 1824) in the same way. While it would be satisfying to know for sure where he read of the murders of the baker in Mannheim and the accountant in Cologne, the absence of such certainty does not mean that he was himself in Mannheim and Cologne in 1825. Burwick has written that 'To search for De Quincey's signature in the registries of Saxony' would be 'a worthwhile enterprise', but if De Quincey used local newspaper accounts, it would be necessary to seach in Cologne and Baden; in Dresden he would have found only what he might equally well have found, and for my money probably did find, in London.

The murderer Williams has a stake driven through his heart, for all the world as though he were a vampire from Gothic romance, but the real point is that 'Williams' is both a petty-criminal real-life murderer and at the same time a persona of De Quincey as his brother William's 'murderer', and thus 'a fictive alter ego through whom he could exact a

---

23 Charlotte Smith, *The Romance of Real Life*, 3 vols (London: T. Cadell, 1787), v-vi.

24 In the sense of writer of *Ritter- und Räuberromane.*

vicarious, imaginary revenge on all those who had tormented him'.[25] De Quincey showed his awareness of the connexion between the *Doppelgänger* and 'murderer' when he wrote 'If I had a *doppel-gänger* who went about personating me, copying me, and pirating me [...] I might [...] be so far carried away by jealousy as to attempt the crime of murder upon his carcase' (11: 460f.). 'Pirating' is elaborated in *Walladmor.*

Of the five tales in Gillies's *German Stories*, it was Kruse's *Oath and Conscience* that meant most to De Quincey, who was clearly moved by it:

> the principal character [...] is urged by conscience and gratitude to discover a murder which he had accidentally witnessed when a child, but is restrained by a superstitious reverence for an oath of secrecy which had been administered to him at that time, and by pious regard to the memory of his father, who had been a participator in the murder, but had since died repentant. A situation of greater trial for a conscientious mind can hardly be imagined

De Quincey's preoccupation with murder can, as these lines show, only have a psychological origin and explanation. There is no need to theorize at length, for the long and the short of it is that he regarded himself as, in some sense(s), a 'murderer'. The reference in the 'reverie upon *Sudden Death*' (13: 304) to being 'self-denounced as a murderer' speaks for itself. Like Kafka, he will have blamed himself for surviving a brother who died early, and in his case there was, in addition, also the death of his beloved sister, for which he also blamed himself; but it was his abandonment of Ann and neglect of his wife Margaret that he regarded as tantamount to murder. His feelings of guilt in this respect get mixed up with his love of mystery and his interest in secret societies, for he lived, on and off, in the world of death and darkness that is personalized in the murderer, but which is also the world of his victim. As pariah, occasional 'notour bankrupt' and debtor on the run, fearful of arrest, his world was, at times, not so far removed from that of the criminal.

His identification with murderers of every historical size and shape is part of his identification with every kind of pariah (the Cagots [Pyrenean pariahs], the Greek Armatoles [banditti, brigands or klephts], the Mainatts [robbers and freebooters, 'the Robin Hoods of Greece'], the Islamic Order of Assassins, highwaymen, and so on. Here too there is a parallel with the contemporary Gothic novel, which exhibits a marked preference for the outcast (Fouqué), highwayman (Ainsworth, G. P. R. James), pirate (Scott), robber (J. Dalton, G. P. R. James), smuggler (John Banim, G. P. R. James), etc. However, this parallel, though striking, is potentially misleading, for the liking for pariahs is, with De Quincey, less a feature of his gothicity, than a personal motif which goes a good deal deeper and even goes a long way to explaining the extraordinary way in which he writes.

The 'Society for the Encouragement of Murder' in *On Murder* may reflect De Quincey's knowledge of the 'Société des Amis du Crime' proposed by the Marquis de Sade in the third volume of his *Juliette* (1797). Secret societies devoted to sexual debauchery were common in the eighteenth century, especially in France, and it was to sexual crimes that the Society for the Friends of Crime was to be devoted; in this country the Hellfire Club went in for sexual debauchery in the context of Black Masses and otherwise, and there was also the Satanic sect of Demoniacs, to which Sterne belonged, who took their name from Milton's 'Demoniack legion'. The Society for the Promotion of Vice, the Society for the

---

[25] A. S. Plumtree, in *Bicentenary Studies*, 150f.

Suppression of Virtue (which successfully prosecuted M. G. Lewis for advocating the publication of a bowdlerized version of the Bible), and the Society of Connoisseurs in Murder listed by De Quincey are all in line with Sade's Society for the Friends of Crime.

The Marquis de Sade not only put into words the monsters within that Fuseli had intuited and which Goya subsequently painted; his attitude towards the novel of his time is also important. Whatever the precise pedigree of the 'modern novel', the term as such was first used in 1800 by Sade (well described by Leslie Fiedler[26] as standing 'almost emblematically at the crossroads of depth psychology and revolution') to characterize the Gothic romance as opposed to the eighteenth-century novel in which 'everything seemed to have been done'. Strictly speaking a form of romance, the Gothic novel is perhaps best regarded as a revolutionary sub-genre of the novel. In terms of its popularity, though not of its origins, it was the product of the French Revolution, although it was, of course, revolutionary in other ways as well in that it subverted the idea of the Richardsonian novel and the bourgeois ideology on which it was based, to say nothing of being opposed to realism and the claim of reason to explain reality. 'What ardent imagination', Schedoni asks in Ann Radcliffe's *The Italian*, 'ever was contented to trust to plain reasoning?' Confronted with a reality more traumatic and terrifying than ever, the novel for a time reverted to the older romance and indeed to fairytale: the ultimate ogres are the Grand Inquisitor and Robespierre.

It is one of the anomalies with which the present story is littered that De Quincey, while noting that 'Germany [...] found her new literature the mere creation and rebound of this great moral tempest [the French Revolution]', had so little to say of the 'great moral tempest' that left so many deep marks on his time and its literature, not least among them the way in which it is reflected in the Gothic novels and tales that he seems to have read in a remarkably uncritical way. In a general way the Gothic novel was inspired by what Michael Sadleir, writing in 1927, called 'the instinct to liberty'.[27] Although the earliest Gothic novels and their immediate precursors went back a generation, the craze for the Gothic was one of the consequences of the French Revolution and, more distantly and less directly, of the English Puritan Revolution that fed into it. Without the Terror, the vogue for the novel of terror would not have grown as it did. It may seem ironical that the storming of the Bastille, that most Gothic of Gothic castles, built to house heretics, in which 'le citoyen S[ade]' wrote his *Aline et Valcour* (1793),[28] should have triggered such a proliferation of imaginary castles, and that the Terror of 1793-4 should have spawned so many imaginary terrors, but the novel of terror is the appropriate novel of the age of Terror. This at all events was the view of Sade, who described the early Gothic novel as the inevitable outcome of the French Revolution and its aftermath. From *The Monk* (1796) onwards the Gothic novel holds up the mirror to post-revolutionary Europe, it being perhaps only thus that novelists could hope to move their readers, who expected the novel to reflect and explain society. That said, the Gothic novel's stance is ambiguous, for the Gothic, as Ian

---

26 Fiedler, 33.

27 M. Sadleir, *The Northanger Novels* (London: English Association), 1927, 20.

28 At the same time time Hubert Robert ('Robert des ruines'), formerly Keeper of the King's Pictures, was imprisoned at Saint Lazare, painting the dark prison corridor (see W. Gaunt, *Bandits in a Landscape* [London: The Studio, 1937], 108-118) that casts its shadow into Kafka's novels.

Duncan has written,[29] 'rehearses a turn against „real life" into the „imagination" that never quite completes the passage into an alternative version of reality', for, while turning its back on the imitation of society, it cannot help looking over its shoulder at the Terror that cast such a long shadow over contemporary society. The inherent instability of the Gothic novel is thus a reflection of the instability of European society at the time.

---

29 Ian Duncan, *Modern Romance and Transformations of the Novel* (Cambridge: Cambridge University Press, 1992), 21.

7. *Rifacimenti*

7.1. De Quincey, Gillies and *rifacimento*

In the High Gothic period from 1790 to 1820 more novels than ever before were translated into English from German and French, and vice versa, the type and quality of translation differing widely, for there was, especially as regards German, more translation work available than there were competent translators to carry it out; translation was badly paid and was expected to be done at speed. Nor did it help when Germans, resident in London, were commissioned to translate into English; the result, as in the case of *The Necromancer,* apparently a translation by Peter Teuthold of *Der Geisterbanner* (Breslau, 1792, 2nd edn 1799) by Lorenz Flammenberg, a pseudonym of Karl Friedrich Kahlert), was liable to be literal translation of German idiom and syntax into English, something that is also much in evidence in Peter Will's translation of *Horrid Mysteries.* To make matters worse, *The Necromancer* is only partly an over-literal translation of Kahlert's novel, for onto it Teuthold has silently grafted a translation of Schiller's *Der Verbrecher aus verlorener Ehre*;[1] so episodic are Gothic novels that this went unnoticed at the time.

Translations ranged from the hit-or-miss (where the translator's knowledge of the foreign language was not really up to the task in hand) or over-literal to the over-free to the sham translation purporting to be what it was not. The idea of free translation, theorized by Dryden a century earlier, resurfaced in the wake of A. F. Tytler's *Essay on the Principles of Translation* (1791) and other complaints about the quality of contemporary translation such as A. F. N. Willich's 'Letter to the editor on the inadequacy of the existing translations from the German' in the *Monthly Magazine* (5[1798], 399). It was Willich who acted as instructor to the famous Edinburgh German Class in 1792, which, according to Scott, whose German confirms the point, involved 'much laughing and little study'.[2] The words 'from the German' or whatever normally meant that the text introduced by those ominous words was either a *rifacimento* (often presented as the 'translator's' own work) or a plagiarism.

Now in the Introduction to his anthology Gillies advocated the 'principle of adaptation, *rifacimento* or *remaniement* :

> that German authors, if anglicized, not as on the present and on other occasions, by the mere process of translation, but subjected to that of a *remaniement* or *rifacimento*, wi ll prove infinitely *more* acceptable than they have ever yet been to the British public, [the translator] is thoroughly convinced [for] it is [...] scarcely possible to imagine two civilized countries, between which there is found a more striking difference in regard to language and moods of mind, than that which exists between Germany and modern England.

---

1 See Alan Menhennet, *Schiller and the 'Germanico-Terrific' Romance* (Leeds: English Goethe Society, 1981), 38-42.

2 On Willich, see Gillies, *Recollections*, 265; and Leslie Stephen, *Studies of a Biographer*, 4 vols (London: Duckworth, 1898-1902), Vol. 2.

I assume that this idea of what would later be called free translation was discussed with De Quincey in advance of publication, and that the conversations in question fed into his ideas on the subject of *rifacimento,* which go beyond what Gillies intended. With De Quincey, *rifacimento* denotes not simply a form of ultra-free translation, an imitation rather than a paraphrase in Dryden's terms, but an almost inveterate literary method that he deploys whether translation is involved or not.

The basic technique is neither De Quincey's invention, nor is it by any means unique to him. He presumably took it over from Gillies because it suited his book, but the term, which he made peculiarly his own, is also used, for instance, by Scott, who calls his 'half-mad German tragedy', *The House of Aspen,* a *rifacimento* of Veit Weber's *Die heilige Vehme*, and by Coleridge, in the first line of his review of Maturin's *Bertram* in the *Biographia Literaria* (ch. 23). The technique, though not the term for it, is basic to the work of M. G. Lewis. Walter Scott's version of Goethe, *Goetz of Berlichingen with the Iron Hand* (1799) is, because of the limitations of his German, more spirited than correct; but it is scarcely a *rifacimento,* which is just what a second version, which appeared in Liverpool a few weeks later, is. The latter, *Gortz of Berlingen with the Iron Hand*, by Rose d'Aguilar, is very free indeed, often inaccurate, and includes a number of additions to the text, including a description of the meeting-place of the 'Vehmgericht', taken from Benedikte Naubert's *Hermann of Unna* (English translation, 1794). It is likely that De Quincey came across d'Aguilar's version in Everton in 1803; as a book published locally, it would have been available to him, and as a book with both a German and a Gothic (the *Vehmgericht*) dimension, would surely have caught his eye. *Rifacimento* is used particularly by those whose knowledge of the target language is not up to the detail of the original text, although I hasten to add that this does not apply to De Quincey; in a general sense, it stands for the type of free translation shading into plagiarism that is characteristic of the Gothic (Romantic) generation. Even Gothics as well known as M. G. Lewis employed exactly the same method of 'translation'. Lewis's versions of Zschokke's *Abällino* (*The Bravo of Venice*) and Naubert's *Elisabeth, Erbin von Toggenburg* (*Feudal Tyrants*) are both *rifacimenti,* the latter being comparable to *Walladmor* in that Lewis published it under his own name. *The Bravo of Venice* suppressed Zschokke's name on the title-page, which merely proclaimed it to be 'Translated from the German'. The same kind of thing naturally also happened in reverse: in 1797 there appeared in Germany an anonymous work entitled *Der bezauberte Helm, oder der Ritter vom Riesensäbel: eine Geschichte aus dem 12. Jahrhundert,* which turned out to be a *rifacimento* of *The Castle of Otranto* and a plagiarism to boot.

The technique of *rifacimento* is characteristic of De Quincey in the extent to which he uses it, which goes way beyond 'translation' as such, and in the way in which it epitomizes his whole approach to writing, for he uses translation as a metaphor that comes to stand for his work as a whole. In his own day he was, of course, known for his skill as a translator and for the fact that he could never resist the temptation to 'improve' the original. Charles Knight, editor of *Knight's Quarterly,* said that De Quincey was incapable of going about this sort of work without improving all he touched.[3] He used free translation or *rifacimento*

[3] Charles Knight, *Passages of a Working Life During Half a Century,* 2 vols (London: Bradbury & Evans, 1864), I, 327.

both as a way of constructing his work out of that of others, vitiating both his work and his reputation in the process, and as a way of reconstructing his own work. Though he seems to be what Dryden calls a 'scholarlike kind of man', he is really more journalist than scholar, but also more editor than creative writer. The idea of refurbishment, recycling, transforming, transplanting is central to his 'creative' process, and, although he pretends to be, and sometimes is, echoing himself, he is frequently echoing others. As Alina Clej has written,

> When he has no topic to write on, he translates [...] There is abundant evidence throughout De Quincey's work that he adopts on a large scale the method of translating or 'transplanting' [...] This method of creative translation is evident not only in his essays and tales, but is also at work in his confessions [...] De Quincey's idea of free translation or *rifacimento,* which refers to a creative rewriting of the original [...] could be [...] applied to some of [his] own writings, where translation in both its literal and metaphorical senses takes precedence over invention.[4]

Indeed, it could be argued that with De Quincey 'invention' is liable to have its original Latin meaning of finding or discovery.

One of the contexts in which his work arises is therefore that of literary forgery, it being no chance that one of his least revealing, most disappointing essays is entitled 'Great Forgers: Chatterton, Walpole, and „Junius"' (Japp, I, 125-31). Elsewhere he refers to the Shakespeare forger W. H. Ireland (11: 270). In referring to Defoe as a forger, he has in mind Defoe's practice of passing off as reality what is only fiction. Given that what he himself does is not so different, the criticism belongs together with his criticism of Coleridge for plagiarism. That he identifies with Chatterton, and feels that he was shabbily treated by Walpole, is understandable. The difference between De Quincey and his eighteenth-century forebears (Walpole, MacPherson, Chatterton) is that whereas they present work which appears to be by another, but is in fact their own, De Quincey does the opposite, presenting as his own work that is, in part or in a sense, arguably by another, so much so that he appears to be most comfortable when generating text by means of a process of supplementarity. *Walladmor* is a case in point, for however much De Quincey may have changed the original novel, forging the work of another in the process and thereby compounding Alexis's forgery of Scott, the novel belongs to Alexis; to pretend that it is an original work by De Quincey is to compound a felony. Alexis's novel pretends to be by Scott, but is in fact wholly his own; De Quincey's 'translation' not only pretends to be by Alexis, but is indeed largely so.

De Quincey forges his own work because he lacks the self-confidence to be his own man, hence his relative inability to write fiction. There is an astonishingly close parallel between De Quincey and Coleridge in this respect. Richard Holmes has said[5] that between 1811 and 1816 Coleridge incorporated dozens of unacknowledged passages from German authors, either literally translated or freeely adapted, in his lectures and published works, and is surely right to connect this plagiaristic habit with the mendacious habits of his drug-addiction, his astonishing lack of self-worth, and the moral humiliations of his private life, not least as regards his relationship with the Wordsworth circle. How much truer must just

---

4 Clej, 216.

5 Holmes, 2: 280n.

this be of De Quincey, who does himself much less justice in his writings. As he writes – indeed, by writing – the pariah seeks to don a cloak of respectability. Under the guise of *rifacimento*, the method became endemic with De Quincey, who, after the early *Confessions*, mostly remakes or forges his own work and its literary foundations. Ironically, the more he did so, the more he became the *non-ens* he was so afraid of being. It is hard to avoid the conclusion that he was, as a writer, hoist with his own petard.

7.2. *The Somnambulist* (1824)

First published in the August-November number of *Knight's Quarterly Magazine* for 1824 , *The Somnambulist* is a *rifacimento* of a tale, 'Die Nachtwandlerin', from Laun's *Seifenblasen* (2 vols, Tübingen, 1809-10), which De Quincey read at Bohte's in 1821: 'The basis of this story is to be found in the *Seifenblasen* of Dr. Schulz' (as usual, De Quincey misspells Laun's real name, which is Schulze). In Laun's tale the character whom De Quincey has transmogrified into 'our main hero – wicked Dick, witty Dick, dear Dick, Sixteen-string Dick, Slippery Dick' is simply a rogue; in De Quincey's hands he becomes De Quincey's collaborator and hoaxing alter ego, so that the tale is best read as a kind of prelude to *Walladmor*. It is a comic hoax-tale which includes motifs (ghost-seeing, hoaxing, masquerading, confusion of identity, and so on) that occur in some of De Quincey's Gothic tales, but which, because the treatment (as Laun's title – *Seifenblasen* means soap-bubbles – indicates) is Aristophanic rather than Gothic, mean that it is closer to P. G. Wodehouse than to Ann Radcliffe.

7.3. *Niels Klim's Journey to the World Under-Ground* (1822-28)

Despite an 1822 watermark, De Quincey's fragmentary translation of Ludvig Holberg's *Nicolai Klimii Iter Subterraneum* (1741), or, rather (and more puzzlingly) of Jens Baggesen's 1789 Danish version of it (*Niels Klims Underjordiske Reise*, probably dates from 1827-28. It was most likely begun, at Gillies's suggestion, for publication in the *Foreign Quarterly Review*, with which Gillies was closely associated, and which ran from 1827 to 1834, although it should not be forgotten that *Blackwood's* had been carrying a series of 'Horae Danicae' since 1820. De Quincey probably chose to translate Holberg's work from the Danish rather than the Latin (of which he had a much better knowledge) because he knew that the Danish version was superior to the original Latin one. The work was first translated into English in 1742 (*A Journey to the World Under-Ground,* by Nicholas Klimius [London: T. Astley]). This translation was reprinted by Scott's protégé Henry Weber in a volume entitled *Popular Romances: Consisting of Imaginary Voyages and Travels* (Edinburgh: W. & R. Chambers, 1833) and, more recently (with some revisions) as *Journey of Niels Klim to the World Underground* (ed. James I. McNelis, Jr, Lincoln, Nebraska: University of Nebraska Press, 1960). A second anonymous English translation, *Journey to the World Under-Ground; Being the Subterraneous Travels of Niels Klim* (London: Thomas North) came out in 1828.

Woodhouse, in 1821, wrote that De Quincey was 'a slight Danish scholar'. It was his brother 'Pink's' imprisonment by the Danes (who had been on the receiving end of his naval activities) that prompted De Quincey to learn some Danish. When he discovered that Gillies knew Danish, he probably decided to emulate his friend by teaching himself some more. Translating Holberg would, however, have been a major undertaking. It seems likely that the appearance of Holberg's *Memoirs* in 1827, coinciding with the inception of the *Foreign Quarterly Review*, caused Gillies to suggest that De Quincey might care to prepare a version of the 'Subterraneous Travels', and that the appearance of a complete new translation in 1828, which meant that his market had disappeared, led De Quincey to abandon the project. His incomplete version, edited by S. Musgrove in 1953, is a *rifacimento:*

> De Quincey's version begins as a faithful, though never literal, translation of the original, but very soon he starts to compress, to transfer details, and even to expand, so that in parts he produces what is rather an adaptation than a translation [...] De Quincey was [...] translating Holberg [...] in order to produce a readable English version for publication.

Niels Klim is accordingly one of De Quincey's first translations of the kind called for by Gillies and discussed by De Quincey at the end of his review of 'Gillies's German Stories', where he urges translators to escape from the thraldom of the text.

Niels Klim or *A Journey to the World Under-Ground* is one of the earliest and most successful imitations of *Gulliver's Travels.* The experiences of this Norwegian Gulliver are closely modelled on those of his prototype, but are more explicit and thus less imaginative. Having entered the world underground (underworld) through a cavern, like Alice after him, Klim finds himself among the Potuites, a race of animated trees (cf. Lucian's Arboreals) who mistake him for a monkey because, though quick in apprehension, he appears weak and unstable of judgment, which is reminiscent of the way in which the Houyhnhnms mistake Gulliver for a Yahoo; the Monkeys themselves regard him as of their kind. Expelled from this arboreal realm, Klim is carried by a huge Post-Bird to Martinia, the aristocratic realm of a race of learned monkeys who are as quick-witted as they as giddy, trifling and talkative. And so on. While there is nothing in Holberg's text that is overtly Gothic, the uncertainty and instability of Klim's life in the subterraneous world, which De Quincey will rightly have associated with the *Arabian Nights,* are Gothic enough.

In the present context Holberg's satire is important for two reasons: because in literary historical terms it belongs in the imaginary voyage or journey tradition of Lucian, Cyrano de Bergerac, Swift, Munchausen and the *Arabian Nights*, which held De Quincey spellbound as a child, and in literary and psychological terms because it promises to be an exploration of the most profound and most Gothic of De Quincey's spatial images, that of the cavern. If he did not abandon his project because of the 1828 translation, he is likely to have given it up because it did not deliver the journey into the depths of the mind or exploration of the inner world (the subconscious) that he had anticipated. Had he known it, he would have found more to hold his attention in Athanasius Kircher's *Mundus Subterraneus* (1665) with its accounts of subterraneous (interior) giants, beasts and demons. In making Klim set out on his journey in 1665, Holberg was saluting Kircher's work.

7.4. *Walladmor* (1825)

7.4.1. The German *Walladmor*

De Quincey's *Walladmor* is a *rifacimento* in the sense of a remake or, in plain English, an adaptation of a first novel of the same title by a young German writer, Willibald Alexis (pseudonym of Georg Wilhelm Häring, 1798-1871),[6] who grew up with Gothic in its German manifestations (*Ritter-, Räuber-, Geister-* and *Schauerroman*: chivalric romance, novel of banditti, ghost/ghost-seer novel, horror/terror novel) in the persons of Christian Heinrich Spieß, Karl Gottlob Cramer, Karl Friedrich Kahlert, Laurids Kruse, Johann Andreas, Karl Hildebrand, and the like, and had connexions with the Dresden writers of whom De Quincey probably first heard through his Oxford friend Schwartzburg. Alexis was twenty-five when he wrote this prank-novel, the first of two.

Born in Breslau in Prussian Lower Silesia (now Wroclaw in Poland), Alexis later said that in his boyhood he had poisoned his imagination with the 'schauderhaften Ritterromanen' (chivalric penny dreadfuls) of the time, epitomized by Schiller as 'geistlos, geschmack- und sittenverderbend' (witless, tasteless, and a bad influence),[7] which he swallowed in such numbers largely because they were forbidden reading. Once they were no longer forbidden, he stopped reading them. He began writing at about sixteen, one of his first works being a lurid revenge-story, *Die Vergeltung,* the sub-title of which ('Eine Sage der Vorzeit') proclaimed him an admirer of Veit Weber's *Sagen der Vorzeit*;[8] for good measure, one of the characters in the tale is named Veit. In 1825, one year after *Walladmor*, he published a short outlaw-novel, *Die Geächteten.* If I add that Alexis had enjoyed a classical education and was given to quoting classical tags, shared De Quincey's interest in criminal psychology (there are a number of criminal characters in his novels), and learned his irony from Jean Paul, it will be obvious that he has so much in common with De Quincey that the Opium-Eater's decision to review and then rewrite his first novel is hardly surprising. At university Alexis translated Scott's *The Lady of the Lake* and *The Lay of the Last Minstrel,* and in 1823 published in the *Wiener Jahrbücher der Literatur* (22 [1823], 1-75)[9] a long article, 'The Romances of Walter Scott', that showed him trying to come to terms with Scott's novels, which had recently begun appearing in German, and led to his decision to make his first novel an imitation of Scott.

Walladmor. Frei nach dem Englischen des Walter Scott. Von W[illibald Alexi]s (Berlin: Herbig, 1824; 2nd edn, 1825), hastily written, in summer 1823, was a high-spirited 'hum' or hoax (in German, a *Jux*) designed to deceive the public and critics. As such it points back, within the Gothic convention, to Horace Walpole's similar hoax. The hope was that it

---

6 In this section I am indebted to the late L.H.C. Thomas's 'Walladmor: A Pseudo-Translation of Sir Walter Scott,' *Modern Language Review,* 46 (1951), 218-231. Thomas wrote his Leeds PhD on *Walladmor,* assembling in the process all the relevant material except that concerning J. H. Bohte. He includes (ibid., 220f.) a summary, in English, of the plot of Alexis's novel. Alexis's real name is Wilhelm Häring, not Ewald Hering (WTDQ, 4: 524).

7 Schiller, *Sämtliche Werke*, ed. K. Goedeke, 15 vols (Stuttgart: Cotta, 1867-76), XIII, 166.

8 In 1806, the 'whole of the works of [Veit] Weber' were said to be in process of translation by J. Powell. Announced as 'shortly to be published', they failed to appear, and in 1823 Scott named Weber as still needing to be translated. He still is.

9 In the same journal (15 [1821], 105-45) he had previously published a comparison of Scott and Byron.

would, initially, be accepted as a 'free translation' of a new work by Scott. In that its aim was not to make money, it was not exactly a 'forgery' as such, or so Alexis must have argued, although Scott would not have agreed. Besides, the hoax was to be revealed, in a knowing, literary version of the explained supernatural, in the third volume. Nor was it a forgery from another point of view: 'It was [Alexis's] unwillingness to repress an ironic tampering with the very processes of narrative illusion that ultimately made his *Walladmor* a spoof rather than a [...] forgery.'[10] By the time it appeared, some well-known German critics had been fooled. The first volume appeared in December 1823, the remaining two volumes followed shortly afterwards. Seen in retrospect, the words 'Frei nach dem Englischen' were, for those with eyes to see, an indication that the work was not a translation as such. They are found on the title-page of most of the many German imitations of Ann Radcliffe,[11] some of which Alexis will probably have known, and are comparable to the words 'From the German' on the title-page of not a few English Gothic novels. Alexis's *Walladmor* belongs to that popular Gothic genus, the sham translation, and more especially the sham translation of Scott, for it is one of a number of novels which appeared in Germany between 1822 and 1827, purporting to be translations or adaptations of Scott; the others were by minor, long since forgotten writers of the day (F. P. E. Richter, K. H. L. Reinhardt, Heinrich Müller, August Schäfer).[12] F. P. E. Richter (pseudonym of Wilhelmine von Gersdorf) produced a novel, *Jacobine oder die Ritter des Geheimnisses,* purporting to be 'Ein historischer Roman, nach dem Englischen des Walter Scott' (An historical novel, adapted from the English of Walter Scott), which was in fact an adaptation of an anonymous novel of the time, *Jacobine von Holland.* Such facts, typical of the Gothic period, puts Alexis's *Walladmor* into perspective. In 1823-24 Heinrich Müller published no less than five supposed'adaptations of Scott'!

There are two versions of the story of how it came to be written, one from each author of our twin-authored novel. When discussing with friends in Breslau at Easter 1823 how an acquaintance who had just been sentenced to six months' imprisonment for taking part in a duel could best while away his time in jail, Alexis said that if he ever found himself in that position, he would set about writing a novel in the style of Scott, whereupon one his friends, Baron S. von G., remarked that Alexis need not be imprisoned to put the idea into practice.[13] De Quincey, in his autobiographical 'Walladmor. A Pseudo-Waverley Novel', has another version of the story:

> After the Author of 'Waverley' had for a considerable succession of years delighted the world with one or two novels annually, the demand for Waverley novels came to be felt as a periodical craving all over Europe [...] Now it happened in 1823 that no Waverley novel was in readiness, or likely to be in readiness for the Leipsic fair at Michaelmas. Upon which a cry arose amongst the German booksellers – *Forge one!* 'Presumptuous enough that,' the reader will say. Doubtless. However, the thing was done. A German, and (to better the case) a German of ultradulness, set to work upon a novel. He called it 'Walladmor'. [...] Well, this book – this 'Walladmor' – made its appearance in the German language, not as what it really was – a German novel, written by a German novelist – but as a translation from an English original of Sir Walter Scott. In this character it ap-

10 Frederick Burwick, 'How to Translate a Waverley Novel: Sir Walter Scott, Willibald Alexis, and Thomas De Quincey', *The Wordsworth Circle* (Spring 1994), 94.

11 See Trainer, 24f.

12 See Frederick Wilhelm Bachmann, *Some German Imitators of Scott*, Diss. Chicago, 1933.

13 Alexis, *Erinnerungen,* ed. Max Ewert, new edn (Berlin: Concordia, 1905), 267f.

peared at Leipsic; in this character it was instantly dispersed over the length and breadth of Germany; and in this character it crossed the sea to London.

No doubt both stories are true, although the link between them is missing. It seems likely that Alexis approached Herbig with a scheme that was welcomed as timely, rather than vice versa. Be this as it may, the storm with which the novel opens was prompted by the stormy conditions encountered by Alexis when out boating the day before he began writing it. The opening episode was written in the public house *Zum deutschen Hause* in Greifswald. Otherwise, *Walladmor* was mostly written on the island of Rügen, which helps to explain its geographical vagaries.

Viewing the *Walladmor* hoax through the rose-coloured spectacles of retrospect, Alexis wrote of it, in his memoirs, as an unqualified success. The truth lies somewhere between this overestimate and De Quincey's underestimate of the novel, the publication of which had a mixed effect on Alexis's subsequent career as a writer: on the one hand it brought him publicity, much of it positive, but on the other hand it lumbered him with the reputation of a joker rather than that of the serious historical novelist – a Prussian Scott – that he sought to be.[14] It needs to be stressed from the outset that, although Alexis only went on to become a minor historical novelist, the way in which De Quincey, for his own reasions, dismisses him out of hand as a writer has neither justification nor historical validity. Whether the schoolboy refrain of which Alexis writes in his memoirs, 'Wer hebt den Klopfer? Wer schlägt ans Tor? / Heben kann ihn nur ein Walladmor' (Who's that knocking on the door? Only a Walladmor can knock like that) is fact or fiction, is, at this distance in time, unclear.

In his memoirs Alexis describes the plan in more detail:

In allerhand krause, buntromantische Begebenheiten mußten zwei Personen verwickelt werden, ein junger Deutscher und ein mystischer Engländer. Beide erscheinen als Sammler. Jener geht darauf aus, zu einem englischen Roman in neuer Manier Stoffe aufzufinden und stößt dabei überall auf einen Unbekannten, der ihm in die Quere kommt, weil er dasselbe will, bis es zum Schluß sich ergiebt, daß es der große Unbekannte selbst ist. Nun handelte es sich um die Frage, ob der kleine Unbekannte nicht dasselbe Recht zur Herausgabe habe, als der große Unbekannte.[15]

(Two people were to be involved in all sorts of complicated, highly romantic events, a young German and a high-minded Briton. Both are collectors. The German sets out to collect material for an English novel in the manner of Scott, and keeps on stumbling across a stranger, who gets in the way because he is doing the same thing himself, until eventually it turns out that he is the Great Unknown [Scott]. Now it was a matter of deciding whether the little unknown [Alexis] had the same right to the material as the great one.)

In Alexis's novel the 'große Unbekannte' (Great Unknown) reveals himself to be Walter Scott. The novel, a *jeu d'esprit*, succeeded, from Alexis's point of view, beyond its young author's wildest expectations, although there are two other points of view involved, Scott's and De Quincey's, to which we come presently. Seen from the point of view of Alexis's budding literary career, *Walladmor* has been said to reveal

---

14 See L. H. C. Thomas, 'The Literary Reputation of Willibald Alexis as an Historical Novelist, *Modern Language Review,* 45 (1950), 195-214.

15 Alexis, *Erinnerungen*, 269.

> the hand of the master rather than the pupil. Alexis rarely departed from the style of Walter Scott. When he deviated he did so consciously and with a definite purpose. The accuracy of his touch in this tour de force promised much for his future development.[16]

While this is not entirely accurate as regards the 'style' of Alexis's *Walladmor*, it rightly suggests that it was always wrong to take Alexis at De Quincey's valuation; there is no excuse for continuing to do so. Delighted with his novel's success, Alexis himself compounded the hoax by reviewing it together with *St. Ronans's Well*,[17] quoting passages from the work to illustrate Scott's literary ideas, and then, carried away by his own cleverness, proceeded to write an article addressed to the public by 'the author of *Walladmor*'.[18] Nor, as we shall see (in 7.5.), did his preoccupation with Scott end there.

By this time Scott was engaged on *The Betrothed*, one of his weakest novels, the manuscript of which had been slated by his publisher, and was wondering whether or not to abandon it. According to Lockhart, he was initially alarmed by reports of the German fabrication:

> While he hesitated, the German newspapers announced 'a new romance by the author of Waverley', as about to issue from the press of Leipzig. There was some ground for suspecting that a set of suspended sheets might have been purloined and sold to a pirate and this consideration put an end to his scruples. And when the German did publish the fabrication, entitled Walladmor, it could no longer be doubtful that some reader of Scott's sheets had communicated at least the fact that he was breaking ground in Wales.[19]

Lockhart's suspicions are, however, contradicted by the facts, for while *Walladmor* completed publication in the new year of 1824, *The Betrothed* was not begun until June 1824. It was in spring 1825 that the sheets of *The Betrothed* were hung up in Ballantyne's wearehouse, waiting for Scott to decide whether to scrap or complete the novel. The truth of the matter is therefore that in choosing to set *The Betrothed* in Wales, Scott was 'flinging down the gauntlet to that insolent forgery, *Walladmor*',[20] showing Alexis what could be done by a writer who really knew the country in which he had set his novel, as opposed to one who had never set foot in it.

It must have been because he had not received the copy of the novel that Alexis supposedly sent him in February that Scott asked Bohn (or was it Bohte?) to obtain a copy of *Walladmor* for him. In a letter to Lady Abercorn of 4 March 1824 Scott took exception to 'the publication of a German novel professing to be translated from the English, and bearing my name at full length on the title-page.'[21] Johnson takes this up, writing of *Walladmor* as an 'impudent forgery, brazenly bearing Scott's name on the title-page'.[22] De

---

16 L. M. Price, *The Reception of English Literature in Germany* (New York & London: Benjamin Blom, 1968), 379f.

17 *Literarisches Conversations-Blatt,* 12 (1824). See Thomas, *MLR*, 46 (1951), 219.

18 'An Einige Schwache Seelen. Ein Brief vom Übersetzer des Walladmor,' *Abendzeitung, Wegweiser,* No. 80, quoted from Thomas, *MLR*, 46 (1951), 219f.

19 J. G. Lockhart, *Memoirs of the Life of Sir Walter Scott* (Edinburgh: A. & C. Black, 1851), 550.

20 Edgar Johnson, *Sir Walter Scott. TheGreat Unknown, 2 vols* (London: Hamish Hamilton, 1970), II, 866.

21 *Familiar Letters of Sir Walter Scott,* 2 vols (Edinburgh: David Douglass, 1894), II, 191f.

22 Johnson, II, 857.

Quincey, with his nose for books, heard that a copy of the novel had reached London, and wrote to Hessey asking him to try to get his hands on it:

> we must have 'Walladmor' [...] if Heaven or Earth can get it. An abstract of the novel, which I will make in 24 hours, will be of universal interest from the circumstances. – Pray send if you can to Bohn's. They have promised to lend Sir W. Scott's copy in default of any other, on condition of a speedy return. And within 36 hours of receiving it at most I will pledge my word for returning it. What I fear is that the copy should be snapped up by somebody on the spot.[23]

Whether it was Bohn or Bohte who obtained the novel for Scott and lent it to De Quincey is not clear. If it was Bohn, why did De Quincey not first approach his friend Bohte? It may be that De Quincey, who had his ear to the ground, heard that Bohn had ordered a copy for Scott, and that he used that copy, the pages of which had to remain uncut, until Bohte came to the rescue with another copy whose pages he could cut. Otherwise it will have been Bohte (whom Scott knew) and not Bohn (who at the time was a secondhand bookseller) who obtained a copy of the novel for Scott. The point is immaterial.

That *Walladmor* and *The Betrothed* are quite different, is there for all to see. However, when *The Betrothed* appeared the following year (1825), *Walladmor* was mentioned, in somewhat Peacockian manner, in the Introduction, which implied it to be the work of the Devil:

> 'I am inclined [says the Rev. Mr. Lawrence Templeton] to suppose the late publication of Walladmor to have been the work of Dousterswivel, by the help of the steam-engine.'
>
> 'For shame, Mr. Templeton,' said the Preses. 'There are good things in Walladmor, I assure you, had the writer known anything about the country in which he laid the scene.'
>
> 'Or had he had the wit, like some of ourselves, to lay the scene in such a remote or distant country that nobody should be able to back-speer [cross-examine] him,' said Mr. Oldbuck
>
> 'Why, as to that,' said the Preses, 'you must consider the thing was got up for the German market, where folks are no better judges of Welsh manners than of Welsh crw [ale].'

A footnote adds that 'The character of this work [*The Betrothed*] is given with tolerable fairness in the text', which is true only if character is understood in a vague geographical sense. Dousterswivel, the gigantic Harz demon of *The Antiquary* (ch. 18), has been shown to come from Germany,[24] and is, not to put too fine a point upon it, a charlatan and a swindler, which Alexis certainly was not.

Walladmor should be read together with the article on 'The Romances of Walter Scott', which illustrates at greater length than its own Foreword what Alexis considered to be Scott's characteristic strengths and weaknesses. It is mainly indebted to *Guy Mannering* and *The Pirate.* In his memoirs Alexis claimed to have based his novel on *Waverley* and *Guy Mannering.* This is disingenuous, for there is little of *Waverley* in it and not a little of *The Pirate*. Although he denied that he had known *The Pirate* before writing *Walladmor*, the plain fact of the matter is that he had himself reviewed it in the *Wiener Jahrbücher* for April/May/June 1823. *Walladmor* was written immediately after this, in July – September.

---

23 Quoted from Lindop, 273.

24 F. Holthusen & Max F. Mann, 'Die Geschichte von Martin Waldeck in W. Scotts „The Antiquary",' *Beiblatt zur Anglia,* XXIX (1918), 280-3, 375-6.

These facts speak for themselves. In *Walladmor* Alexis made considerable use of *The Pirate.* The steam-packet Halcyon, the wrecking of which opens the novel, takes its name from the frigate of the same name. The cast of the novel includes Gillie Godber (cf. Norna of the Fitful Head, but also Meg Merrilies of *Guy Mannering*),[25] Captain le Harnois (cf. jury-captain Goffe), and Master Dulberry (cf. Triptolemus Yellowley), who was Alexis's favourite – because most original (least Scott-like!) – character. If he had read *The Devil's Elixir,* De Quincey would have recognized that Alexis had modelled Dulberry on the Irishman Ewson in Hoffmann's novel. Bertram, whose name goes back, in part, to *Guy Mannering*) is the negative hero, Ginievra the negative heroine. There is in the novel the same paradigmatic pattern of doubling that has been said to characterize *The Pirate.*[26] In order to achieve the three-volume format that was necessary if the work was to have any chance of passing for Scott's, Alexis had to insert not a little unnecessary material, which tends to read like De Quincey's digressions, and which De Quincey, with nice irony, later removed.

The first mention of *Walladmor* in the British press occurred in a footnote appended to a review of *St. Ronan's Well* in the *Literary Gazette* for December 1823:

> It is a curiosity of literature that a pseudo-translation of this novel reached London before the original. It is entitled *Walladmor* and published by Herbig, Berlin. The first chapter is an account of the explosion and wreck of the Steam-packet Halcyon, off Bristol; and details with some attempt at effect, the struggles of two of the passsengers in endeavouring to save their lives on the same cask! The whole is indeed a Tale of a Tub.

In order to be able to write his own review for the *London Magazine,* De Quincey borrowed the copy of the book that Scott had ordered, and is said to have read it, or begun reading it (the story is surely apocryphal, emanating from some wit in the Blackwood circle), without cutting the pages, for fear of offending Scott. It is a good story, and one which, if true, would do much to explain the differences between Alexis's and De Quincey's respective hoaxes.

Alexis was impressed by a review in the *Monthly Magazine* (February 1825, 64), which he wrongly believed to be by Scott. In his memoirs he wrote of Scott's 'launige Anzeige des *Walladmor*', and quoted the view that Walladmor was 'de[r] kühnste Vexirstreich unserer Zeiten', which he attributed to Scott. In fact it was De Quincey, in his *London Magazine* review, who described *Walladmor* as 'the boldest hoax of our times'.

7.4.2. De Quincey's View of the German *Walladmor*

We therefore come to De Quincey's views of Alexis's hoax novel. I say 'views' because there are two pieces in question. In the first place there is his original review, headed 'Walladmor: Sir Walter Scott's German Novel' (a punning title which managed to imply, by analogy with 'German silver', which is not silver at all, but a white alloy of nickel, zinc

25 A writer friend of Alexis, Sophie Mai, thought Gillie Godber closer to Hogg's spaewives than to anything in Scott.

26 Marilyn Orr, 'Repetition, Reversal and the Gothic: *The Pirate* and *St. Ronan's Well,' English Studies in Canada,* 26 (1990), 187-99.

and copper (better known nowadays as Chinese silver), that the novel was 'A cheap substitute for the real thing' [L 273]), which appeared in the *London Magazine* (10 [1824], 353-382). Then there is another piece, entitled 'Walladmor. A Pseudo-Waverley Novel' (14: 132-45), which originally appeared in *Tait's Magazine* for September 1838 (559-63) as part of the 'Autobiography of an English Opium-Eater. Recollections of Charles Lamb'. Reading De Quincey's 1824 review, it is easy to see how he came to write his *Walladmor*, much of which is there anticipated, for his review of Alexis's novel consists, once he has got to the point, of translations, some twenty-five in all, mostly of passages in the first two volumes of Alexis's novel, with linking passages of various lengths. He quickly enters into the spirit of his subject:

> *Freely translated!* Yes, no want of freedom! All free and easy! impossible to complain on that score. Verily, this is the boldest hoax of our times. [...] A hoax was bespoke in three volumes; and a hoaxer was bespoke to make it. And the grave publishers throughout Germany, Moravians and all, subscribed for reams of hoax. A great *Hum* was inflated at Leipzig and sent floating all over the fields of Germany [...] Bubbled Germany laughed because it knew not that it was a bubble: and bubbling Germany laughed because it knew full well that it was.

Here, in passing, is the key to his subtitle for one of his translations (also published in 1824) of Laun, *The Incognito, or: Count Fitz-Hum.* The prefix Fitz- denotes the illegitimate son of a nobleman, so that Fitz-Hum is a doubly dubious name (Hum = hoax); but it also amounts to an incognito of De Quincey, who himself has a number of incognitos, as author of the pseudo-*Walladmor*. There are some surprises in De Quincey's summary of the novel (as opposed to his own version of the novel itself), among them the fact that some Gothic details, including the important revenge-motif, which takes several forms in the novel, are omitted. That said, it gives a tolerably fair, if truncated, view of Alexis's novel, and some idea of what the reader is likely to find in De Quincey's own *Walladmor*.

De Quincey's attitude changed, however: from regarding it as a harmless hoax that he had compounded and, in his own view, trumped, by piling on top of it a further hoax of his own, he came, partly as a result of the hassle he had with his 'translation', and partly as a consequence of hostile reviews, to wish it to the Devil. It was Masson who, unwarrantably, spoke of Alexis's novel as 'the wretched German abortion', a term which is not only totally unwarranted (quite apart from the fact that there is no reason to think that Masson had read it, or was capable of reading it, in the original), but also in effect belittles De Quincey's version. While De Quincey would hardly have expressed himself in those particular terms, there can be no doubt that he refused to reprint his *Walladmor* not just because he was fed up with the whole affair, but because he was also afraid of the damage that a republication could do to his reputation. By then his life's work was virtually complete and could be seen to involve quite enough *rifacimenti* without bringing *Walladmor* into the equation.

In his autobiographical writings ('Walladmor: A Pseudo-Translation of Sir Walter Scott', 14: 132-45) De Quincey describes the circumstances under which he agreed to 'translate' the novel, and summarizes what this involved:

> mending and retouching into something like common sense wherever that was possible; but far more frequently forging new materials, in pure despair of mending the old; and reconstructing, very nearly, the whole edifice from the foundation upwards. And hence arose this singular result: that, withou any original intention

to do so, I had been gradually led by circumstances to build upon this German hoax a second and equally complete English hoax. The German 'Walladmor' professed to be a translation from the English of Sir Walter Scott – my 'Walladmor' professed to be a translation from the German; but [...] it was no more a translation from the German than the German from the English.

He adds, in the most revealing comment of all, that 'writing into the framework of another man's story fearfully cramped the freedom of my movements.' Clearly he regarded himself as being involved in producing a work of his own. Alexis's novel was also translated into Dutch, Swedish, Polish, and French, the French translation (*Walladmor,* roman attribué en Allemagne à Sir Walter Scott, traduit de l'anglais par M. A. J. B. Defauconpret [Paris: Charles Gosselin, 1825], which initiated a new series, the Bibliothèque des meilleurs Romans modernes Anglais et Américains) being, in a further ironical twist, a version not of Alexis's *Walladmor*, but of De Quincey's, which was not a translation at all in the normal sense, but a matter of 'writing into the framework of another man's story', in the course of which De Quincey claimed to have made a silk purse out of the proverbial sow's ear:

Sir John Cutler had a pair of silk stockings, which his house-keeper, Dolly, darned for a long term of years with worsted; at the end of which time the last gleam if silk had vanished, and Sir John's *silk* stockings were found to have degenerated into *worsted* [...] I must not have you interpret the precedent of Sir John and Dolly too strictly. Sir John's stockings were originally of silk, and darned with worsted; but don't you conceit *that* to be the case here. No, no! I flatter myself the case between us is just the other way. Your *worsted* stockings it is that I have darned with silk

In Germany, the publication of Alexis's *Walladmor* led to a dispute as to whether it was what it proclaimed itself to be. It was taken for a deliberate forgery, for a *jeu d'esprit* from the pen of Washington Irving (whom Alexis mentions in his text)[27] or Coleridge,[28] and so on. The critic of the *Brockhausische Blätter,* Wilhelm Müller, first regarded it as spurious, but eventually changed his mind and apologized for his mistake, whereupon the third volume appeared, showing beyond all doubt that it was a spoof. On the other hand the *Heidelberger Jahrbücher* reviewed it as a genuine Scott novel a year after the first edition had appeared. There is a close parallel here with the reception, in 1843, of Wilhelm Meinhold's *Maria Schweidler*, *die Bernsteinhexe*, which was mistaken for an original historical document, as its author had intended it should be.[29] Meinhold 'forged' his own work, claiming to have found the manuscript under the choirstalls in the parish church of Kosertow on Usedom,[30] and, like Chatterton and Alexis, was disbelieved when he owned up to his authorship, leaving at least one well-known, if gullible, critic out of face. Perhaps the most significant tribute to Alexis's 'ironical *Walladmor*' came from the poet Heinrich Heine, a man of the highest literary standards who knew England well. In *Reisebilder II* ('Die Nordsee III') he commended the Scott-imitations of Alexis, Alexander August Ferdinand von Oppeln-Bronikowski (who in a series of historical novels published between 1825 and 1834 did for Poland what Alexis did for Prussia) and James Fenimore Cooper.

27 *Abendzeitung, Wegweiser* (1824), No. 11.

28 *Zeitung für die elegante Welt* (1824), No. 176.

29 See Patrick Bridgwater, *Anglo-German Interactions in the Literature of the 1890s* (Oxford: Legenda, 1999), 76.

30 Bridgwater, *Anglo-German Interactions,* 91.

Heine's commendation can serve as a warning against accepting De Quincey's strictures against Alexis at face value. There is little in the present story that can be taken at face value.

7.4.3. The German *Walladmor* as Gothic Novel

However much De Quincey may have come to lament his folly in agreeing to translate *Walladmor* against the clock, it was, in some ways, a happy chance that led him to do so, for seldom have two novelists from different countries had more in common than Thomas De Quincey, who knew as well as anyone the North Wales area in which Alexis chose to set his novel (without knowing the area himself, for he knew England, as De Quincey knew Germany, at second hand) and Wilhelm Häring. For both of them the novel meant, in 1824, the Gothic popular novel with which they both grew up. 'Gothic' is the only narrative language with which they are familiar. For their first piece of extended fiction they both automatically had recourse to what they knew best, with the addition of a large dose of Romantic irony and not a little Gothic cross-generic shenanigans. To see Alexis's *Walladmor* for what it really is, and get away from the elaborate smokescreen created by De Quincey, we need to take a closer look at the novel, the literary, as opposed to satiric, portion of which is, not surprisingly (given that the sham translation is a common Gothic form) Gothic. But then of course Scott is himself close to Gothic:

> The outmoded motifs and properties of Gothic romance were replaced by Scott in a manner that afforded similar excitement but added to it the colour and conviction of reality. The wicked Montoni, the scheming Schedoni, the savage banditti and spectres of Gothic romance, became in the works of Scott genuine outlaws, monks, highland chiefs, and phantoms of Scottish tradition. For the Salvator Rosa landscapes were substituted real mountains, forest-vistas, valleys and caves, and the impregnable castles of Scotland.[31]

The text of *Walladmor* contains a number of references to other Gothic writings. Its starting-point seems to have been Alexis's memory of Maturin's *Bertram* and Vulpius's *Rinaldo Rinaldini.* The opening shipwreck, which probably reminded De Quincey of the opening of one of his favourite Gothic novels, Mary Pilkington's *The Accusing Spirit* (1802), and of Schiller's *The Ghost-Seer,* is in fact borrowed from Maturin's overwrought drama of 1817, *Bertram*, which also furnished Alexis with the name of his centre of consciousness in the text, Bertram. In *Walladmor*, as in *Bertram*, the shipwreck is, in Coleridge's words, 'a mere supernatural effect without even a hint of any supernatural agency; a prodigy without any circumstance'.[32] The opening is also reminiscent of Christian Vulpius's once-famous 'tale of the last century', *Rinaldo Rinaldini*, which opens with the robber-captain sitting at the foot of a sheer cliff-face, talking to two other characters, one of whom is named Nicolo. Alexis later referred to himself as being 'mit dem Rinaldo geboren', in other words, as having grown up with *Rinaldo Rinaldini*.[33] Here already are the names of Alexis's two most important characters, linked in the text by being *Doppelgänger*

---

31 Varma, 175.
32 Coleridge, *Biographia Literaria,* ch. 23.
33 *Blätter für literarische Unterhaltung,* 13 Feb. 1834.

one of the other. In Maturin's tragedy the hero-villain Bertram is a robber; in Alexis's novel he is a literary bandit and *persifleur*. Alexis's robber-leader Niklas (Nichols, Niccolo) belongs, in some respects, in the sublime mould of the Gothic novel; but, although his wild, stormy character reflects the stormy wildness of nature, he is not exactly the honourable robber who has performed the noble actions that prompt Vulpius's Altaverde to argue that 'The devil himself might act nobly, although he be a devil'. References to the *Vorzeit* (olden days) invoke Veit Weber's famous *Sagen der Vorzeit* series of impassioned improbable tales. They are appropriate in that the style (discourse) of the novel is straightaway closer to Veit Weber (or Beit Weber, as Scott always called him, with unconscious irony) and company than to Scott – unless it be to the Scott of *The House of Aspen,* that 'sort of a half-mad German tragedy' that is a *rifacimento* of Veit Weber's *Die heilige Vehme.* If *Walladmor*, as a parody of Scott, belongs together with *The Pirate,* as a spaghetti-Gothic novel it belongs together with Peacock's *Nightmare Abbey* (1818) and Eaton Stannard Barrett's *The Heroine* (1817).

The underground vault in which Bertram is held at the beginning of the novel is reminiscent of the lair of the banditti in Karl Friedrich Kahlert's *Der Geisterbanner*, the English rewrite of which, *The Necromancer; or, The Tale of the Black Forest*, one of the Northanger Abbey 'horrid' novels, De Quincey probably had in mind when he wrote his lost tale of the Black Forest, *The Curse*; the curse is a motif in his *Walladmor. The Necromancer* is not simply the barbarous, over-literal translation it seems to be, in which English words perform (unbeknown to the translator) to the conventions of German idiom and syntax, with often hilarious results, but a *rifacimento* made by fusing together Karl Friedrich Kahlert's *Der Geisterbanner*, of which it purports to be a translation, and Schiller's *Der Verbrecher aus verlorener Ehre.* In *Walladmor* there are a number of references to Schiller. Niklas, as the 'noble criminal' ('Welche Seelengröße leuchtet aus der Nacht seiner Sünden', Vol. 3, I: 9) is of the legion of Gothic heroes based on Schiller's Karl Moor in *Die Räuber* and ultimately on Milton's Satan (cf. Old Nick), the hero-villain of *Paradise Lost*, although Coleridge would not have mistaken him for the 'horrible wielder of heart-withering virtues', as he did Karl Moor. The 'ghostseers' in the text go back to *Der Geisterseher*, and 'Der Verbrecher' (Niklas) to *Der Verbrecher aus verlorener Ehr*e, the first English translation of which appeared in the *German Museum* (II, 144ff.) in 1801. Niklas, the hero-villain, is one of two heroes in the novel, the other being the negative hero, Bertram; the two are related as lookalikes and in being, both of them, 'robbers' and alter egos of the author, Bertram representing Alexis as pseudo-Scott, while Niklas stands for Alexis as Gothic robber (of Scott). As a name, Walladmor happens to echo Schiller's Wallenstein and Maturin's Aldobrand, but it is perhaps more plausibly based on Cadwallader (featured in Peacock's *Headlong Hall* in 1816) with the addition of the O.Engl. suffix *mor* (mountain). The falcon (Vol. 1, ch. 2) comes from the *Ritterroman.* The reference to 'Miß Ratkliffs Romanen' (sic: Vol. II, ch. 3), meaning the novels of Mrs Radcliffe, speaks for itself; the context is the ruined abbey or 'verfallenes Raubnest' (banditti-infested ruin) of Griffith ap Gauvon. What such detail means is that the young Alexis had recourse to his own reading when he was filling in the detail of his supposed Scott-imitation, which is at the same time a novel in the *Ritter-*, *Räuber-, Geister- und Schauerroman* convention(s).

In the novel there are, too, a number of references to Salvator Rosa (1615-1673), who became in some ways the exemplar of the Romantic artist; De Quincey was familiar with his work (E 354f). In *Walladmor* we see the crags and cliffs that Salvator made his own, and the pirate ship moored in a cove beneath a perpendicular cliff surrounded by that Gothic castle is straight out of Salvator. The human and geographical wildness that we associate with Salvator, the picturesque landscapes with rocky settings and figures of witches, redcoats and brigands, are present in full measure in Alexis's *Walladmor*, which, like Salvator's own work, contains memories of his short-lived bandit role.[34] In his review De Quincey draws attention to a passage (Vol. II, ch. 4) where

> Bertram [...] is busy with the picturesque; wishing that Merlin or some other Welsh wizard would call up Salvator Rosa from his grave to sketch the fine composition arranged by the prodigious shadows of Snowdon – the moonlight and the armed men carousing by their pine-wood fire within the gloomy shades of the abbey

The German *Walladmor* opens with a highly Gothic sudden event that comes like a bolt from the blue and spells the end of the relative security that preceded it, in this case a shipwreck that leaves the *dramatis personae* at the mercy of the sea, making this less a tale of a tub than a tall story of a barrel (How is someone supposed to lie on a barrel?). Is Alexis toying with the reader in the deconstructive way in which Kafka later did, in this case suggesting, via the metaphor *das schlägt dem Faß den Boden aus* (that takes the biscuit), that his tale is an unlikely one, as characters representing Alexis (Bertram) and Scott (Malburne) engage in a life-and-death struggle in the sea, until they reach an accommodation and agree to take turns on the tub? The shipwreck is even repeated in the third volume, with (melo)dramatic results that set in train the ending of the novel. Once on terra firma, Bertram finds himself in the hands of Gillie Godber, who is described as a witch, but also as a Medusa and (later) a Fury. In her capacity as witch, she goes back to similar Gothic figures in Scott, notably Meg Merrilies and Norna of the Fitful Head; though in her way a 'dark lady', she in no way goes beyond the typical Scott self-deluded female enthusiast, completely lacking the mythical depth of Our Lady of Darkness, whom De Quincey would not have been capable of envisioning at this time. Alexis is close to Scott in respect of the (mostly explained) supernatural.[35] Bertram finds himself not only in the hands of an apparent witch, but in a subterranean cavern or 'recess' with, for company, a skeleton seated on a chair. His situation is itself 'no canny' (*unheimlich*), and he seeems to be paralyzed, powerless to move even when a door that is bolted on the inside opens from the outside, unless he is dreaming and therefore subject to sleep paralysis. The Gothic cavern, a leitmotif of the novel, recurs in the form of the 'Mörderhöhle' (Walladmor Castle is described as a 'Mördergrube' and 'Räuberhöhle); such nests of murderous brigands and robbers infest the pages of the popular fiction of the time, English and German and French alike.

It is above all the spatialities of the novel that are Gothic. The precipitous cliffs, dizzying heights and yawning chasms that are much in evidence represent both the

---

34 See, especially, W. Gaunt, *Bandits in a Landscape. A Study of Romantic Painting from Caravaggio to Delacroix* (London & New York: The Studio. 1937), 29-33.

35 See Coleman O. Parsons, *Witchcraft and Demonology in Scott's Fiction* (Edinburgh & London: Oliver & Boyd, 1964).

insecurity and precarious balance of the world into which Bertram finds himself projected, but also the fine line between success and abject failure that Alexis is all the time treading. Notwithstanding De Quincey's criticisms, in which self-interest was involved, the balance, as we have seen, came down in favour of success. The smugglers who play such a large part in the novel are, similarly, both figures from Scott and the pages of Gothic fiction and, at the same time, continual reminders of Alexis's 'Schleichhandel' (smuggling) and the fact that he, as author, is 'auf dem Schleichweg' (engaged in underhand business), hence Bertram as 'brother' of Niklas: the author (or 'translator') as smuggler. It is Alexis's self-depiction as a robber or smuggler that makes his *Walladmor* such a perfect choice, but also such a challenge, for De Quincey, whose subconscious feelings of guilt are conjured up. The idea of the writer as transgressor, and indeed smuggler, was bound to appeal to De Quincey, bound to provoke an evasively idiosyncratic reaction.

Walladmor Castle, a large but (gothically) shapeless (indeterminate) pile perched on a beetling cliff above a raging sea, is described as a 'gefeite(s), mit Geistersehern und allem Romanenapparat versehene(s) Schloß' (an enchanted castle furnished with ghost-seers and the [Gothic] novelist's whole bag of tricks). It is a typical Gothic castle, not least in possessing a memorably terrible and claustrophobic prison, subterranean passage, and so on; but this 'wunderbar gebautes Schloß' (prodigious castle) with its 'Zauberturm' (magic tower) is also the magic castle of folklore and superstition, home of Sir Morgan Walladmor, who represents the superstitious, Gothic world of the medieval ancestors he never tires of invoking. Equally Gothic is the 'verfallene(s) Raubnest' (robber-infested ruin) of Griffith ap Gauvon, a ruined abbey with the phantasmagorically shifting outline of Gothic convention and a tower that makes it a kind of spectral double of Walladmor Castle. The Romantic/Gothic figures of the mysterious Stranger and the solitary Wanderer (traveller) are present too, as is the pariah that features in other work by both Alexis and De Quincey. Here too are the Gothic motifs of murder, revenge, incarceration and execution. The preliminary hearing of the 'Inquisit' (accused; cf. Inquisition) and his trial belong in the context of the tension between law and lawlessness, initially invoked by the storm, that characterizes Gothic. The confusion of identities in the novel, including the question of the identity of the author (reflected in the novel as the question of the identity of several of the main characters) is wholly Gothic, as is the whole mystery regarding the status of the manuscript. The novel is cross-generic in being, intentionally, a parody of Scott, and, intentionally or otherwise, a parody of a Gothic novel or *Räuberroman,* whose means and motifs provide the individual trees in this vast Hercynian forest of a novel. In De Quincey's hands it then becomes even more generically indeterminate, even the identity of the author being uncertain. In short, Alexis's Gothic masquerade parallels De Quincey's. The only question is whether De Quincey's *Walladmor* will turn out to be more or less Gothic than Alexis's.

7.4.4. De Quincey's *Walladmor* (1825)

The makings of De Quincey's *Walladmor* are there for all to see in his 1824 review of Alexis's novel: 'all' he needs to do, it seems, is contrive a 'better' (which from Alexis's point of view means worse) framework from which to hang his translations, which means, in effect, cutting out what he calls Alexis's 'rigmarole', concentrating on altering and condensing the last two volumes (from the third volume he includes only the trial-scene). Alexis's novel is itself episodic. When De Quincey has further concentrated on the tableaux translated in his review, the result is a novel that is episodic in the manner of Grosse's *Horrid Mysteries*, which both Alexis and De Quincey may safely be assumed to have known, and which we have come to see as a caricature of the novel at its most unspeakably 'Gothick'. Goldman is right to say that De Quincey has 'conceived his story not so much as a narrative of events, or a study of characters, but as a sequence of romantic tableaux, elaborately put together in the manner of theatrical scenery'.[36] Once the mixture has been given a further spin and has been further distanced by means of satire, *Walladmor* is there for the writing.

In 'translating' *Walladmor*, De Quincey stretches the concept of *rifacimento* first to and then past the limit. It would have been less mystifying if he had inscribed it 'altered from the German', as Thomas Dibdin did with his version of Kotzebue's *The Will for the Deed* in 1805, or 'Taken from the German', a wording that was also used at the time. Alexis's novel comprised 3 volumes totalling 883 pages, arranged in 26 chapters. De Quincey reduces this to 2 volumes totalling 542 pages, arranged in 21 chapters. He follows the original fairly closely in his first volume, which includes most of the material in Alexis's first volume, a good deal of which he had included in his review. His second volume represents a severely pruned and modified version of Alexis's second and third volumes (of the third volume little survives), written as De Quincey got hoist with his own petard. He excises the digresssions on Welsh history that Alexis had inserted to bulk out his novel to Scott-like proportions, and changes the names of some of the characters to make them seem genuinely English, thereby turning a spoof into a forgery.

The idea that De Quincey has simply tightened up and generally improved the original is a suspect notion, given that he is tinkering with another's work, not revising his own. Because of his own respect for Scott, De Quincey omitted Alexis's Malburne (= Scott), and did not present Bertram (= Alexis) as a budding author 'der in die Welt läuft, um einen Scottischen Roman zu schreiben' (who is setting out to write a Scott novel). Alexis, who naturally regarded the ironical Bertram-Malburne relationship – the relationship between himself and Scott – as the core of the novel, thought the English translation must have been done by a friend of Scott, if indeed Scott himself did not have a hand in it. He could hardly recognize his original in the translation, because the element of 'well-intentioned parody' had been omitted altogether. Seen from Alexis's point of view, De Quincey had taken one liberty too many. He had not produced a translation at all; in building an English hoax upon a German one, he had deconstructed the German hoax, substituting a 'Gothick' concoction of his own for Alexis's pastiche of Scott.

The process of encapsulation is typically Gothic: Alexis writes a novel amounting to a caricature of the typical Scott novel as he sees it. De Quincey then summarizes that novel (and there is a clear difference between Alexis's Foreword, which puts all the emphasis on radical politics, and De Quincey's reading of the novel, which foregrounds its Gothic elements), subjecting it to his own wit and preconceptions of various kinds, and then finally goes one step further in writing what is less a translation (or even a *rifacimento*) of a

---

[36] Goldman, 97.

pseudo-Waverley novel, than a further refracted and ironized counterfeit of an original counterfeit. The more he 'corrects' Alexis's novel, the more of a forgery his own novel becomes. Both the process of literary 'coining' and the cross-generic product of it are Gothic in today's terms, while much of the detail both of Alexis's novel and of De Quincey's is Gothic in terms of their time. It needs to be borne in mind all the time that we are dealing not with one but with two writers who grew up with Gothic. Alexis, in 1823, has not yet outgrown it; De Quincey never will. Alexis's *Walladmor*, while purporting to be a new novel by Scott, was less a pseudo-Waverley novel than a *Räuberroman* translated to Wales and attributed to Scott. In other words, it was a *Räuberroman* masquerading as a Waverley novel. The padding, which often extends to whole chapters, was there for all to see, but so too were the motifs and machinery of Gothic and the style of German popular novels of the *Ritter-, Räuber- und Schauerroman* type. There were, it is true, echoes of Scott and his prepossessions and character types, but the discourse as such was not that of Scott.

De Quincey's summary of Alexis's novel represents his idiosyncratic reading of an already idioynscratic work. In making his own version of *Walladmor*, De Quincey excises much more than what he calls 'the rubbish – political, astrological, and diabolical'. He cuts most of what might be deemed padding, but not all; the funeral of Le Harnois, a smokescreen and seeming digression, is retained because it is an important part of the 'smuggling' motif, which is in turn part of the ship metaphor, with which De Quincey makes brilliant play. Malburne (Scott) is deleted, as is the relationship between Bertram and Malburne, and Bertram (Alexis) is further diminished by losing his relationship with Ginievra, thus enabling the second shipwreck to be deleted too. In refocussing the novel De Quincey plays down the 'pseudo-Waverley' element, concentrating instead on the underlying Gothic Romantic (Chatterton, Ireland, De Quincey) idea of the writer as 'coiner', which serves to link the novel with his own Gothic works.

In rewriting the novel, De Quincey anglicizes, 'improves' and 'corrects' it, changing and upgrading its style, which is no longer that of Veit Weber and the *Räuberroman*, but is now closer to the style of Lee's *Kruitzner* and De Quincey's *Klosterheim,* which the motif of the stranger (a dissembler wearing a masque and with an 'extraordinary talent for personating') prefigures. The 'Falken' deriving from the *Ritterroman* is also deleted. De Quincey inserts a good deal of detail in support of his rewrite, but more important at this point is the fact that, for stylistic reasons, he cuts some details that would have been in line with his refocussing of the novel. This shows that, while he enhances the gothicity of the novel, his motivation is aesthetic, not a matter of gothification for its own sake. He excises everything smacking of bad taste, coarseness, crassness, or ignorance. For Alexis's mottoes he substitutes ones of his own choosing to match his refocussing of the novel. Alexis's mottoes (copied and/or imitated from Percy, etc.) were in line with the ballad material favoured by Scott. De Quincey's, by contrast, mostly come, like Ann Radcliffe's, from Shakespeare and other older dramatists, this underlining the even more episodic, dramatic nature of De Quincey's novel, although Alexis's novel, which De Quincey described as opening 'with the following *scena*', was already dramatically conceived. One of Alexis's models, Vulpius's *Rinaldo Rinaldini*, is, after all, a Gothic 'tale' in dramatic form. De Quincey emphasizes the element of drama, breaking chapters not at Alexis's endings, but at dramatically suitable points, ending, for the most part, on a note of suspense. Nicholas

(Niklas), a nobler character than in Alexis's novel, is now closer to Schiller's Karl Moor. Moreover De Quincey

> translates his hero into the identical twin of his Byronic antagonist, surrounds him with impersonators, has him accused of forging his 'papers', and while he is incarcerated, pictures him reading 'the *first* volume of *Walladmor,* a novel, 2 vols [...] the second being not then finished,' in Borgesian reinscription of periodical desire.[37]

Miss Walladmor, as she now becomes, no longer resembles the heroine of a German sentimental romance, and 'Where Alexis has her whisper sweet words of encouragement to her parting lover, De Quincey has her perish in his arms.'[38] Burwick argues that De Quincey had done something similar in translating *Der Freischütz,* when he restored the death and madness of the original ending, but in fact De Quincey simply translated Johann Apel's original tale rather than the harmless libretto that Friedrich Kind had produced from it.

Having ridiculed the pseudo-Scott's evident lack of familiarity with the Welsh countryside and Welsh customs, De Quincey set out in his 'translation' to 'outhoax the hoaxer' by depicting the Welsh setting and political events 'more accurately'. He not only much 'improves' (at the expense of Alexis, who had unwittingly imputed to Scott considerable ignorance of English manners and Welsh geography) the English and Welsh background; he takes advantage of his much greater experience as a writer to tighten up Alexis's narrative in countless small ways that affect the quality of the novel rather than its nature, thereby making the novel his own in a qualitative stylistic sense.

7.4.5. *Walladmor* as Gothic Novel

More significant than De Quincey's deletions from Alexis's text are his additions to it, which is where our consideration of the greater or lesser gothicity of his *Walladmor* must begin. For a start, he develops the ship metaphor, which should be understood to include what Maturin calls the 'plague-ship of German letters'; the shipwreck, which includes shipwrecked hopes and wrecked lives (throughout his work he uses the word wreck revealingly often, always with subliminal reference to his own wrecked life) and piracy (hence the 'derelict, wrecker and plundering vessel') and pirating, which applies to both (pirated) versions of the novel, as does the smuggler/smuggling complex, which carries the idea of Scott's proofs being carried to Germany, but also the shipment of Alexis's 'pirated' novel into Britain. It is steam – hot air – that enables the novel. The steam-packet Halcyont parallels the steam-press, with the aid of which Scott, entering into the fun, supposed Alexis's novel to have been written by the Devil (cf. printer's devil, but also devil in the sense of a 'mischievously clever person'). De Quincey, who had a devil of a time of it in trying to produce copy for the printer, will have had his own take on this. The motif of the 'strange ship' carrying one supposed dead links with the legend of the Demon Frigate

---

37 Russett, 112.

38 Burwick, *The Wordsworth Circle*, XXV/2 (Spring 1994), 96.

(Scott, *Rokeby* [1813], II: ix) or Phantom Ship/Flying Dutchman that spanned the century following its appearance as 'Vanderdecken's Message Home' in *Blackwood's* in 1821.

In the German *Walladmor,* which is, technically, an involuted novel in that the text includes a metafictional account of its own genesis, Bertram is Alexis's 'focus' in the text, while Niklas stands for Alexis as 'robber', 'pirate' and 'smuggler', but also as the devil (cf. Old Nick) in question. In the English version of the novel, by contrast, in which the involuted element is not present in the narrative proper, Bertram and Edward Nicholas represent De Quincey himself. Bertram's upbringing in Germany represents the fact that De Quincey, like Alexis, grew up with the Gothic fiction that at its most horrid was popularly – and to a considerable extent falsely, for there is little in the German equivalent that is more horrid than Lewis's *The Monk* – associated with Germany. Edward Nicholas, for his part, represents De Quincey as 'robber,'pirate' and 'smuggler', although now it is Alexis, not Scott, who has been robbed, De Quincey who has smuggled a text of his own into Alexis's *Urtext.* De Quincey hollows out Alexis's novel in order to insert himself, parasitically, at its core. He uses Alexis's text as so much material out of which to construct a neo-Gothic counter-text of his own devising. The writer as ghost-crab, then, inhabiting the house of another's imagination, or as a parasite supported by a tree without which it could not exist This points forward to a passage in *Suspira de Profundis* in which De Quincey wrote that 'The whole course of this narrative resembles [...] a tree's stem hung round and surmounted with some vagrant parasitical plant',[39] which in turn invokes the machinery for dreaming planted in that mighty palimpsest, the human brain. It is not the least of the ironies surrounding this text/counter-text that, whereas Alexis's *Walladmor* is remembered, if at all, as an unfortunate prank that did its author's subsequent literary career no good, De Quincey's, which is the more truly parasitical of the two, still enjoys a kind of literary half-life. In an essay entitled 'De Quincey as Gothic Parasite: The Dynamic of Supplementarity',[40] Jan B. Gordon has examined the 'Gothic parasite' theme, but unfortunately did so (so far as *Walladmor* is concerned) on the strength of De Quincey's review-summary of Alexis's novel rather than his own version of the novel, into the text of which De Quincey smuggles a reference to that other, better known and more successful example of the Gothic novelist as coiner, W. H. Ireland, forger of the Shakespeare manuscripts and other documents that fooled the general public and caused Boswell to salute the master-forger's work.

De Quincey develops the motif of the double or *Doppelgänger*, which he spreads into further corners of the text, and emphasizes those of the outcast and the labyrinth. At every opportunity he applies the concept of the sublime (to which Alexis did less than justice) to the Snowdonian rockscape, emphasizing not just the 'tumultuous assemblage of mountains'(WTDQ, 4: 303), but, more especially, 'how majestically [the ruins] stand upon the naked peaks of the rocks; and how boldly the pointed [Gothic] arches rise into the air and throw themselves over the unfathomable chasms!' (WTDQ, 4: 312). It is as though the very arches are tempted to suicide by the grandiose image of descent and fall that invokes the Fall. There is a similar description later in the text: 'Dazzled by the grandeur of the spectacle, Bertram [...] overlooked the spacious ruins of the entire monastery, as its highest

---

[39] De Quincey, *Confessions of an English Opium-Eaterand Other Writings*, ed. G. Lindop (Oxford: Oxford University Press, 1996), 94.

[40] In *Bicentenary Studies*, 239-62.

points silvered over by moonlight shot up from amidst the illimitable night of ravines, chasms and rocky peaks' (WTDQ, 4: 362f). It is mostly the sublime of terror that is invoked, for De Quincey draws attention less to the awe-inspiring peaks than to the life-threatening ravines and chasms that complement them. Alexis's references to Salvator Rosa are given additional point by this added emphasis on the sublime. De Quincey re-emphasizes the Gothic/fantastic nature of Walladmor Castle and its double, the ruined abbey of Griffth ap Gauvon, the description of which is enhanced by the addition of a reference to a 'subterraneous church of vast dimensions, such as are sometimes found in the old monasteries below the ordinary chapel of the order'. The 'vast dimensions' of both edifices are emphasized, and a 'faery' element is added: Sir Morgan is presented as the 'old dragon' in the fairy-castle of Walladmor, so that he and Gillie Godber are as it were ghosts of the ogre/wicked count and witch/wicked stepmother of Gothic and fairytale convention. What De Quincey has in mind is probably not the dragon as a metaphor for the Devil, for he claimed to have excised the diabolical, but the dragon as the symbol of Old Wales embodied in Sir Morgan and, by extension, the dragon as the embodiment of patriarchy that hunts down Edward Nicholas. In the final confrontation Miss Walladmor – the dragon's traditional maiden-prey – is killed.

In De Quincey's hands *Walladmor* becomes an avenger-novel motivated by Gillie Godber's burning desire for revenge, a fact that immediately links it with his other Gothic works, and more especially with *The Avenger*. The wreck topos links it with *The Household Wreck*. The Masque and his appearances and disappearances resurface, in further developed form, in *Klosterheim*. The outcast theme, the descent/abyss motif and the 'dream' connect the novel with *Confessions*, while the heights and depths of the Snowdonian landscape prefigure those of *Suspira de Profundis*. Two of De Quincey's translations are also invoked, 'The Fatal Marksman' and 'The Incognito, or Count Fitz-Hum'. The robber, murderer and stranger are familiar figures in De Quincey's Gothic/autobiographical works.

More generally, *Walladmor* has many Gothic features. As a counterfeit tale, a counterfeit copy of an existing counterfeit, the novel stands in the convention established by Walpole's counterfeit medieval tale. The resultant generic instability is matched by the spatial instability that is much in evidence in the novel, for instance in the phantasmagorically shifting appearance of the ruined abbey (tower) of Griffth ap Gauvon. The use of antiquated space (Gillie Godber's cottage in a quarry, the ruined abbey and the antiquated castle) and claustrophobic or fear-inspiring spatialities (again, the abbey and castle, but more especially the extraordinary prison in the latter, the *ne plus ultra* of gothicism) correspond to and parallel the sublime, banditti-infested Snowdonian landscape with its spectral spaces. Both the landscape and the figures in it are haunted by their past, their hidden secrets. The sense of loss analysed by Sedgwick is exemplified in the way in which Gillie Godber and Sir Morgan Walladmor are possessed by their lost sons, or the way in which Edward Nicholas (unlike Bertram, who is relatively incurious about his) is driven by his own past. The ghosts that flit in and out of the text are not only shades from the Gothic past with its belief in ghosts and from the literarily Gothic present, which, as in the person of Walter Scott, is unable to shake off that belief; at the same time they are reminders of the more solid and familiar ghosts by which the main figures in the novel are haunted. Nicholas embodies the inbetween-state of Gothic: he is very much alive in another identity, but, until the end, as good as dead in his own. At the same time he stands in for

Gillie Godber's son, killed by Sir Morgan and thus abjected by him. Problematical identity is an aspect of the instability that is quintessentially Gothic; more especially it is a feature of late High Gothic, as exemplified in Francis Lathom's *Italian Mysteries* of 1820.

Equally Gothic is the blurring of lines and values symbolized in the blurred outline of the tower of Griffth ap Gauvon, or the way in which the gallows with their own dark secrets and abjected identities well up out of the mist. The line between law and lawlessness is deliberately blurred, so that the wicked deed is liable to take on the colouring of a noble one. Such instability, so characteristic of Gothic, is built into these two novels with their cross-generic status: Alexis's text as *Räuberroman* and pseudo-Waverley novel, the two versions of *Walladmor*, both of them pretending to be something they are not, one somewhere between a *Räuberroman* and a Waverley novel, the other somewhere between that and a Gothic novel by De Quincey. Both involve, in different degrees, the combination of and tension between high and low culture, but the most significant Gothic feature of Alexis's novel, and even more of De Quincey's, is its 'insistent artificiality', the fact that it exaggerates and parades its own fictionality, and that 'its representations and even its gothicism are [...] pointedly fake and counterfeit from the beginning'.[41] Alexis's work is populated by ghosts from Scott; De Quincey's, populated by ghosts of ghosts, is by definition the more Gothic.

7.5. *Schloß Avalon* (1827)

For a time Alexis remained obsessed with Scott. Having written *Walladmor* (1823-24), he translated a novel that was, like *Walladmor*, in part a burlesque of Scott's *The Pirate*, James Kirke Paulding's *Koningsmarke, the Long Finn* (1823: *Königsmark, der lange Finne* [Berlin: Herbig, 1824]), and followed that up by writing a second Scott-pastiche of his own, *Schloß Avalon* (1827),[42] of which Scott-scholarship appears not to know. He later wrote that whereas *Walladmor* was 'ein Spiel' (a sport), *Schloß Avalon* was 'ein Werk' (a [serious] work). As we have seen, the name Königsmark has its own place in the history of the Gothic novel, for H. J. Sarrett published, in 1803, a romance, *Koenigsmark the Robber; or, The Terror of Bohemia*, which was said to be translated or adapted from the German of R. E. Raspe, and which was followed by a chapbook of the same title, published in 1815 and spuriously attributed to M. G. Lewis. Königsmark was a captain of banditti. At the same time Alexis translated Thomas Colley Grattan's *Highways and Byways* (1825: *Heer- und Querstraßen*, 1824-8), so it seems that he even shared De Quincey's predilection for the company of 'walking gentlemen', particularly when they also go in for gothified historical tales, as Grattan did in *The Heiress of Bruges* (1830), the German translation of which Alexis reviewed.[43]

In 1826 Alexis was on a satirical high, even planning to bring out an English translation of *Schloß Avalon* before the original had appeared, to say nothing of planning a further instalment of the *Walladmor* hoax in the form of an article entitled '„Seltsames Abenteuer

41 Hogle, *Cambridge Companion*, 14f.

42 Cf. Catherine Smith's *The Castle of Arragon; or The Banditti of the Forest* , 4 vols (London: Henry Colburn, 1809).

43 In *Blätter für literarische Unterhaltung*, 1831, 657ff.

eines deutschen Reisenden in England", Kritische Novelle vom übersetzer des Walladmor' ('Strange Adventure of a German Traveller in England', a Critical Afterthought by the Translator of *Walladmor*).[44] On 5 July 1826 the publisher Brockhaus wrote to Alexis, trying to put the brakes on his enthusiasm:

> You seem to attach great importance to an English translation and almost to regard this as the main object; I have no such favourable opinion of the idea. It is certainly true that *Walladmor* has evoked no small interest in England, but we shall have to wait and see whether [*Schloß Avalon*] does likewise.
>
> However, if I know my English booksellers, I believe that none of them will enter into a contract with me to buy the final proofs [...] We have no wish to bring out an English translation.[45]

When it appeared in June 1827, *Schloß Avalon, frei nach dem Englischen des Walter Scott vom Übersetzer des Walladmor* (Leipzig: Brockhaus) shows that Alexis had by then also gone several steps further in learning from his study of Scott's style:

> he did not, as before, merely expose the weaknesses of Scott's novels, but [...] attempted to carry through actual betterments. He chose the subject matter which Scott had always avoided, the fall of the house of Stuart; he let the action extend over a long period of years in order to introduce the necessary historical perspective; and, finally, he made use of a second passive hero, while Scott employed regularly but one. Alexis made use, in this novel, of several character types and situations that belonged to Scott's stock, but [his] aim was [...] different: he wished to write a historical novel, rather than a novel of cultural history.[46]

If Alexis was by now 'paying little more than lip service to a hoax diluted by repetition', and wanting his work to be judged on its own merits, as Thomas claims,[47] it may seem odd that he not only used a pseudonym, but once again donned the emperor's clothes; in doing so he will have had in mind both the success of his *Walladmor* and the vogue for Scott-imitations in Germany at the time. If Heinrich Müller could offload five Scott-imitations onto the market in the course of two years he may have thought, surely he could get away with a second one himself. This time the whole procedure is much more transparent, as is shown by the long introduction in which Scott and Alexis discuss possible titles for the novel. Suggestions from Alexis include 'Die rieselnde Blutspur unter den Trümmern des westlichen Thurmes' (The Trail of Blood Among the Ruins of the West Tower), which would have indicated that this novel too was as much a satirical *Schauerroman* as another pseudo-Waverley novel. Eventually Scott suggests 'Schloß Avalon', after the Isle of Avalon (Ynys Avallach), the final resting-place of King Arthur and home of Morgan le Fay. By this time Avalon had come to be seen as an Earthly Paradise (cf. its early alternative name, the Island of Apples) and a place of escape (cf. the world of the romance, which includes the Gothic novel) from the modern world. The title is in line with the folklore interests attested by Scott's German books.

---

44 See *Blätter für literarische Unterhaltung*, 9 Nov. 1826, 429-31; 10 Nov. 1826, 433-5; 11 Nov. 1826, 437-9; 13 Nov. 1826, 441-4.

45 Quoted from Lionel Thomas, *Willibald Alexis. A Biography* (Oxford: Blackwell, 1964), 38.

46 Price, 380.

47 Lionel Thomas, 'Schloß Avalon', *German Life & Letters*, X (1957), 97 (-105).

Thomas argues that *Schloß Avalon,* though a 'magnificent failure',[48] stands comparison with those of Scott's novels composed against a foreign background, such as *Quentin Durward*, but Alexis, who here earns his spurs as an historical novelist, would surely have done better to write in his own right instead of posing as a translator (and rival) of Scott. German booksellers and readers were evidently confused as to the identity of the author of *Schloß Avalon.* Alexis himself noted[49] that the novel was included in a Viennese edition of the Waverley Novels, and that he had been assured by a bookseller in Teplitz that it was a genuine work by Scott. The edition of Scott's *Werke* in 75 vols published in Grätz by Kienreich in 1828-34 included *Schloß Avalon*, but not *Walladmor*, which had become known as the work of Alexis. De Quincey, for his part, seems not to have known about *Schloß Avalon.* While it may simply be that he did not wish to be involved again, the more likely explanation is that, following Bohte's death in 1824 and the liquidation of J. H. Bohte & Co. in 1826, he did not get to know about this second Scott-imitation, which was only once noticed in England (*The Foreign Review*, 1 (1828), 219-223). By that time De Quincey, living mostly in Edinburgh, was no longer in touch with contemporary German literature in the way in which he had been in 1821.

7.6. *The Spanish Military Nun* (1847-54)

To the 'military robber' of *Klosterheim* De Quincey now adds the 'military nun'. The *Spanish Military Nun* is, in Masson's words, 'a cooked, and spiced, and De Quinceyfied (which means electrified and glorified) translation from the French' (13: 245). In other words, it is a characteristic *remaniement* or *rifacimento*, in this case involving the fictionalization of a piece by Alexis de Valon, entitled 'Catalina de Erauso', which appeared in the *Revue des Deux Mondes* on 15 February 1847. Valon's article was itself a *remaniement,* based on an autobiographical account, *Historia de la Monja Alferez Donna Catalina de Erauso, escrita par ella misma*, the second part of Valon's essay being an account of the history of this history, which he was continuing, and which De Quincey was to continue in his turn; nor did the story end there, for either Valon's article or De Quincey's recast of it inspired a further encapsulation in the form of a minor Gothic novel, *Catalina; or, The Spaniard's Revenge* (London: Dicks, 1847) by one William Hillyard. Two and a half months after Valon's essay had appeared, De Quincey's version began to be serialized in *Tait's Edinburgh Magazine* in May 1847 (it was completed in the July number). *The Spanish Military Nun*, the story of a young woman, Catalina de Erauso (1592-1635), who served as a cavalry lieutenant in the Spanish army, goes back to a Spanish account written by Goya's friend Joaquín Ferrer and published in Paris (where he was at the time in political exile) in 1830. Goya, who was himself in exile in France from 1824 until his death in 1828, was friendly with Joaquín María Ferrer and his wife, whose portraits he painted.

The story of the 'Spanish Military Nun' or 'nun-lieutenant', though set in the early seventeenth century, belongs in the historical context of the savage war of Spanish

48 Thomas, ibid., 103.
49 Alexis, *Erinnerungen*, 281.

Independence, known in English as the Peninsular War, which is commemorated in Goya's *Disasters of War* series, and in the literary context of *The Peasant of Portugal* and *The Caçadore* and of De Quincey's Gothic tales generally, with which it has a number of key elements in common. Catalina's whole life is, like De Quincey's own, a masquerade; she (whom he calls Kate after Kate Wordsworth) is another Masque, another Max. Here are the avenger-motif, murder, mystery and mystification, secrecy, even the visionary element as 'Kate begins to descend the Mighty Staircase' that we all descend in the end. The whole rigmarole of a translation that is not a translation, and of successive encapsulations, is thoroughly Gothic.

8. Fictions

What is shown by the course of reading that De Quincey followed in Everton in spring 1803 is not his interest in the novel, as Eaton argues, for, far from showing any real interest in the novel as such, he shows a marked lack of interest in it. Defoe he dismisses as a 'forger'. Of Richardson, Fielding and Smollett he has nothing to say. Of Scott – *Walladmor* notwithstanding – he did not have a particularly high opinion; when he mentions a work by Scott, it is the *Letters on Demonology and Witchcraft*. What his early reading shows is, rather, his interest in Gothic as such, regardless of genre (novel, tale, ghost-story, tragedy, ballad), chiefly as a method of encryption of the ultra-personal. However, Eaton's comments, though outdated in most respects, still point to the problems posed by De Quincey's fictions:

> De Quincey's desire to write fiction was a lifelong prepossession [...] As literature, all his attempts at fiction are [...] merely curiosities. They are one and all conceived in the old-fashioned mode of the late eighteenth and early nineteenth centuries, that mode which produced so many sentimental and mysterious narratives unreadable by our sophisticated age. His models were the romantic works of German writers, of whom Schiller and Tieck are the most famous; and the greater number of De Quincey's stories are merely translations and free adaptations. So persistent was his habit of borrowing, that one may well suspect that even for *The Household Wreck, The Avenger,* and *Klosterheim*, which are generally accepted as De Quincey's own inventions, some obscure German originals may still be discovered. (E 348f.)

Leaving aside the fact that it is precisely the 'mysterious [Gothic] narratives' of the late eighteenth and early nineteenth centuries that are hugely popular in our own perhaps over-sophisticated age, what needs challenging is the idea that the 'greater number' of De Quincey's stories are translations or *rifacimenti.* This is simply not true.

That early Gothic is parasitical, is shown by the legion of the unreadable, the second- and third-rate novelists whose very titles proclaim their unoriginality. This applies even to a work as famous as *Horrid Mysteries*, which lives off Schiller's *The Ghost-Seer.* However, while much of his non-fictional work is parasitical in the sense of being over-indebted to the work of others, without which it would not exist, De Quincey is, contrary to much received opinion, at his most original in his fictional work. The view that his fictional works were parasitical was sustainable only on the basis of the idea, propagated by critics from Eaton onwards, that it was based on supposed German models. That idea, it is now clear, was false save in relation to *Walladmor.* Goldman proved the parasitism of De Quincey's essayistic work, but failed to show that the fictional work was parasitic. All five of the fictions by De Quincey discussed in this chapter are original works. The idea that *The Avenger, The Household Wreck*, and *Klosterheim* are unoriginal did De Quincey a grave disservice. Their relation to comparable German works known to me is discussed below. The 'known to me' is a necessary proviso, for German 'Gothic' texts, like English ones, were many, often by minor writers, and have often not survived; indeed, because of the traditional German disdain for popular literature, an even smaller percentage have survived than of their English counterparts. While I am confident that the works discussed in this chapter are not copies or imitations of German works, this may never be proved one way or another.

The idea that De Quincey's models, in a far more general sense, were 'the romantic works of German writers, of whom Schiller and Tieck are the most famous', is also misleading. De Quincey read Schiller's *The Ghost-Seer* in 1803, and was doubtless impressed by it, but he never commented on it, and his own fictions are not 'ghost-seer' stories, although the device of the Masque in *Klosterheim* may, it is true, go back to his early reading of *The Ghost-Seer*. He translated 'Ein Spiel des Schicksals', but did not use it as a model. Of Tieck he may not have known much at all, though he was familiar with *Phantasus*, and may have read *Der Geheimnißvolle* at Bohte's. Of 'romantic works of German writers', let alone works by German Romantic writers, there is relatively little trace in his works. He was, on the other hand, clearly familiar with many supposedly 'German(-type)' Gothic tales written in English. It was the fashion at this time for English Gothic tales to masquerade as German, and vice-versa, to say nothing of masquerading as the work of others: *Walladmor* is the tip of a sizeable iceberg. What he did know was the work of the Dresden-based *Pseudoromantiker*, notably Friedrich Laun, and in 1821, while staying with Bohte, he read widely in contemporary German fiction (but apparently not that of the major Romantics, with the possible exception of Tieck). What he may have read can be ascertained from J. H. Bohte & Co.'s catalogues; what he actually read, can only be guessed at. What is certain is that neither his literary interests nor his reading in English and German equipped him to be a novelist of consequence. He evinced little interest in the novel as such: in the index to his collected works the names of the great novelists of the time are conspicuous by their absence.

For Eaton the essential defect of De Quincey's tales lies in the unreality of the plots and the lack of 'reality of character'; he scorns De Quincey's stereotypes. Most of this can be discounted, given the change in literary fashion, for it means little more than that Eaton scorns romances because they are not novels of a particular historically conditioned and therefore now dated kind. It may well be that De Quincey did not fully appreciate the fact that the 'romantic stories' of his youth were outmoded, but on the other hand there is no sign of Eaton realizing that Gothic is still alive in the second quarter of the nineteenth century, not least in the work of Scott and Dickens, or, down market, in that of W. H. Ainsworth and G. P. R. James. Besides, there is infinitely more to fiction than social realism, including the psychological realism that is so much in evidence in P. B. Shelley's Gothic novellas and in the fictional work of De Quincey, who was fully aware that 'every man has two-edged tendencies lurking within himself' (4: 298). We must not lose sight of the fact that in 1830, in a rare comment on the novel, De Quincey wrote that 'What [novelists] are striving after [...] is to realize an ideal, and to reproduce the actual world under more harmonious arrangements' (14: 371). This may seem a far cry from *Klosterheim*, but it is not, for one of the things De Quincey does in that novel is to present himself and his life in a quasi-heroic light: Prince Max is his super-ego. Elsewhere he remarks that 'All novels [...] have faded almost with the generation that produced them', and goes on to speak of the 'faded histrionic masqueraders' he will himself be joining (4: 297). Presumably he has his own Gothic masquerade in mind as he writes. He may appear to be mentally and imaginatively arrested in the early Gothic period, but he belongs to post-

1820 Gothic, in which imitation gives way to pastiche and writers use Gothic not for its own sake, but for their own mostly autobiographical ends. He uses the Gothic convention because it is the only fictional convention with which he is familiar and because it provides the mask without which he could not have written autobiographical fiction. More especially, it provides him with a convention within which the imagery of his mental life is perfectly at home, hidden in the safest of places, on the surface of the text.

However, there is more to this question than literary taste and history. There remains his narrative as such. He belongs together with Carlyle not only as a writer on German literature and an expert on Jean Paul, but also as a fiction writer *malgré soi.* His fictional writings, which are generally agreed to show that he 'lacked the novelistic imagination'[1] may be compared with Carlyle's novel fragment *Wotton Reinfred* of 1827 (in his *Last Words* of 1892). If Carlyle, 'Unpractised in writing fiction, [...] forces autobiographical traits and personal experiences into the framework of a novel',[2] De Quincey does much the same thing: 'Lacking the fictional imagination, De Quincey tended, when he wrote a story, to flesh out some basic plot with detail borrowed from his own past' (L 304). His characters are what he, in a different context, calls 'sham and make-believe men [and women]', not 'authentic men of flesh and blood' (1: 63). In the essay in *London Reminiscences* on William Godwin, of whom he says that 'most people felt of Mr. Godwin with the same alienation and horror as of a ghoul, or a bloodless vampyre,[3] or the monster created by Frankenstein', he refers to the difficulties faced by the writer of fiction who, like himself, is not a born novelist:

> of all men who can ever have lived, he [...] must have found the labour most irksome of creating incidents, and making the narrative continue to move [...] Is there anything disgraceful in this dearth of incident – this palsy of the fable-creating faculty? [*In a footnote he adds*: to produce a fable (i.e. the outline or framework of a nexus of incidents) is not very difficult; the true difficulty is in making the fable move – in calling up the secondary incidents through which and by which this fable is to revolve] (3: 23f.)

The ostensible context here is *Caleb Williams*, which De Quincey found 'stagnant' and 'sluggish in motion', but the real subject is his own difficulty in articulating historical or autobiographical material into a fictional narrative. His daughter wrote to H. S. Salt in 1907 that her father's early reading involved 'mysteries, murders, highway-men, mysterious people and dark corners' (E 223), and Japp quotes her as saying that

> He simply lived in the romances of his youth. He cared nothing for delineations of character, and I do not think he cared much for pictures of modern life [...] Dark-lanterns, and Spanish cloaks [...] and a mysterious villain with dagger or stiletto were the *sine-qua-nons* in the novels of his youth; and he seemed to favour this kind of work to the end. 'Klosterheim', indeed, is conceived much in this vein. (Japp, 439)

The very fact that he apparently never outgrew his early Gothic reading, and read very little of what his daughter's generation would have thought of as proper fiction, was, ostensibly, the worst possible starting-point when it came to trying his hand at fiction, for

[1] Lindop, in *Bicentenary Studies*, 213.
[2] J. W. Smeed, *German Influence on Thomas Carlyle* (Edinburgh: The Carlyle Society, 1964), 4.
[3] The spelling suggests, given the context, that De Quincey knew John Polidori's *The Vampyre.*

> [De Quincey's] adherence to the conventions of Gothic fiction strengthened his tendency to rely upon stereotyped characterization and stylized settings while also curbing those energies of his prose which the discursive essay, with its lack of narrative constraints, set free [...] The novel belongs to the Gothic tradition and may owe much to the youthful De Quincey's avid reading of violent and sentimental fiction.[4] (L 213)

It can therefore be argued that De Quincey owes both the best and the worst aspects of his work to Gothic convention.

8.1. *The Stranger's Grave* (1823)

The Stranger's Grave. A Tale (London: Longman, 1823), first attributed to De Quincey in 1870 by Mortimer Collins, canonized by Axon in 1914, and recently decanonized by Symonds, is a short novel in the early Gothic sentimental mode, with a burlesque twist. In it aspects of autobiography, artlessly fictionalized, appear, it seems, within an artful Gothic framework. As the title implies, it involves the early Gothic trope of 'The Mysterious Stranger' that features in the anonymous German vampire-tale of that title, which, appearing in translation in 1860, was a precursor of *Dracula;* it also features in Sophia Reeve's *The Mysterious Wanderer* (3 vols, 1807), Hoffmann's abandoned or lost novel of 1796, *Der Geheimnisvolle,* Tieck's 'Der Fremde' and 'Der Geheimnisvolle' (1805), Washington Irving's 'The Adventure of the Mysterious Stranger' (in *Tales of a Traveller,* 1824), Mark Twain's *The Mysterious Stranger* (1916), and a dozen similar titles in Montague Summers's *A Gothic Bibliography*. As a title, *The Stranger's Grave* is as Gothic as it gets. In the context of De Quincey's fiction, the Stranger might seem to point to the narrator of *Klosterheim*, with which the present text is thereby connected, although his forename goes back to De Quincey's *Walladmor*.

Set partly in Wetheral (Cumbria), where De Quincey is thought to have stayed with his brother Richard in 1814-15, this being one of the main reasons for the attribution (originally by local people) to De Quincey, and partly in an imaginary Peninsular landscape that appears to link it with *The Caçadore* and *The Peasant of Portugal,* this harrowing, maudlin, melodramatic sensation-novel with an admixture of Gothic elements has as its hero one Edward Stanley, who may be supposed to be the author's representative and part of his tripartite centre of consciousness. The background of the novel appears to reflect some of the main events in the author's early life,[5] but its subject is the incestuous relationship between Stanley and his niece Emily that has been taken as a fictional composite of De Quincey's relationship with his artless young wife Margaret, which began as an affair at Wetheral in 1813 and was condemned by the Wordsworths, and his love for his dead sister Elizabeth. In the novel Stanley has a sister named Margaret, and his niece Emily falls in love with him shortly before his death; incest is not uncommon in Gothic fiction. Thrown together by the 'Editor' in 1823, and describing events that the protagonist was unable to throw off, the novel describes events that took place thirty years previously, when De Quincey was seven, a clear reference, it was thought, to the death of his sister Elizabeth, the melancholy pomp of whose funeral he never forgot. There is no need to rehearse all the

---

4 Lindop, in *Bicentenary Studies*, 213.
5 See Lindop, 264f.

supposedly autobiographical detail in the tale. The 'autobiographical' hero with his involuted relationship and sense of guilt is of less interest than his 'death', which could be thought to stand for the death of De Quincey's super-ego.

The narrative is preceded by an Advertisement or notice to the reader by the 'more than sexagenarian' Editor, who reveals that the manuscript consists of an introduction by the late Perpetual Curate of Wetheral, followed by 'the disjointed tale, with which he [the Editor] has taken no other liberty than merely to throw it into language of his own, [that] appears to have been penned by the ill-fated hero himself.' There is also a brief Conclusion by the Editor. The author thus appears in threefold guise: as editor, narrator and hero. That the hero's testament is recast, in a kind of notional *rifacimento*, into a third-person narrrative, means that an essentially autobiographical work is translated into a fiction, and that the figures in the tale are the stereotypes of those in low-grade sentimental Gothic. However, given that the hero of this Gothic novel confesses, on his death-bed, to being 'an incestuous person, a murderer and a parricide', it also has an important third meaning:

> In that the reading of the 'lost' text of Stanley's testament negates its purpose as a confession designed to exculpate its author, there is something inherently destructive in this recasting [...] the translation of this confession turns him into a character in a novel, containing and obliterating his identity.[6]

In a psychological sense this short, hastily written novel, about experiences that the author and his protagonist were unable to throw off, and which the Editor says, in a most undequinceyan phrase, is 'thrown into' language of his own and 'thrown into' order, is 'Gothic' not least in being a classic case of abjection in Julia Kristeva's sense.[7]

Read thus, the novel might be thought to reflect (i) De Quincey's full awareness of the fatal damage he did to himself as man and would-be author in his early life, which left him with writing as the only way open to him, but one which consisted of crisis after crisis, any one of which might be fatal, and (ii) his awareness that his writing, being autobiographical in nature, was itself a form of dying. His self-mockery, his implicit view of himself as 'emotional zombie and moral imbecile',[8] may be refreshing and even entertaining (and there are humorous touches in this depressing tale), but there is, as in Laun's work, a serious undertone; in this case it is deadly serious. The short novel includes a number of Gothic motifs: the mysterious stranger who goes incognito (which also applies to Emily; there are two mysterious strangers, two Stranger's Graves), transgressive desire and the transgression (in the additionally Gothic form of incest) to which it leads, with those concerned haunted by the guilt that turns them into pariahs, the marital masquerade, and the way in which death runs rampant. Stanley, haunted by his once-innocent self, appears as an apparition, as his own zombie, so that the village folk see him as possessed (by an evil spirit in the form of his familiar, Flora), as 'no gentleman, but mayhap a murderer, or a warlock'. Edward Stanley's inner world is Gothic, and the tale is Gothic not least in that it would turn, if De Quincey were the author, on a sense of guilt arising from a tragic flaw in his character that left him with no alternative to writing, but which also ensured that his writing was but a

---

6 Thomas De Quincey, *The Stranger's Grave,* ed. Edmund Baxter (London: Aporia Press, 1988), 7.
7 Admirably summarized by the Editor in *The Cambridge Companion to Gothic Fiction,* 7.
8 Edmund Baxter, in his Introduction to Thomas De Quincey, *The Peasant of Portugal* (London: Aporia Press, 1985), 6.

pale shadow of what it could have been. There is, I repeat, a sense in which the real De Quincey died in or before Oxford, leaving his zombie to circumnavigate literature as best he could.

Notwithstanding the various parallels between the lives of Edward Stanley and Thomas De Quincey, clearly set forth by Lindop, the attribution of the novel to De Quincey was always questionable on stylistic grounds, for the plain fact is that the style of the novel is simply not that of De Quincey. Hogg was right to say that 'there are *no De Quincey fangs* in this story'. To compare it to the style of *Walladmor*, is fanciful; *Walladmor* is altogether better written. However, all this is academic, for in 1993 it was established by Barry Symonds, through incontrovertible evidence from the Longman archives, that the author of the novel is in fact George Robert Gleig (1796-1888),[9] who served in the Peninsular War and the American War of 1814 before taking orders in 1820; he went on to write a number of novels, among them *The Subaltern* (1825. German translation: *Soldatenleben. Kriegsabentheuer in den Pyrenäen und Süd-Frankreich*, 1830) and *The Country Curate* (1830), and became chaplain-general of the forces (1844-75).

What *The Stranger's Grave* shows is simply that much fiction of the time either is or can be read as vaguely Gothic.

8.2. *The Peasant of Portugal* (1827) and *The Caçadore* (1828)

Ostensibly a Gothic tale of revenge, the events of which are revealed as problems of the text, *The Peasant of Portugal*, rediscovered and identified as De Quincey's by Grevel Lindop in 1985, combines elements of early Gothic (notably the motif of the secret avenger, which it shares with *Klosterheim* and *The Avenger*) with a late Gothic preoccupation with textual instability. First appearing, anonymously, in *The Literary Souvenir; or, Cabinet of Poetry & Romance,* ed. Alaric A. Watts (London: Longman, 1823), it relates 'An Episode of the Peninsular War', in which De Quincey, who must have remembered something of his father's 'Portuguese recollections' (1: 86), and may have read some of the spate of autobiographical novels published in the 1820s by those like Gleig who had served in the Peninsula, took a keen interest. He did so not because he admired Napoleon, who was, for him, an upstart, a sciolist, 'in a most polished age, and in a nation of [...] great refinement [...] the sole barbarian of his time; presenting in his deficiencies the picture of a low mechanic, and in his positive qualities the violence and brutality of a savage' (5: 363, 365). The 'violence and brutality of a savage' were nowhere more apparent than in the cruel war in Spain and Portugal, in the fires of which Goya forged a new, Gothic art for the new times to come.[10] *The Disasters of War* series speaks for itself as the background to De Quincey's tales set on the Spanish Peninsula

The Peasant of Portugal focuses on a young peasant, Juan Taxillo, whose wife Marguerita is raped and killed by French cavalrymen. In a way that prefigures the series of assassinations in *The Avenger*, Juan takes to the mountains, and, acting like a latterday old man of the mountain, or, better, like 'some fiend possessed of supernatural powers', starts

---

[9] See Barry Symonds, 'The Stranger's Grave: Laying a De Quinceyan Ghost', *The Charles Lamb Bulletin*, 83 (July 19930, 105ff.

[10] Pierre Gassier, *Goya* (New York: Skira, 1955), 83, and, more generally, 85-124.

secretly assassinating members of the French unit in question. Eventually he is betrayed, and when the surviving members of the French unit enter his Gothic lair or 'fastness', a cave in a cliff face high above a yawning chasm, totally unsupported from beneath, he destroys them and himself. The tale is thus a shorter variant of *The Avenger*, with the setting changed; the Gothic fastness resembles the aerial dungeon at Walladmor Castle, and the central avenger-figure is similar. The tale has a number of Gothic elements: the 'supernatural' avenger, the secret campaign of terror, the rape and murder, the cave and the 'dread abyss' that guards it, the *frisson* that accompanies the act that signals the end for all concerned, and so on. When viewed with the wisdom of hindsight, both Juan Taxillo and the French cuirassiers represent De Quincey, for the tale reveals both his protectiveness towards his young wife and foreknowledge that he would prove responsible for her death; but the model for the hero who 'commits brutal acts in affirmation of virtue and justice' (L 226), thereby becoming no less guilty than his victims, is Schiller's Karl Moor, with whom De Quincey had identified at the age of sixteen. Written in 1827, *The Peasant of Portugal* – a dry run or precursor of *The Avenger* – seems to show De Quincey moving away from German Gothic, unless, that is, the idea for it came from *Rache für Weiberraub* (1796) by the Viennese playwright Friedrich Wilhelm Ziegler (1760-1827), whose penchant for violence he shared. He is, however, unlikely to have known Ziegler's work.

The Caçadore (The Portuguese Light Infantryman) first appeared, anonymously, in a volume entitled *Friendship's Offering* (1828), edited by the Gothic novelist and miscellaneous writer Leitch Ritchie, who was then at the beginning of his literary career; it was reprinted and attributed to De Quincey by Edmund Baxter in 1988. If it is by De Quincey, which is by no means certain, it is no more than a potboiler, for it is in effect a recast of *The Peasant of Portugal,* with an ending that leaves the narrator alive. This time the avenger is named Velasquez, presumably with reference to the famous seventeenth Spanish painter whose battle-pieces anticipated Goya's war-paintings.

8.3. *Klosterheim* (1832)

When De Quincey wrote *Klosterheim* in order to claim the £100 Blackwood had promised him for a work of fiction, he chose the Gothic form, or elements of it, not 'because it was popular',[11] which was no longer the case in 1832, but because it was the only form of fiction with which he was conversant, and the only form in which he was personally involved: his imagination had been caught and held by it, and the more he tried to define his standpoint, to write about his oppressive inner world without seeming to do anything of the sort, the more he had resort to Gothic. One cannot imagine him writing in any form lacking the involutes and convolutes of Gothic with its textual and hermeneutic layering.

The background to the novel must have chosen itself, for the Thirty Years' War had been treated both historically and dramatically by Schiller, whose *Wallenstein*, which De Quincey greatly admired ('an immortal drama', he called it, 'and, beyond all competition, the nearest in point of excellence to the dramas of Shakspere', 4: 437), Coleridge had translated in 1800. De Quincey knew Coleridge's translation, of which he remarked that it

---

[11] *Klosterheim,* ed. John Weeks (Santa Barbara [CA]: Woodbridge Press, 1982), vii.

contained 'some inaccuracies', but that Coleridge's 'valuation of many [...] German words or phrases was delicate, and sometimes profound', 5: 200f.). And then there was Schiller's *The History of the Thirty Years' War in Germany* (first published in German, 1791-93), that he also knew, of which three translations existed, one by Capt. Blaquiere (1799), another by J. M. Duncan (1828), and, the most interesting in this context, *Historical Works of Schiller* (*The Thirty Years' War; The trial and execution of Counts Egmont and Horn; Siege of Antwerp*), translated by George Moir (Edinburgh: Constable, 1828), who had also just translated (anonymously) *Piccolomini* and *Wallenstein* (1827). A number of De Quincey's historical characters (Wallenstein, Pappenheim [whose name he invariably misspells], Butler, Holk) appeared in *Wallenstein.* Prince Max, De Quincey's super-hero (and super-ego), is based on Max Piccolomini (with a touch of Karl Moor from *The Robbers,* with whom De Quincey was still identifying thirty years after first encountering him), and the relationship between Max and Countess (Princess) Paulina is reminiscent of that between the idealist young colonel, Max Piccolomini, and Countess (Princess) Thekla in *Wallenstein*, by which De Quincey was deeply moved, and also of Laun's *Des Fürsten Geliebte* (1823).

There was also the work of Tromlitz, a Thirty Years' War specialist, whose *Siege of Antwerp* De Quincey also greatly admired. A. von Tromlitz is the pseudonym of Johann Wilhelm Karl Ernst von Witzleben (1773-1839), who attended the Pagenschule in Weimar, where he was taught by Musäus and Herder. He subsequently held commissions in the Prussian, French and Russian armies; captured by the French in 1806, he subsequently served under Murat, then served in Spain in 1811, and on Blücher's General Staff in 1815. In 1818 he was appointed Adjutant-General of the Prussian army, and from 1833 to 1835 was Prussian Minister of War. Encouraged by Schiller, he began writing in the early 1790s. Forgotten now, he is the author of numerous once-popular historical novels à la Scott, mainly set during the Thirty Years's War, the history of which he followed Schiller in treating freely. But if *Klosterheim* is set in Tromlitz's period of choice, and includes some of the same historical characters (e.g. Colonel Count Holk of the Holksche Reiter, who was promoted Field Marshal after the Battle of Lützen in 1632, and died in 1633, the year in which *Klosterheim* is set), there is no evidence that De Quincey was unduly influenced by Tromlitz, although it may have been from him that he learned to pack his work with detail. Unlike De Quincey, Tromlitz writes as a professional soldier.

More important, as a model, than any of these, was De Quincey's favourite novel, Harriet Lee's *Kruitzner.* Published originally in Vol. 4 (1801) of Harriet and Sophia Lee's *Canterbury Tales*, *Kruitzner* was published as a separate volume in 1822, by Byron's publisher John Murray, on the occasion of the publication of *Werner*, which, as Byron himself stated, was 'taken entirely from *The German's Tale, Kruitzner*', which makes *Werner* another *rifacimento.* Set in much the same place and period, *Klosterheim* is, generically, much closer to *Kruitzner* than to anything by Tromlitz. This is hardly surprising, for it is all that was ever written of De Quincey's projected *New Canterbury Tales*, intended as a tribute to the author of his favourite work of fiction.

An extended Gothic tale in the manner of *Kruitzner*, *Klosterheim, or: The Masque* is set, like Harriet Lee's novella, in which Kruitzner is a masque for Count Siegendorf, during the Thirty Years' War. *Kruitzner* opens with 'a winter memorably severe'; De Quincey signals his admiration for *Kruitzner* by having *Klosterheim* open with a winter of 'unusual severity'. Harriet Lee describes the danger facing Lady Paulina's party in the forest: 'For more than twenty years, all Germany had been a theatre of warfare and desolation; where numerous hordes of banditti, lurking in the fastnesses of mountains, or in the recesses of forests, were ready to pour down upon the weak and unguarded'.[12] De Quincey personalizes the danger in the person of 'Holkerstein, the military robber', probably named after Peter Halkerston, author of the recently published *A Treatise on the History, Law and Privileges of the Palace and Sanctuary of Holyroodhouse* (Edinburgh: Maclachlan & Stewart, 1831). The extensive gardens, open to intruders, of the convent in which Paulina finds refuge, have rightly been associated with the spacious garden with a wall so low as almost to invite intruders of the house at M. in which Kruitzner and his wife similarly find refuge (WTDQ, 8: 439, n. 78) after a nameless malady had attacked Kruitzner and forced him to look 'into the chasm which no ray [...] ever yet penetrated', which, given his early love of the tale, may be one of the many sources of De Quincey's chasm-imagery. The name Klosterheim I assume to derive from 'Kempferhausen', the sobriquet given to De Quincey's Germanophile friend R. P. Gillies in John Wilson's *Noctes Ambrosianae,* although it also foregrounds the convent-cum-castle that is its most important, Gothic spatiality.

To the limited extent to which De Quincey had models for aspects of *Klosterheim*, two of them are named consecutively, under the heading of 'Estrangement from Wordsworth', in his *London Reminiscences.* Having come to the conclusion that Wordsworth is *einseitig* (biased), he reveals that it is Wordsworth's failure to appreciate *Kruitzner* and *Wallenstein* that has led him to this conclusion. He calls Harriet Lee's *The Landlady's Tale* and *The German's* [*Tale. Kruitzner*, or *Kruitzner. The German's Tale;* both forms occur] 'absolutely unrivalled as specimens of fine narration'. *The German's Tale* in particular is 'inimitable', 'a tale in which so very much depends upon the plot', which, it must be said, is somewhat involved. He praises 'the whole colossal exhibition of fiendish grandeur in Conrad, the fine delineation of mixed power and weakness in Siegendorf, and the exquisite relief given to the whole by the truly Shaksperian portrait of feminine innocence and nobility in Josephine' (3: 204f.), and then goes on, showing that the two passages are linked in his mind, to write of *Wallenstein*:

> Most people have been enraptured with the beautiful group of Max Piccolomini and the Princess Thekla [...] because they furnish a sweet relief to the general harsh impression from so many worldly-minded, scheming, treacherous, malignant ruffians, meeting together in one camp as friends, or rivals, or betrayers (3: 205f.)

So impressed was De Quincey that he repeats what he has been saying, in the context of Gilfillan's Literary Portraits (Shelley):

> Everybody who has read with understanding the 'Wallenstein' of Schiller is aware of the repose and the divine relief arising upon a background of so much darkness, such a tumult of ruffians, bloody intriguers, and assassins, from the situation of the two lovers, Max Piccolomini and the Princess Thekla, both yearning so profoundly after peace, both so noble, both so young, and both destined to be so unhappy. (11: 376)

Here, then, are De Quincey's profound admiration of these two works with a similar historical background to *Klosterheim,* and the fact that they are linked in his mind, not least

---

12 Sophia and Harriet Lee,*Canterbury Tales* (London: Colburn & Bentley, 1832), 240f.

as works that were lost on Wordsworth with his deplorable aversion to Gothic. When De Quincey came to try his hand at an original piece of extended fiction, it was always likely that the memory of these two works would supervene. As, indeed, it did. Schiller also provided him (in *Die Räuber*) with the motif, central to *Klosterheim* and *The Avenger,* of a disguised son who sets out to avenge a father murdered or supposed murdered. Christian August Vulpius's 'phantastischer Räuberroman', *Rinaldo Rinaldini, der Räuberhauptmann* (1798: *Rinaldo Rinaldini, the Robber Captain*, tr. John Hinckley, 1800), on the other hand, though a strong influence on Alexis's *Walladmor*, has no connexion with *Klosterheim.*

Criticism, it has to be said, has made uncommonly heavy weather of De Quincey's 'models'. In reality the situation is clear. He is indebted to Harriet Lee for the background and generic type (gothified history) of *Klosterheim*, which in a general, stylistic way is closer to *Kruitzner* than to any other work. Thematically he owes more to Heinrich Zschokke's *Abällino der große Bandit* (1793) as remade by M. G. Lewis into *Abällino, The Bravo of Venice* (1805). To *Abällino*, which he will have read in 1821, at Bohte's, if not much earlier, De Quincey owes his basic story, including the nobleman-hero as 'apparition', in disguise until the end, when he reclaims the estates of which he had been dispossessed, and reveals his true identity; the notices that appear, addressed to the populace; the idea of 'Venetian dissimulation', and the name Adorni (Adorno in Lewis). Ian Jack was right to say, forty years ago, that *Klosterheim* is 'in the genre established by [...] *Abällino* [in which] a bandit, who is really a nobleman and who employs many disguises, strikes down the enemies of Venice and thus saves the state'.[13] However, if, 'In certain of his moods and habits, the Masque bears a likenesss to Lewis's „Bravo", [...] the setting of De Quincey's story is very different'.[14] Besides, *Abällino* is a tale of assassins and assassination, which *Klosterheim* is not. Lewis's *rifacimento* of Zschokke's work appears to have given De Quincey the basic storyline and the idea of a climactic grand wedding, but we must not lose sight of Schiller's *The Robbers*, which also profoundly impressed him, and was itself the model for Zschokke (and indeed for Vulpius). *The Robbers* is an avenger-tragedy ('Avenging Power! thy hand is here! [...] Here consecrate this sword to the avenging God, whose ways are incomprehensible', 'Vengeance is mine', 'Revenge! revenge! revenge! – this violated, profaned, this hoary head!' – the words are all Karl Moor's), and the forest sequence in *Klosterheim* is coloured by De Quincey's memory of such scenes in *The Robbers*. The hero of *Klosterheim* bears the same name as old Moor (Maximilian Count de Moor) and of Max Piccolomini in Schiller's *Wallenstein,* and Maximilian, who, like Karl Moor, is the avenger of his father, enters his father's castle in disguise.

This amalgam of Lee, Zschokke/Lewis and Schiller explains everything that needs explaining. There is no substantial debt to any other work, German or otherwise, and De Quincey's debt to Lee and company should put an end to the hunting for a non-existent source that has gone on far too long. Even if it is true that De Quincey uses all or most of the stock ingredients of the *Schauerroman* or Gothic novel, the fact serves only to link the tale to the Gothic convention as such; it simply does not follow that he 'probably

13 Ian Jack, *English Literature, 1815-1832* (Oxford: Clarendon Press, 1963), 394.

14 Edith Birkhead, *The Tale of Terror* (London: Constable, 1921, repr. New York: Russell & Russell, 1963), 174.

plagiarized a German source'.[15] Such vague generalizations are unhelpful. Besides, the Gothic novel as such is essentially 'plagiaristic'; almost everyone copies everyone else, so that plagiarism is a feature of Gothic – but also of the non-Gothic writing of the time. Thus Maximilian resembles Theodore in *The Castle of Otranto* in that he is 'the [...] noble scion [...] disenfranchised by a corrupt figure of hostile authority'; this makes him decide to play the outcast, disguising himself as „The Masque", and enduring the obloquy associated with the hoax, so that he ultimately might expose [...] the true impostor.'[16] Otherwise, De Quincey's echoes of *The Castle of Otranto* and *The Mysteries of Udolpho* (see WTDQ, 8: 436, n. 40; 437, n. 62; 438f., n. 77) are extremely modest by comparison. I would argue that, faced with such clear evidence as to De Quincey's real models in *Klosterheim*, there was never any need to surmise that *Klosterheim* might be a *rifacimento* of some obscure German original,[17] which was not only a red herring, but meant overlooking the stylistic characteristics that distinguish it so clearly from the vast majority of German tales of the kind that Goldman seems to have had in mind.

There remain the names of De Quincey's characters, some of which point to his likely Gothic reading. Max, as I have said, is taken from Schiller's Max Piccolomini, and the *Wallenstein* trilogy also shares with Klosterheim a number of historical characters, indluding Gustavus Adolphus, Wallenstein, Horn, Butler, Tilly, Holk, and Pappenheim. Countess Paulina of Hohenhelder (a counterfeit, implausible German name of the sort so common in Gothic; Hohenelbe, used in 1803, is more plausible) has a forename used in Charlotte Dacre's *The Libertine* (1807) and in Francis Lathom's *Italian Mysteries* (1820), although this does not mean that it betrays De Quincey's knowledge of either work, for the name is common in the English and French Gothic novel. In fact, De Quincey probably took it from a German Gothic novel, *Gräfin Pauline* (1800), that he read at Bohte's. (Princess/Countess) Adeline bears a name that is common in Gothic novels, including Radcliffe's *The Romance of the Forest*, which De Quincey knew. The White Lady, Agnes von der Weißenburg, comes from Benedikte Naubert's fairy tale 'Die weiße Frau', most likely via M. G. Lewis's *The Monk.* Graf St Aldenheim may owe his name, in part, to Graf St Aldegonde in Tromlitz's 'The Siege of Antwerp', which De Quincey read in 1826. The name *Holkerstein*, a translation of that of (Peter) Halkerston, is a reminder that the world of the novel is, behind the Gothic masque, De Quincey's own inner world. Father Anselm may have been suggested by the Father Anselmo in Mary Picard's *The Castle of Roviego; or, Retribution* (1805 and/or Hannah Parkhouse's *The Italian Marauders* (1810). Madeline is common in early Gothic (Isabella Kelly's *Madeline* [1794], Elizabeth Bonhote's *Bungay Castle* [1796], Regina Maria Roche's *Clermont* [1798]). Of place-names, Falkenberg is the name of a ruined castle in Lippe; as Fauconberg, a personal name, it appeared in Catherine Cuthbertson's *The Hut and the Castle* (1823). Falkenstein is a place in Bavaria with a castle ruin of the same name; the French form of the name, Faulconstein, appeared in *Faulconstein Forest* (1810). There is a Waldhausen in Upper Austria; De Quincey's Waldenhausen is 'coined', perhaps by analogy with Munchausen. And so on. Many of the

---

[15] Goldman shows that he is out of his depth when he refers only to one outdated, American piece of research on the German Gothic novel.

[16] Snyder , *Research Studies*, 49 (1981), 134.

[17] Eaton, 349; Albert Goldman, *The Mine and the Mint: Sources for the Writings of Thomas De Quincey* (Carbondale: Southern Illinois University Press, 1965), 156f.

names used by De Quincey have Gothic precedents, and the Stranger, who narrates the tale, is, of course, an omnipresent Gothic figure. The wealth of Gothic surface detail both links *Klosterheim* with numerous early Gothic novels and serves (unless I am wrong to attribute to De Quincey a Kafkaesque reserve; his shyness is well-attested, though not necesssarily to be taken wholly at face value) to arrest any eye inclined to look too closely beneath the surface; indeed, it amounted to a way of making the (autobiographical) surface invisible.

Rightly described by F. S. Frank as 'heavily Gothic', *Klosterheim* appears to belong to the type of historical Gothic. It has many Gothic features and motifs. Most obviously Gothic is the Castle-cum-convent to which the name Klosterheim owes its prefix. *Kloster* (monastery, convent) comes from Latin *claustrum*, which also means frontier post or point of control. De Quincey breathes fresh life into the convent as a Gothic setting,[18] not least by combining it with the Castle. Other Gothic motifs include the mysterious stranger (The Masque, which may go back to De Quincey's reading in 1803 of Schiller's *The Ghost-Seer,* in which the Prince goes masked), the avenger-motif, the mask-motif and the question of identity, the tyrannical aristocrat (the usurping Landgraf is an 'illustrious profligate' [M. G. Lewis, in *Abællino*] if ever there was one), the persecuted heroine, the lawlessness of the ruffianly mercenaries and the apparent lawlessness of the Masque's actions, the 'nefarious conspiracies and unavenged crimes', Adorni's 'Venetian' dissimulation and duplicity (Adorni is the almost obligatory Italian villain of early Gothic; he is reminiscent of Schedoni in Ann Radcliffe's *The Italian*, and of figures based on Schedoni in down-market Radcliffe-imitations), the manhunt, violence and apparent violence, the subterranean passsage, the quest for justice, the trial-scene, the punishment of the usurper,[19] the explained supernatural à la Radcliffe, the 'fairy- tale' element, and, last but by no means least, the narrative and stylistic instability of the text. The labyrinth is ever-present, in forms varying from 'labyrinths of the forest', 'labyrinths of tortuous passages' and 'labyrinths of passages [in] the interior of the convent' (12: 54, 72, 122) to 'the most tortuous labyrinths of political manoeuvring' (12: 49), all of these reflecting and reflected in the labyrinthine nature of the text and the author's mind. The forest scene (ch. 3) takes the reader back to the famous proto-Gothic scene in *Ferdinand Count Fathom* (cf. 21) in which 'every shadow of a tree became the apparition of a ruffian eager for blood'. The only major feature of Gothic that is absent is arguably the use of claustrophobic space, although the underground passages must have become pretty claustrophobic as a whole army was spirited into Klosterheim through them. De Quincey may seem to ignore the Gothic potential of the 'subterraneous passages [...] of surprising extent', but he does not really do so: they, like the purple passages in the text, serve a subversive purpose, subverting and destroying the security of the defenders and bringing death to them, just as the stylized passages subvert and destroy the seeming certainty of the text.

Ever since De Quincey declined to allow this Gothic novella to be included in the collected edition of his works published in his lifetime, it has been supposed that he had something to hide in terms of too close a model, but this was a canard. The real reason was that he knew *Klosterheim* both to be far more personal than it seems, and to expose his main weakness as a writer, by which I mean the fact that his imagination was that of the

18 On this and the numerous Gothic features of the work, see R. L. Snyder, 'Klosterheim: De Quincey's Gothic Masque,' *Research Studies,* 49 (1981), 129-42.

19 Cf. *The Castle de Albani; or, The Usurper Punished* (London: John Arliss, n.d.).

‘schoolman’ and historian rather than the creative writer; the opium-eating is explicable, in part, as an attempt to remedy this deficiency. In the shorter tales this shows less than in *Klosterheim*, where he is forced to make good by unnecessary elaboration. The evidence suggests that *Klosterheim* is the work of the Latin schoolman and polyhistor, not the plagiarist. I know of no Gothic novelist, German or otherwise, who deploys as scholarly a style as De Quincey. *Klosterheim* is overwritten, whereas almost all Gothic romances – let alone the average German Gothic potboiler – are underwritten, often vilely so. In this case the passages of purple (‘impassioned’) prose seem inappropriate. The very strength of the work, identified by Coleridge:

> I have read nothing since the *Quentin Durward* which would compare in interest with *Klosterheim*; and in purity of style and idiom, in which the scholar is ever implied, and the scholarly never obtrudes itself, it reaches an excellence to which Sir W. Scott [...] appears never to have aspired

can be read as a weakness, but if *Klosterheim* is weak, it is so not because De Quincey has donned an outmoded (‘Gothic’) imaginative straightjacket, but because he has shown himself unable to do so anything so straightforward. The ostensibly inappropriate style of the novel, the clash between style and content, is accordingly explicable as an example of the textual instability of Gothic.

One’s first impression of *Klosterheim* is that for a Gothic novel it is uncommonly well written, so much so that its style and stylishness arguably proclaim it to be not a belated run-of-the-mill Gothic novel, but a pastiche of such: the stylishness is subversive. Given that self-parody is an element both of late early and of later Gothic, the question is whether it really is a belated Gothic novel, or in large measure a work of a different kind masquerading under Gothic colours. Insofar as it is Gothic, it is so less because it, like *Kruitzner*, has an admixture of Gothic motifs, than because the text is destabilized by the manner of its telling. In terms of style or discourse it is, in short, too well written. The elaborate, digressive style strongly suggests that De Quincey was concerned to fill space, not save it as he would have wanted and needed to do if paraphrasing a German original. The style is pure De Quincey. The novel is elaborately written in the sense that he elaborates on everything: it is full of historical detail. Such wealth of detail, appropriate in Tromlitz’s *trompe-l’oeil* historical novellas, is uncalled for in what is less an historical novel than a gothified exercise in symbolical autobiography. If De Quincey is plagiarizing anyone, it is himself, this being shown by the echoes of other works (*The Revolt of the Tartars, The English Mail-Coach, The Avenger, Confessions, The Incognito, The King of Hayti*). *Klosterheim* is short, and would have been shorter but for De Quincey’s tendency to prolixity. Rhetorical laxity and prolixity replace imaginative necessity. De Quincey’s besetting sin as a writer – his failure to get to and stick to the point – is much in evidence: he misjudges the pace of the book, starting in so leisurely a way that he is eventually obliged to conclude too swiftly, abbreviating the grand climax of the novel. He is content to develop his sentences with little regard for textual necessity; he has no sense of urgency. The style is too heavy for the dramatically conceived text, which it thereby subverts. The dissonance between content and style, which destabilizes both the text itself and the reader’s reaction to it, means that the tale is Gothic not in the backward-looking way that has caused many critics to disregard and undervalue it, but in a knowing way that points forward to 20th-century Gothic. De Quincey, like Kafka, cuts the ground from under his feet as he writes. Readers will decide for themselves whether he does so intentionally or unintentionally.

It was Mario Praz who wrote, fifty years ago, that De Quincey 'seems like the last, imitative survivor of a moribund school, that of the „tales of terror"':

> The sensationalism of *Klosterheim* (1832) [...] derives from Mrs Radcliffe, combined with historical scenes in the manner of Scott. Like Mrs Radcliffe, De Quincey makes an effort to create an atmosphere of terror, only to dissipate the 'terrific' elements in incidents that are very far from supernatural. In works of this kind De Quincey is doing no more than echo a defunct manner'.[20]

That was in 1956, but if it ever existed, the time is long since past when *Klosterheim* was adequately described as a belated example of the *Schauerroman*. It was probably Praz's misreading of it that caused *Klosterheim* to be underrated by De Quincey scholars, though not by those who know the Gothic novel. Alethea Hayter's disparaging reference to 'one inconsiderable Gothick novel' merely pointed to the question she did not ask: whether *Klosterheim* really is a 'Gothick' novel, or rather an archetypal Gothic novel, or – like *Kruitzner* – an historical novel with Gothic trappings, or a cross-generic mixture of Gothic novel, historical novella and fairy tale, or perhaps an exercise in Gothic autobiography and the Piranesi-like construction and dynamics of text. In reality it is all of these. It is, of course, true that

On one level, the novel is a highly conventional if belated example of Radcliffean Gothic romance: lovers are reunited, guilt is punished, rights are restored, and the supernatural is conveniently explained away as the product of rumours, shadows, and overheated imaginations. (WTDQ, 8:224)

This level is, however, not much more than a masquerade, and it is immediately apparent that there is a good deal more to this 'novel' than the Gothic masquerade that is foregounded. *Klosterheim*, as its subtitle indicates, hinges on the theme of disguise or dissimulation. The primary masquerade in the tale is that of De Quincey himself'. Snyder is right to speak of 'De Quincey's self-masking and self-mythologizing'.[21] The masked ball is, in a way that is characteristic of De Quincey, a literal masquerade within a literary one. The crux of the matter is that while *Klosterheim*

> 'relies freely on many of the trappings that have become virtual clichés of the genre[,] what actively focuses the novel [...] is not this set of borrowed contrivances, but rather De Quincey's implicit identification with the hero and his self-impersonation through the fantasy.'[22]

It is this that makes *Klosterheim* so much more than an 'inconsiderable gothick novel' echoing a defunct manner.

At the beginning of the novel De Quincey writes of war threatening to convert the vast central provinces of Germany,

---

[20] Mario Praz, *The Hero in Eclipse in Victorian Fiction,* tr. Angus Davidson (London: Oxford University Press, 1956), 76.

[21] Snyder , *Research Studies, 49* (1981), 129, 134.

[22] Snyder, ibid., 131.

so recently blooming Edens of peace and expanding prosperity – into a howling wilderness; and which had already converted immense tracts into one universal aceldama, reviving to the recollection at every step the extent of past happiess in the endless memorials of its destruction.

The word aceldama comes straight from the Grecian De Quincey's inner world and is separated by a stylistic and conceptual gulf from the *Schauerroman* with which Goldman sought to associate *Klosterheim*. From this it is a short step to a passage in the memorial on Sir William Hamilton, in which De Quincey 'descends' some forty years [into memory] and is prompted to write that

Of all curses, that which searches deepest is the violent revelation through infinite darkness [...] of a happiness or a glory which once and for ever has perished. Martyrdom it is, and no less, to revivify by effect of your own, or passively to see revivified, in defiance of your own fierce resistance, the gorgeous spectacles of your visionary morning life, or of your too rapturous noontide, relieved upon a background of funeral darkness (5: 304f.)

De Quincey begins his novel by 'positing the fictional equivalent for „the aboriginal fall" [13: 304], the pivotal event in his own spiritual history';[23] those 'Edens of peace' point all the way back to his prelapsarian early childhood. Like Maximilian, De Quincey

is abruptly cut off from his patrimony; like the Landgrave, the autocratic Hall is depicted as governed by 'vindictive malice' [3: 365n.]; and again like his Gothic surrogate, De Quincey endures various privations and goes underground supposedly as a result of that oppression. These correspondences define the autobiographical core of his novel.[24]

De Quincey's overall aim as a 'novelist' is to 'realize an ideal, and to reproduce the actual world under more harmonious arrangements' (14: 371). What makes and characterizes *Klosterheim* is 'his tacit identification with the Gothic hero who surmounts the various pitfalls of a fallen world.'[25]

The final tableau involves a rewriting of history in the form of the ending of *Confessions*, and therefore a rewriting by De Quincey of his own life:

The scaffold, the corpse, and the other images of sorrow, were then withdrawn; seven thousand Imperial troops presented arms to the youthful Landgrave and the future Landgravine, the brilliant favourites of the Emperer; the immense area of St. Agnes resounded with the congratulations of Klosterheim; and as the magnificent cortege moved off to the interior of the *schloss*, the swell of the Coronation anthem rising in peals upon the ear from the choir of St. Agnes, and from the military bands of the Imperial troops, awoke the promise of happier days, and of more equitable government, to the long-harassed inhabitants of Kosterheim. (12: 152)

It is impossible not to agree with Snyder, who writes:

The reappearance of such oneiric elements as the sonorous anthem, the reunion of the protagonist with the idealized female figure, and, most importantly, the restoration and jubilant vindication of Maximilian as hero

---

23 Snyder, ibid.,132.
24 Snyder, ibid.,137.
25 Snyder, ibid.,134.

> all testify to a direct line of relationship with the autobiographical narrative, and at the center of this tableau stands De Quincey himself, transmuting the fragmentary incompleteness of his life into the ordered congruities of literature.[26]

This is the real point: that the apotheosis of Maximilian represents the literary sublimation of the outcast into king, the imaginative attainment of the 'sublimity' of which De Quincey had been dreaming for half a century.

As an exercise in 'the making of experience into fiction',[27] *Klosterheim* is a kind of authorial half-way house between the autobiographical *Confessions* and the mythopoeic *Suspira de Profundis:*

> gothic is akin to myth, and akin to dream, providing on the level of fiction an entry to the opium world of illusion and equivocal truth. In its twilight realm of the distant past, the town of Klosterheim is a 'picture within a picture' of human life, into which writer and reader descend [...] there is a sense of the mind descending into its own inner depths [...] Klosterheim [..] strangely resembles the mind of the opium-eater, isolated from its surroundings, controlled in its waking consciousness, yet taking on by night an anarchic aspect at once threatening and creative.[28]

The *Confessions* are, after all, related both to Gothic and to the autobiographical novel, and little is more Gothic than life – and genre – in disarray. It is easy to imagine De Quincey writing the novel, surrounded by the darkness shading away into deeper darkness mirroring the layers of the mind, the text that is generated being a palimpsest in reverse in which the disguised subjective meaning is hidden beneath the surface levels of meaning it supersedes. The figures and events of the novel belong in the world not of the popular novel but of dream, fairytale and myth. De Quincey is mythologizing, 'realizing an ideal' unattainable in reality; he is reproducing his actual life 'under more harmonious arrangements'. In a word, he is 'coining' his own life.

That *Klosterheim* is a text of more than one kind is shown in a number of ways, one of them being the fact that Prince Max, De Quincey's Gothic super-hero, who also represents his super-ego, is modelled on figures from Schiller and from fairy tale (including the *Arabian Nights*), for the ending of the work is pure fairy tale: the heroine rescued from durance vile by a prince in disguise, the Masque revealed to be the son whose father the *Landgraf* was murdered by the usurper, and so on, to say nothing of the magic way in which an Imperial army, complete with band, is spirited into Klosterheim, a piece of imaginative sleight of hand worthy of the *Arabian Nights.* It is shown, too, by the fact that the town of *Klosterheim* stands within an apparently boundless forest that points to the 'vast Hercynian forest' of the 1856 revision of the *Confessions*, and therefore to the idea that

> every intricate and untried path in life, where it was from the first a matter of arbitrary choice to enter upon it or avoid it, is effectually a path through a vast Hercycian forest, unexplored and unmapped, where each several turn in your advance leaves you open to new anticipations of what is next to be expected, and consequently open to altered valuations of all that has been already traversed. (*Conf.*, ed. Hayter, 182)

---

26 Snyder, ibid.,139f.

27 *Klosterheim,* ed. Jonathan Wordsworth (Oxford & New York Woodstock Books, 1992), vii.

28 *Klosterheim,* ed.Wordsworth, x.

This passage shows that *Klosterheim* is indeed 'informed by considerations of autobiography',[29] for it is above all to autobiography that the 'altered valuations of all that has already been traversed (sc. in life's journey) refers. But the forest carries other meanings as well. In terms of the Gothic fantasy that is *Klosterheim* it denotes the threat (both to the Klosterheimers and to the incoming travellers) that obtains at such a time of lawlessness and uncertainty. That this historical meaning applies to nineteenth-century Europe is shown by De Quincey's comment in an article entitled 'Political Anticipations' (in *Blackwood's Magazine,* 28 [Nov. 1830], 720): 'Now, in 1830 [...] Europe is overshadowed, as by some great Hercynian forest, with a rank growth of anti-social desires and disorganizing principles.' The historical parallel explains, in part, why De Quincey set *Klosterheim* in the seventeenth century, but this too does not exhaust the meaning of the forest, which also has metaphysical implications, as can be seen via the parallel with Caspar David Friedrich's *Early Snow*, painted about two years before *Klosterheim* was written, which was discussed in 4.2 above. This 'vast Hercynian forest,'[30] to which De Quincey is so attached, has multiple connotations. In the first instance it stands for 'the sense of loss and fear of oblivion that torments the town's inhabitants',[31] who find it reduplicated in the 'impenetrable blackness' of the cathedral (forest and cathedral resemble and stand for one another; they are in some ways symbolically interchangeable) and their own future. More generally it stands for the impenetrable meaning of life and the metaphysical quandry in which De Quincey is joined by the reader, but also, as De Quincey reveals elsewhere, for 'the pathless forests of literature' and the hermeneutic forest of meaning and literary evaluation, interpretation and misinterpretation, a point to which I return in the next chapter in relation to Kafka.

The 'vast Hercynian forest' is also the tangle of De Quincey's life with all its involutions and convolutions; it is the horizontal equivalent of the vertical imagery of the chasm. What is lurking in the darkness of the forest-as-subconscious is death, although it must be added that in the midst of the forest-like 'mob' Max is safe from death. Klosterheim, a fictional town in seventeent-century southern 'Germany', represents De Quincey's own world, a 'refraction of the opium-eater's experience'; it is essentially a later, literary version of the Gombroon of his childhood.[32] Prince Max and his *Doppelgänger,* the Masque, are a (double) mask for De Quincey and his opium-eating double or Gothic self, while Klosterheim itself is not only a 'picture within a picture', but is presented as 'a series of theaters within theaters'[33] that are also the horizontal equivalent and expression of the vertical levels, the depths within depths or conceptual doubling of the text. Even the female lead (Paulina) has a double (Adeline). In sum, the novel so far transcends the Gothic novel that the question of its weakness as such a novel does not arise.

---

29 Baxter, 116.

30 Hercynia [silva] means the thickly forested areas of central Germany, especially the Thüringer Wald and the Erzgebirge. The classical name is out of place here, although it has to be said that it appears in a Gothic chapbook, Frederick Chamberlain's *Lucretia, or: The Robbers of the Hyrcanean [sic]Forest* (London, n.d.), which may have prompted De Quincey's robbers, although he may have met it in Caesar's *Commentaries.*

31 Baxter, 116.

32 Thomas De Quincey, *Klosterheim*, ed. Jonathan Wordsworth (Oxford & New York: Woodstock Books, 1992), ii, vii.

33 Lindop, in *Bicentenary Studies*, 229.

8.4. *The Household Wreck*

'The Household Wreck' (first published in *Blackwood's Magazine* in January 1838) has been described as 'a distinctly Kafka-esque piece',[34] and has been linked with Kafka on several different grounds. The way in which the heroine, Agnes (modelled on De Quincey's wife Margaret, who died in 1837, leaving her husband feeling guilty of neglecting her, which he construed, in psychological terms, into murder, but based on a Mrs Perrot, charged with shoplifting in Somerset in 1799[35]) is arrested without, initially, being able to discover the reason why, is sufficiently close to the case of Josef K. in *Der Proceß* for the epithet to be justifiable, particularly when the mysterious, trumped-up guilt (which finally leads to a charge of shoplifting, that reflects De Quincey's feeling of guilt at not having done more to support his wife financially) leads to the heroine's death. Kafka too is condemning himself, in his case for his 'heresy' (in the form of disobeying his father's 'commandments') and supposed sexual self-indulgence, through his protagonist. Both Agnes (→ Latin *agnus*, lamb) and Josef K. are sacrificial lambs or scapegoats, into which both De Quincey and Kafka construct themselves. In either case what counts is less guilt as such than a sense of guilt. The point has been well made by A. S. Plumtree:

> In both De Quincey and Kafka we find the imaginative expression of the inexorable Kierkegaardian formula: 'The individual in dread, not of becoming guilty, but of being regarded as guilty, becomes guilty.' For most of his adult life De Quincey was rarely free of this dread of guilt stemming from 'the sad anxieties, the degrading fears, the miserable dependencies of guilt' (2: 292). Hence his close identification with the outcast and the persecuted, developed in early childhood, was intensified by experiences which conferred on him the stigma of criminality.[36]

The real 'robber' in 'The Household Wreck' is not the innocent lamb (Agnes ↔ *agnus [dei]*) of a wife, on to whom, in calling her 'My Eve, partner in my paradise' (12: 185), De Quincey projects his feelings of guilt vis-à-vis his own wife, than the narrator, with whom he identifies, who 'innocently' incurs real guilt. The wretched Barratt, who, reduced to a 'disfigured wreck' after being attacked by the angry mob, confesses on his deathbed, represents the narrator's Gothic, Satanic self. The text is Gothic in its layering: behind the innocent wife and the guilty husband stand the author's innocent and guilty selves, good and evil, God and Devil.

The guilt in question, like the robbery in *Walladmor*, has an important literary dimension. De Quincey not only took the frame of the story from Milton's *Paradise Lost,*[37] but was clearly aware that the *rifacimento* which underlies so much of his work is at times barely distinguishable from plagiarism, hence the clearly self-critical feeling that went into his denunciation of Coleridge on this score. Not to put too fine a point upon it, theft lies at the heart of De Quincey's literary enterprise. *The Household Wreck* signals his tacit awareness of the fact.

---

34 Lindop, 327

35 W. J. B. Owen, 'De Quincey and Shoplifting,' *Wordsworth Circle,* 21/2 (1990, 72-6.

36 In *Bicentenary Studies*, 146.

37 See Clej, 240f.

The importance of the Fall to De Quincey is emphasized by the 'Daughter of Lebanon' fragment with which the 1856 version of the *Confessions* concludes. This establishes as historical parallel the Miltonic expulsion of Adam and Eve from Eden, looking back on their lost paradise (or, in De Quincey's case, the false paradise offered by his dreams) as a region 'with dreadful faces thronged and fiery arms' (3: 449). In the background is the lost paradise of De Quincey's early childhood, ringed by the faces of the dead and the uplifted arm of the avenging 'elder nurse', so like the figure on the Statue of 'Liberty' at the beginning of Kafka's *Der Verschollene* (*America*), who, with sword upraised, is clearly ready to put mankind (in the person of the Everyman figure Karl Rossmann) to the sword. The link between *Confessions* and *The Household Wreck* is shown by the palace of memory: 'Yet in the lowest deep there still yawns a lower deep; and in the vast halls of man's frailty there are separate and more glooomy chambers of a frailty more exquisite and consummate' (12: 158). This descent from deep to deep is both an enactment of his fall and a search for the meaning that he will never reach because ultimately there is no meaning save death. To remember is to be reminded of one's fallen nature; the deeper one descends (falls) into the unconscious or depths of the personality, the clearer the extent of the fall becomes. To be is to be fallen. To be is to be no more.

That De Quincey's confessional and Gothic works are related is underlined by the idea for a new work with which he was toying in October 1822 when the *Confessions* appeared in book form:

> One night in high summer, when I lay [...] sleepless for want of opium, – I amused myself with composing the imaginary *Confessions of a Murderer;* which, I think, might be made a true German bit of horror, the subject being exquisitely diabolical; and, if I do not flatter myself, some few dozens of useless old women I could frighten out of their wits and this wicked world. – Yet do not mention this, if you please, to anybody: for if I begin to write imaginary *Confessions,* I shall seem to many as no better than a pseudo-confessor in my own too real confessions.[38]

Clearly all the German horror tales he had swallowed at Bohte's were on his mind, no doubt dissolving into terrifying hypnagogic images as he lay on the edge of the sleep that was denied him. His reasons for not wanting to go down the road of imaginary confessions that would implicitly identify him as the murderer always in question are wholly understandable, but, given the way in which his work was to develop, imaginary, counterfeit confessions and the way in which they would have destabilized and thus further gothified the real ones, would arguably have been at least as appropriate as the road he actually took, which continually led back into his own childhood rather than deeper into the brave new world of Romantic and post-romantic Gothic. As his German Romantic contemporary Novalis put it, 'Nach innen geht der geheimnisvolle Weg. In uns, oder nirgends, ist die Ewigkeit mit ihren Welten, die Vergangenheit und Zukunft. Die Außenwelt ist die Schattenwelt' (Inward lies the secret way. Within ourselves, or nowhere, is eternity with its worlds, the past and future. The outside world is the shadow-world).[39]

The burden of guilt that De Quincey had been dragging around with him ever since 1792 acquired a huge incremental weight when he found himself in the debtors' sanctuary

---

38 Quoted from Lindop, 258.

39 Novalis, Sixteenth Fragment of 'Blütenstaub'.

at Holyrood, afraid of finding himself imprisoned like a common criminal. Given that *Der Proceß* is the record of a dreamlike process going on in the mind of the author and thence of the protagonist, there is a parallel with Agnes's dream as re-experienced by De Quincey's narrator (= himself):

> at last all the solemnities of a great trial would shape themselves and fall into settled images. The audience was assembled, the judges were arrayed, the court was set. The prisoner was cited. Inquest was made, witnesses were called; and false witnesses came tumultuously to the bar. (12: 228f.)

This dream, and, more generally, the whole story, would have been even more interesting if De Quincey had been familiar with Kant's description of the secret tribunal of conscience in the *Critique of Practical Reason*, which provided Kafka with a model for his Court:

> The consciousness of an internal *tribunal* in man (before which 'his thoughts accuse or excuse one another') is Conscience. Every man has a conscience, and finds himself observed by an inward judge which threatens and keeps him in awe (reverence combined with fear); and this power which watches over the laws within him is not something which he himself (arbitrarily) *makes*, but it is incorporated in his being. It follows him like his shadow, when he thinks to escape. He may [...] stupefy himself with pleasures and distractions, but he cannot avoid now and then coming to himself or awaking, and then he at once perceives its awful voice. In his utmost depravity he may, indeed, pay no attention to it, but he cannot avoid *hearing* it. Now this [...] moral capacity, called *conscience*, has this peculiarity in it, that although its business is a business of man with himself, yet he finds himself compelled by his reason to transact it as if at the command of *another person*. For the transaction here is the conduct of a *trial (causa)* before a tribunal. But that he who is *accused* by his conscience should be conceived as *one and the same person* with the judge is an absurd conception of a judicial court; for then the complainant would always lose his case. Therefore in all duties the conscience of the man must regard *another* than himself as the judge of his actions, if it is to avoid self-contradiction [...] this other may be an actual or a merely ideal person which reason frames to itself.[40]

The Household Wreck conveys not only De Quincey's feeling of guilt, but also a deeper anxiety and a heavier burden of anguish. Here too there is a parallel with Kafka, for the juggernaut heard approaching by Charles Lloyd in De Quincey's account of his friend's life (2: 994), which is a projection of his own sense of impending catastrophe, invites comparison with the approaching enemy, who in the final analysis is himself, heard by Kafka's self-projection, the Burrower, in 'Der Bau', who is trapped in his own creation. Both writers are aware that, being their own worst enemy, they are responsible for the loss of control that the juggernaut represents, and which is one of the fundamental features of Gothic: De Quincey in the sense that his life was vitiated by early mistakes (leaving school and home; leaving Oxford without a degree; acquiring there the drug habit that did so much damage to his personal and literary life), Kafka in the sense that he gave himself, for a variety of unnecessary reasons, a very hard time psychologically. Lindop has said elsewhere that the 'bizarre juxtaposition of realistic and Gothic conventions' in [*The Household Wreck*] 'is enough to take [it] into a Kafkaesque realm of the absurd',[41] but there is more to it than that, for if the environment in *The Household Wreck* 'has no qualities

---

40 Kant, *Critque of Practical Reason*, tr. Thomas Kingsmill Abbott, 3rd edn (London: Longmans, Green & Co, 1883), 321ff.

41 In *Bicentenary Studies*, 231.

independent of the narrator's extreme emotional states',[42] the environment in *Der Proceß* has no reality outside the protagonist's mind, of which it is at all times a reification.[43] Parallels between De Quincey and Kafka, in the background in this chapter, are foregrounded in the next.

The Household Wreck has many Gothic features. The court-cum-prison, seat of an unjust tribunal and scene of a trial, is as Gothic (an 'old decaying prison', it is vast, ancient, in parts ruinous, a gloomy pile of a building, a rat-hole) as the dubious administration of the law, which is no longer absolute; shaken by the French Revolution, the system's power over its prisoner-victims is growing less. There is in this respect a close parallel with Kafka's *In der Strafkolonie*. There could hardly be a better example, when De Quincey eventually gets round to it after the depressing and undistinguished preamble, of the Gothic sensing of 'the darkness of our paths' (12: 162) and anticipation of 'some great calamity travelling towards me' (12: 168), the 'sudden desolations' (12: 160), 'sudden horror' (12: 212), and subsequent tightening of the screw, bringing with them the loss of all security and certainty, the wrecking of human lives. Gothic is the idea of an enemy in the house of life, Gothic the shipwreck of all peace and security. The loss of control by all the main characters speaks for itself, as does the venality and 'air of Italian subtlety and dissimulation' of the head jailer's deputy, a Portuguese Jew biblically named Manesseh, and his venality, echoing *Klosterheim,* that goes back to *The Bravo of Venice*. The masque-motif of *Klosterheim is repeated.* The peculiarly De Quinceyan notion of a 'perfect revenge' links the tale with *The Avenger*. The Hungarian woman represents the Gothic figure of the gypsy/outcast (cf. Laun's *Die Zigeunerin*, 1825). From sudden unjust accusation to mockery of a trial and miscarrriage of justice, incarceration in that vast, rambling pile of a prison, and escape via a locked door, a secret door in a fireplace, and an aperture high above the ground (as in *The Peasant of Portugal*), the whole nightmare is wholly Gothic, but the wild tragedy of this pronouncedly Gothic tale again transcends Gothic, this time in its particular applicability to De Quincey and the tragedies of his private life.

8.5. *The Avenger* (1838)

First published in *Blackwood's Magazine* in August 1838, *The Avenger* shows the influence of the *Blackwood's*-type tale of terror in its explicit treatment of multiple murder, but at the same time it is one of De Quincey's most obviously Gothic and 'German' (in the sense in which the word was used in 1797-98), as well as being one of his most certainly personal texts. Sedgwick took the following early passage as 'a good epitome of De Quincey's Gothic elements':

> And the general feeling [...] was, even among the boldest, like that which sometimes takes possession of the mind in dreams – when one feels one's-self sleeping alone, utterly divided from all call or hearing of friends, doors open that should be shut, or unlocked that should be triply secured, the very walls gone, barriers swallowed up by unknown abysses, and a world of illimitable night, whisperings at a distance, correspondence between darkness and darkness, like one deep calling to another, and the dreamer's own heart the centre from

42 Lindop, in *Bicentenary Studies*, 231f.

43 See Patrick Bridgwater, *Kafka's Novels: An Interpretation* (Amsterdam & New York: Rodopi, 2003), passim.

which the whole network of this unimaginable chaos radiates, by means of which the blank *privations* of silence and darkness become powers the most *positive* and awful. (12: 236)

De Quincey is here describing the feelings of an inhabitant of a city terrorized by secret murder, but the significance of his words is altogether wider, for, as Sedgwick says, 'The oppressiveness of this space, the ego's sense of being under it as if underground or underwater, is a profound affinity with the Gothic tradition', and the 'association of depth with sleep and dreams is further reminiscent of the Gothic'.[44] She rightly compares this passage with another in which De Quincey, lying 'under a world's weight of incubus and night-mare' (3: 433), feels

deep-seated anxiety and funereal melancholy, such as are wholly incommunicable by words. I seemed every night to descend – not metaphorically, but literally to descend – into chasms and sunless abysses, depths below depths, from which it seemed hopeless that I could ever re-ascend. Nor did I, by waking, feel that I *had* re-ascended. (3:435)

There is a clear parallel between Gothic and nightmare, for this feeling of oppression and helplessness corresponds to the symptoms of what Erasmus Darwin calls 'the disease we call Night-mare'. Whether De Quincey read either Darwin's *Zoonomia* (1796) or J. Waller's *A Treatise on the Incubus, or Nightmare* (1816), in which, notwithstanding the title, Waller too writes of 'Night-mare', I do not know, but he certainly knew that Wordsworth found in the *Zoonomia* the story on which his 'Goody Blake and Harry Gill' is based. In an interesting note (14: 276) De Quincey writes of Erasmus Darwin's reputation, which may imply that he had not actually read his most important work. On the other hand there is little room for doubt that he knew Robert Macnish's *The Philosophy of Sleep* of 1834. Macnish, a fellow *Blackwood's*-contributor, gives an extremely vivid description of 'the horrors it [night-mare] frequently gives rise to', and one of his descriptions in particular is revealing: 'he [the sufferer from nightmare] is prostrated by inevitable destiny beneath the approaching wheels of the car of Juggernaut'.[45]

Masson suggested that we ought perhaps to reserve 'the possibility of some yet unascertained German suggestion for *The Avenger*', and more recently Goldman has written that 'If one were able to discover the source, [one] would probably find that [*The Avenger*] is much more like a translation than a thorough-going recast'.[46] When asked whether he were the author of *The Avenger*, De Quincey replied that 'he did write *The Avenger*', adding that. it was written under circumstances forcing him to finish it very hurriedly.[47] He did not say he was the author of the tale, but merely implied that he wrote it under circumstances similar to those that obtained when he wrote *Walladmor*. However, while his wording on this occasion does not preclude the possibility that it may be a *rifacimento,* on another occasion he described *The Avenger* as 'A German tale (*scene laid in Germ*, I mean, but entirely of my own invention, turning upon Secret murder'.[48] This

44 Sedgwick, 37f.
45 Macnish, 135.
46 Goldman, 156f.
47 Quoted from Goldman, 157.
48 NLS MS 3112 f.288 (Quoted from De Quincey, *The Stranger's Grave,* ed. Baxter, 5.

statement is so catagorical that the idea of the tale perhaps being a translation should be dropped forthwith. *The Avenger* and *The Household Wreck* are Gothic tales of terror. From 1938 also dates a further Gothic tale, *The Curse,* a 'Tale connected with the Black Forest' that took its starting-point from *The Avenger* and is unfortunately lost; it has no connexion with the anonymous tale of the same title that appeared in *Fraser's Magazine* in November 1832.

The 'avenger' is, of course, a Gothic figure, and vengeance a common theme at the time, so there is no obvious reason why De Quincey should have needed a 'German suggestion'. That said, there are suggestive tales by three German writers who are known to him. Tromlitz, praised by De Quincey in his review of Gillies, has a powerful tale, *Vergeltung* (*Revenge*) which he may have known, and while *The Avenger* is neither a translation nor an imitation of it, the idea of someone returning to the scene of their early life to wreak vengeance in one way and degree or another on those by whom they have been maltreated is common to both tales. There is a also a weak early work by the author of *Walladmor,* Willibald Alexis, also entitled *Vergeltung,* which De Quincey could not have known since, although written in 1814, it was not published until 1901. Then there is Laurids Kruse.

His praise of Laun and Tromlitz notwithstanding, it is a striking fact that De Quincey's real attention is held, in Gillies's *German Stories,* by five tales of secret murder, two of them by a writer, Laurids Kruse, who in 1829 published *Die Rache* (*Revenge*), a tale of revenge, set in Kruse's north-east part of Germany, which he might conceivably have come across, although Bohte did not stock it and De Quincey is unlikely to have seen it elsewhere. There is, however, no reason why he should have found the motif of revenge in a German tale, for it is omnipresent in Gothic from Schiller and Grosse onwards. Maturin's *Fatal Revenge* (1807), a study of 'vengeance as atrocious as the crime that provoked it', was closer at hand, it being precisely this sort of vengeance that held De Quincey's somewhat malicious imagination; Maturin shared De Quincey's preoccupation with guilt (original sin). Laurids Kruse also published six volumes of *Kriminalgeschichten und romantische Erzählungen* (1827), which would have provided De Quincey with models for tales of murder if he had known them, which is, however, unlikely. Although Kruse was once well known in northern Germany – he retired to Wandbek, on the outskirts of Hamburg, in 1820 – his work was (and is) virtually unknown in the English-speaking world.

The Avenger may seem 'At first sight a fairly conventional Gothic tale' (L 233), but it is also a tale, about the exploits of a secret avenger who terrorizes a whole community, whose central motif, linking it to *The Peasant of Portugal* and *Klosterheim*, shows it to be 'fairly conventional' only on the surface. The theme of revenge and the avenger-figure, which are such a feature of De Quincey's Gothic tales, are the product of one of his obsessions:

> This insulated, idyllic space is for De Quincey the perfect settting for a violent tragedy or, given the Miltonic associations, for a scene of fall. The same pattern appears in many of De Quincey's Gothic tales like 'The Household Wreck' and 'The Avenger' or in the novel *Klosterheim.* In each case a small, idyllic community or innocent household is ravaged by an act of 'blank treachery' not unlike the cunning attack carried out by the

serpent on Adam and Eve's 'sacred and sequester'd' bower. With De Quincey the Miltonic myth of the fall of man assumes a Gothic style.[49]

It is, however, not just a 'Gothic style' that is in question, for the Fall is *the* Gothic event:

the Gothic tradition replays with almost infinite variations the myths both of the temptation and fall in Eden and of the perilous experience of the post-lapsarian wilderness. The fruit consumed in Eden turns to poison, withering humanity's world into one of suffering and death rather than opening it into the bloom of divine infinity Satan had promised.[50]

The 'infinite iteration' of the 'aboriginal fall' of which De Quincey wrote in 'The English Mail-Coach' (13: 304) is the key event of Gothic. No doubt the Fall was also the subject of some of Elizabeth Penson Quincey's gloomier evangelistic deliberations. The model for this wrecking of a small, innocent household is the wrecking of De Quincey's childhood and the fall from innocence into tragic knowledge that it entailed.

The Avenger is a tale with obvious autobiographical roots. Maximilian Wyndham, the 'minister of a dreadful retribution', in speaking of 'the great wreck of my life' (12: 164), is speaking for De Quincey, who, however, unlike his alter ego in the text, was never reconciled to the wreck in question. Maximilian is initially presented as an ideal, part-autobiographical, super-ego figure; he shares De Quincey's intellectual brilliance. Like Maximilian in *Klosterheim* he is an officer in the Imperial service, a mysterious figure and the avenger of grievous wrong done to his family. *The Avenger* shares with *Klosterheim* the basic situation of a beleaguered city. Maximilian's 'profound sadness' mirrors the profound sadness and rapacious grief that De Quincey felt following the death of Elizabeth, while his 'freezing gravity' is reminiscent of that of De Quincey's mother. De Quincey is, of course, present as narrator, in the guise of a professor at a university[51] in north-eastern Germany, apparently Göttingen, that turns out to bear a close resemblance to Oxford, where 'ill blood between the city and the University' was not unknown. The narrator's 'monastic abode' with a suite of ten rooms to spare and an English porter's lodge, and with Black Friars nearby, is based on Worcester College and Blackfriars in nearby St. Giles. De Quincey's Oxford friend, the mysterious, presumably Jewish (since he taught De Quincey some Hebrew) and probably (judging by his distinguished name) aristocratic Schwartzburg (or was it Schwarzenberg?), was part-model for Maximilian, and his mother may well have been a Jewess married to an Archduke of Austrian family. Some of the names of Maximilian's victims are telling: Weishaupt is named after the founder of the Illuminati, 'the profoundest conspirator that has ever existed', who adopted as his pseudonym the name of a Thracian bandit, Spartacus;[52] Albernass declares the two old bachelors to be asses (*albern* means assinine), and Münzer (literally coiner) links its owner with De Quincey. Margaret (Liebenheim), who at one point is made to resemble Goethe's Gretchen,

49 Clej, 238.

50 Stephen C. Behrendt, in his Introduction to Shelley's *Zastrozzi and St Irvyne* (Oxford & New York: Oxford University Press, 1986), xiv.

51 In 'Walstein's School of History', Charles Brockden Brown similarly invented a German professorial persona ('Krants of Gotha') for himself.

52 Louis Blanc, quoted by Montague Summers in the Introduction of his edition of Grosse, *Horrid Mysteries,* 2 vols (London: Holden, 1927), I, xvi.

is named after De Quincey's wife Margaret, for whose death the previous year he felt responsible. The number of victims corresponds to the number of De Quincey's close relatives and friends who died in his lifetime. *Blackwood's,* in which this tale of revenge first appeared, was known for its literary assassinations.

De Quincey has a literary model for the avenger in the form of Schiller's Karl Moor and, further back, if he looked there, in the late sixteenth- and early seventeenth-century revenge tragedy of Kyd, Ford, Middleton and Webster. Ford and Webster's *A Late Murder of the Son upon the Mother* (1624) provides the precedent; De Quincey's life adds the context. In *The Avenger* his hero, Maximilian, turns into a multiple murderer whose victims include his wife, Margaret Liebenheim. As in *Klosterheim*, Max/Maximilian is named after Max Piccolomini in Schiller's *Wallenstein*, but the point in that in each case Max(imilian) is a masque for De Quincey himself, who saw himself as fallen man, as sharing in 'the reason of the aboriginal fall' (13: 304), and regarded himself as having murdered his own wife by neglect. It is a pity that this self-proclaimed pundit of German philosophy was apparently unaware of one of the greatest German philosophical works of his lifetime, Arthur Schopenhauer's *Die Welt als Wille und Vorstellung* (1819-44), in which the Fall or 'the guilt of the human race through its [very] existence' is treated as a fundamental fact of human existence. Schopenhauer, who, with Goya, epitomizes Black Romanticism, is as relevant to *The Avenger* and *The Household Wreck* as Goya is to the tales (*The Peasant of Portugal* and *The Caçadore*) reflecting the Peninsular War of 1807-14. '„Vengeance is mine; I will repay,“ saith the Lord' (Rom. XII, 19), read by the preacher in *The Household Wreck (*12: 232), is twice quoted by Schopenhauer in the first (1819) volume of *The World as Will and Idea* (I, 419, 462). The terms in which the rhetorical question asked by the narrator, 'What is life' (12: 158), are answered, are Biblical and Baroque ('vanitas vanitatum, et omnia vanitas') rather than Gothic.

De Quincey relates to the Avenging Lord in the first instance through his own vengeful nature and the fact that he was capable of regarding revenge as 'noble' (1: 132). That the narrator presents his tale as 'a separate chapter in the private history of German manners' immediately indicates his autobiographical nature, for 'German manners' were one of De Quincey's hobby-horses, a subject on which he was given to pontificating in the most preposterous way. The key is hidden away in a reflection on the subject of the Prussian Marshal Blücher which forms a digression in the 'Recollections of Charles Lamb': 'Revenge is a luxury, to those who can rejoice in it at all, so inebriating that possibly a man would be equally liable to madness from the perfect gratification of his vindictive hatred or its perfect defeat' (3: 70). Few men have had so ample a vengeance as Blücher, when holding Paris as a conqueror, he says, writing of the 'intoxicating' 'delirium of his vengeance'. No one would write that but from the depth of personal feeling. De Quincey's attitude contrasts, to his disadvantage, with that of P. B. Shelley, who in one of his early Gothic tales sees vengeance as ignoble, Satanic, the epitome of self-centredness:

> Like Satan, Zastrozzi [is] destroyed from within by an ego grown beyond all bounds of reason; in his role as the self-appointed Avenger he is not unlike the cruel and retributive God of the Old Testament whom Shelley rejected.[53]

De Quincey, by contrast, has a vengeful streak to which the vengeful God of the Old Testament appealed; it is no chance that the multiple murders in *The Avenger* are committed by a son to avenge the dishonour done to his Jewish mother.

53 Behrendt, xvii.

9. De Quincey and Kafka

Notwithstanding his reputation as a Kant scholar, intuitive understanding of the wit, playfulness and delicacy of Jean Paul, enthusiasm for Schiller's *Die Räuber* and *Wallenstein* and for the work of Laun, Tromlitz and Kruse, the German-language – and indeed the Gothic – writer with whom Thomas De Quincey (1785-1859) has most in common is unquestionably Franz Kafka (1883-1924), whose work I have recently shown[1] to belong in the context of Gothic and the closely related fairytale. A comparison of the two men's work shows that De Quincey is, in many often surprising ways, a precursor of Kafka. The two men's times, cultural backgrounds, psychologies, characters, exterior lives, and personal and literary styles may be quite different, but they belong together as Gothic writers and poets in prose whose work is informed by a similar sense of alienation and loss, and as introspective masters of the dream narrative and the autobiographical fragment.

Biographers describe both men as living behind a psychological wall of glass, what De Quincey calls a 'party-wall of crystal' (11: 369), and thus by extension in a house without a door. Kafka's protagonist, K., in *Das Schloß*, can neither (literally) gain entrance to the Castle, nor (metaphorically) escape from his obsessive immurement within it; as a 'castle-in-the-air', it is a Piranesi-like aerial prison-edifice, a metaphorical version of the aerial dungeon of Walladmor Castle, and, as such, symbol of the outlaw's fastness in which De Quincey passed his life. It was because they felt themselves to be outsiders, outcasts, pariahs with a 'dreadful taint of guilt, real or imputed, in ages far remote' (1: 101) that they created such an invisible screen around themselves. Both identify with pariah-figures, De Quincey with the young prostitute, 'Ann the Outcast', and Kafka with witches. At the time of his 'noviciate' in London in late 1802, De Quincey described himself as 'little better than an outcast', and Kafka too was all too aware of the manifold ways in which he was an outsider: rejected by his father, neglected by his mother, a stranger in his native city, writing in the impoverished language of its non-native minority, blaming himself for outliving two brothers who died in infancy, he is in many ways the archetypal Cain-like outcast of Gothic.[2]

Kafka's Gothic, like De Quincey's, is a reflection of his identity problem. However he looked at his genetic inheritance and position, and therefore at his own identity, he could not get away from a sense of alienation. Because his paternal genetic inheritance involved unacceptable characteristics and weaknesses, while his individual characteristics (and the weaknesses into which he construed them) were rejected by his father, self-definition became a major preoccupation. De Quincey, like Kafka, was exposed to the 'terrible uncertainty' of his inner existence. Fearing nonentity, they are both fundamentally concerned with self-definition; everything they write is a means to that end. Writing, for both of them, is a transgressive act, yet transgression as such is, paradoxically, a means of maintaining some sense of identity and authenticity. Defining themselves as writers and

---

1 See Bridgwater, *Kafka, Gothic and Fairytale*.

2 In the Romantic *Umwertung der Werte,* Cain, like the Devil, becomes a heroic figure; see Lowry Nelson, Jr., 'Night Thoughts on the Gothic Novel', *Yale Review*, 52 (1962), 237.

transgressors, it follows that they write in order to explore, but not to redeem or overcome the sense of guilt that is inseparable from the act of writing. Without the sense of guilt that drove them to write, they would be nothing, which is precisely what they both feared themselves to be. Because the negative terms in which they perceive themselves constitute their identity, they have no choice but to cling to their negative self-images, their Satanic Gothic selves.

De Quincey is said to have looked out from his defensive vantage-point behind that wall of glass with affectionate sympathy towards others, as Kafka also did, but to have been unable to receive back any such sympathy that was proffered to him. Kafka, for his part, received much affection from others, but mostly chose to keep them at a distance in order to maintain the lack of distracting emotional involvement that was necessary to him as a writer. He was as much a 'solitary in the fastness of his own personality' (E 510) as De Quincey. In either case the inner man appears to be rigidly concealed from view, and thus forced to exist in the kind of subliminal dungeon (the phrase is Eaton's, but the concept is perfectly applicable to Kafka) that Kafka portrayed in all its horrid (in the Gothic sense) particularity in *Der Bau.* To write is by definition to reveal oneself, but both men were deeply concerned to defend the fastness of personality, the citadel of the self, against intrusion of any kind. Both were surrounded by inhibitions. Eaton wrote (E 511) that De Quincey had a morbid fear lest he should impose on others, but this can be read as a mask for a greater fear: that others might obtrude upon him. Kafka was not so different.

There is a strikingly close parallel between Kafka's frantic Burrower (the writer as giant mole), trapped in his own construct, and De Quincey as Gothic 'coiner' sitting in a 'deep grave-like recess' listening to the steps of the Avenger approaching. De Quincey wrongly fancies himself safe, but in reality he too is trapped (within his Opium-Eater persona), whereas Kafka, who was dying an extraordinarily painful death as he wrote his last Gothic tale, knew that he was doomed because the Avenger was within. Both men hide from view, while at the same time parading themselves for view. Kafka's *Ein Hungerkünstler* is about what he felt to be the element of exhibitionism in any art that goes public, and De Quincey, while hiding behind his most famous persona, simultaneously parades himself for and before the public gaze. Although they both experienced the external world as unreal, they saw its intrusive threat as real enough. They have convoluted, labyrinthine mentalities, the labyrinth image being as pervasive in the work of the one as in that of the other. Hayter commented on 'Those labyrinths [of the self] he [De Quincey] explored with tireless self-scrutiny', adding that 'Perhaps no other writer has combined such vivid and intense subconscious activity with such acute observation of it.'[3] This may be true of English literature, but it ceases to be true if one takes a wider view.

Though they came of families that were, by their time (late Georgian England, late Habsburg Austria), relatively affluent, they were, both of them, psychologically exposed and emotionally deprived, De Quincey as a result of losing, at an early age, his father (whom he barely knew, so much had his father been away from home), elder brother and favourite sister, a loss which left him shattered, and from which he never recovered, and Kafka as a result of losing two brothers in infancy and having a father whose affection for his surviving son was often, or it seemed to him, less apparent than the weight of his

3 *Confessions*, ed. Hayter, 24.

disapproval of someone so fundamentally unlike himself and thus so unintelligible and so challenging. Kafka's father was just as much a 'Harlequin Mephistopheles' as De Quincey's elder brother William, who for a few important years performed the role of father. Both writers, for different reasons, felt abandoned not only by their fathers (hence, on a psychological level, Thomas's reinvention of himself as De Quincey, which meant turning his back on the father who had abandoned him first in life and then in death), but also, albeit to a lesser extent, by their mothers, who withheld from them the affection that their sensitive, vulnerable temperaments craved, leaving their sons to obtain from the family maids (in De Quincey's case) or governess (in Kafka's case) the emotional reassurance that they should have given them themselves.

Both mothers, whose priorities lay elsewhere, were cool and unimaginative, De Quincey's being 'freezing in excess', forbidding in the severity that was the denial of the charity she believed herself to be practising; her son later remarked, probably thinking of the forbidding Abbess of Ann Radcliffe's *The Italian*, that her austerity fitted her for the role of Mother Superior of 'rebellious nunneries' (E 19); the appeal of the 'Female Infidel' lay in the fact that she was in every way the diametric opposite of Mrs Quincey. Kafka's mother, who was by no means as forbidding as Elizabeth Penson Quincey, though her son described her as acting as 'beater' in the family hunt that had himself as its prey, neglected her son while she pandered to her husband, who was more demanding. De Quincey's adoption of the apparently aristocratic 'De' was also a way of distancing himself from a mother whose kingdom was not of this world.

One cannot, of course, imagine Kafka sitting with 'a decanter of laudanum and a book of German metaphysics', or describing himself as doing so, but he too studied the German metaphysics of De Quincey's time, notably the work of the philosopher of Gothic, Schopenhauer, but also Kant, in his student days. The image of De Quincey sitting with a decanter of laudanum (masquerading as claret) and a book of German metaphysics (3: 410) is of a piece with Peacock's image (*Nightmare Abbey*, ch. 2) of Scythrop (P. B. Shelley) sleeping with Grosse's *Horrid Mysteries* under his pillow, dreaming of ghastly confederates holding midnight conventions in subterranean caves. Like the mask worn by Maximilian in *Klosterheim*, itself a reflection of the mask De Quincey felt obliged to wear, it is a pose or 'masque', one of many in De Quincey's autobiographical fragments. 'Little Mr Quincey' was a wearer of masks: Tabitha Quincey, the Opium-Eater, the Dreamer, the Translator, the Eudaemonist, the Old Man as Child, X.Y.Z., etc. Kafka did not go in for self-performance in the same way, although he does privately think of himself as a 'Hungerkünstler' (starvation artist), a 'Nachaffe' (ex-ape), 'der Ewige Jude' (the Wandering Jew [literally the Everlasting Jew]), 'ein unmöglicher Vogel' (an impossible bird),[4] and invariably wears a *Tarnkappe* or mask of invisibility in his fictional writings; even in the diaries he is given to writing about himself in the third person, as De Quincey also did, though less regularly. De Quincey's pose was so successful that he was regarded as a powerful author before he had published a line, and is to this day often taken at his own valuation without his credentials being properly examined. Having reinvented himself in his teens as Thomas De Quincey, he performs the role of gentleman-scholar and man-of-letters that is so important to him because he, like Kafka, who also suffered from spells of what De Quincey dubbed his

4 Kafka's surname represents a German spelling of the Czech *kavka*, jackdaw.

‘Chattertonian melancholia’, is afraid that his work may prove to be a mere literary construct, ‘a tale told by an idiot, full of sound and fury, signifying nothing’.[5] He not only needs to establish a human and literary persona, but needs to hide behind it. One of the attractions of *rifacimento* was that it offered a way of indulging his Gothic or other self without being seen to do so.

In De Quincey we see already the ‘enigma of manner’ assumed by Walter Pater, with whom he has so much in common, both of them ‘gentleman-scholars’ with a secret fascination with violence, their work an autobiographical masquerade. Pater was to use dead writers as a way of writing about, and thus secretly defining, himself; De Quincey uses living writers, notably Wordsworth and Coleridge, but also Godwin and others, in much the same way; it is of a piece with his Kafkaesque technique of hiding away important passages of self-revelation in unlikely places. Like Kafka after him, De Quincey is riven by self-doubt. His refusal to come at the heart of the matter, his penchant for digression, is a reflection of this. Kafka, by contrast, always sticks strictly to the point; his inability to complete his novels has a different cause. De Quincey’s inveterate rewriting implies an over-awareness that no text is final, and while Kafka’s unfinished novels might be thought to imply the same thing, with Kafka it is less a matter of a failure of technique than a failure of nerve, a wise refusal to look too steadily into the Pit. Gothic famously resists closure.

For De Quincey at least the elixir of literature was, in some ways, a devil’s elixir, although it is Kafka who (in a letter dated 5 July 1922) actually defines writing as ‘service to the Devil’. For Kafka writing is, in the end, a religious act. For De Quincey it is an aesthetic one; that is why *rifacimento*, the aesthetic-linguistic improvement of another’s work, is so characteristic of him. Kafka, who was no less certain in his literary judgments, would have regarded *rifacimento* as a hubristic waste of time. De Quincey’s work is original in its unoriginality; Kafka’s is wholly original. If De Quincey had become the good lawyer that Eaton fancied he might have become (whatever that is meant to mean), and thus a half-time writer like Kafka, who successfully combined writing with a ‘legal’ career, he might also have been a better writer, but, as it is, he became – like all of us – what he always was. Happening to resemble Kafka in so many even personal ways, he was in the final analysis an altogether different person; in particular he lacked the personal and literary self-discipline that was the bedrock of Kafka’s life.

It was the sense of inadequacy and guilt imposed on them by their upbringings, and especially the sense that they were unworthy of their worthy businessmen fathers, whose material values they rejected, that turned them into Cain-figures. Cain, that ‘Satan clad in human flesh’,[6] is an importamt figure in Kafka’s work and scheme of things. He originally planned to write his first novel on the Cain-and-Abel or ‘hostile brothers’ theme that had loomed so large in German Pre-Romanticism (Sturm und Drang), most notably in Schiller’s *Die Räuber*, one of the two works, the other being *Der Geisterseher*, that caused Schiller to be regarded, in the Anglo-American and French worlds, as a father of the Gothic, and was also a common fairytale motif (cf. the Grimms’ ‘Die zwei Brüder’ [The Two Brothers]). Kafka’s diaries and letters make it abundantly clear that he, like Byron, saw himself as a Cain-like and therefore devilish marked man; it is this fact that accounts for his interest in

5 Shakespeare, *Macbeth* (1606), V, ii: 44.

6 Rudwin, *The Devil in Legend and Literature*, 305.

Byron's letters and journals, a selection from which he possessed. Kafka's *Der Verschollene* (*America* is the outdated, misleading title of the English translation) opens with the floating Gothic world of the liner (a version of the pirate-ship, for on board it Kafka is smuggling himself into an imaginary world) arriving in a New York harbour of the imagination dominated by a gigantic figure on Manhattan Island – a deformed version of the Statue of Liberty – whose upheld sword threatens the transgressive new arrival. There is a telling parallel with De Quincey's vision of the 'elder nurse' with 'fiery' arm similarly upheld: in either case the avenger-God of the Old Testament is near the surface of the mind. De Quincey, for his part, apparently still set on shocking his mother, described Cain (in the First Paper in 'On Murder considered as one of the Fine Arts') as 'a man of first-rate genius', a phrase Kafka would have been incapable of using, not least because he identified with Cain and was by nature humble to the point of self-effacement. It is De Quincey's subversive Gothic self speaking.

The 'infinite iteration' of the 'aboriginal fall', of which De Quincey wrote in 'The English Mail-Coach' (13: 304), and which has been seen as the key event of Gothic, is the centrestone of *Der Verschollene* and a leitmotif of Kafka's thoughts in his unhappiest periods, when he felt that he understood the Fall, by which he was obsessed at such times, better than anyone else. No doubt the Fall was also the subject of some of Elizabeth Penson Quincey's gloomier evangelistic lucubrations; one of the few intellectually positive things she did for her son was to introduce him to Milton's *Paradise Lost* in 1799. The 'suspicions of some inveterate discontinuity, randomness, or errancy in the order of things',[7] by which De Quincey was haunted, are linked both to the minor writings that were associated, for him, with feelings of guilt, and to the confessional heart of his work, for his addiction stood in his mind for that 'infinite iteration' of the 'aboriginal fall' at Oxford and the false paradise it opened up to him. Just as 'With De Quincey the Miltonic myth of the fall of man assumes a Gothic style',[8] so with Kafka's *Der Verschollene* the Biblical myth of the Fall assumes a Gothic style. German-language parallels English-language Gothic in many ways, but, the influence of Milton on Schiller's *Die Räuber* notwithstanding , it tends to take its concern with the Fall from the Bible (and, later, from Schopenhauer, in whose Gothic philosophy it is central) rather than from Milton, and its notion of the sublime from Kant rather than from Burke. The importance of the 'aboriginal fall' to De Quincey is emphasized by the 'Daughter of Lebanon' fragment with which the 1856 version of the *Confessions* concludes. This establishes as historical parallel the Miltonic expulsion of Adam and Eve from Eden (cf. the Eden valley in Cumberland), looking back on their lost paradise (or, for De Quincey, the false paradise offered by his dreams) as a region 'with dreadful faces thronged and fiery arms' (3: 449). Kafka's *Der Verschollene*, a paradise lost novel that also features a threefold false paradise, has its starting-point in Kafka's awareness, which came on less suddenly than De Quincey's, in puberty, of his own 'fallen' condition.

When the poet Charles Lloyd, on the run from The Retreat at York, turned up on his doorstep announcing that he was being pursued, De Quincey will have been horrified by what Lloyd proceeded to say to him shortly afterwards:

---

7 Snyder, in *Bicentenary Studies,* xvii.

8 Clej, 238.

I dare say you think you know me; but you do not, and you cannot. I am the author of all evil; Sir, I am the Devil . [...] I know who you are; you are a nobody, a nonentity, you have no being. You will not agree with me, and [...] will attempt to argue with me, and thus to prove that you do exist; but it is not so, you do not exist at all. (L 217)

To this visitation by 'the Devil' must be added a comparable one by 'a sort of demon' (one of the tribe of cacodemons of Romantic mythology)[9] in the guise of 'the Malay' that happened shortly afterwards. De Quincey was probably less affected by these visitations than Kafka would have been, but he will have been deeply affected by the self-proclaimed Devil's pronouncement that he, De Quincey was a nonentity and therefore did not exist, which cut to the quick of his angst and self-doubt. K., in *Das Schloß* (*The Castle*) fails in the end to overcome the very same awareness of nonentity and therefore superfluity, which drives the whole novel. Given all the cultural differences between the two men and their times, it is a strange fact that they both not only identified with the Wandering Jew, but regarded themselves as being possessed by demons, and indeed by the Devil, although Kafka went further than De Quincey in this respect.

Notwithstanding the fact that between *Paradise Lost* (1667) and *Der Verschollene* (1912) the Devil passed from being seen as a part of the divine creation to being recognized as a creation of the human mind, Milton's belief in a personal Devil was shared by Kafka, whose identification with the arch-rebel derives in large measure from his bedevilled relationship with his father, and by De Quincey. On the Freudian view spelled out by Ernest Jones, the Devil is simply the personification of the repressed, unconscious instinctual life. Belief in the Devil, said to be attributable, as in Kafka's case, to 'infantile experiences of fear', represents

in the main an exteriorization of two sets of repressed wishes, both of which are ultimately derived from the infantile Oedipal situation: the wish to imitate certain attributes of the father, and the wish to defy the father; in other words, an alternating emulation of and hostility against the father.[10]

The Devil, that is to say, represents unconscious aspects of the Father-Son complex. More specifically he represents both the father against whom hostility is felt, and the son who defies the father, each party seeing the other as diabolical. From the son's point of view, Kafka *père* was the very devil to live with: he exhibited to the full the diabolical characteristics of arbitrariness, unjustness, petty tyranny and general unreasonableness, all of them documented to the full in the *Brief an den Vater* (*Letter to My Father*); he mocked his son's endeavours and derided his literary ambitions and achievements. Kafka therefore had a double reason for identifying with the 'devil' his father declared him to be: because in reacting against and defying his father he was performing the rôle of the Devil as arch-rebel that he felt was expected of him, and because he could not help letting his father's unjust censure get to him, coming to see himself, in the upshot, as in some way diabolical, whereas in reality he was closer to being saintly.

---

9 *Kakodämon der Schrekliche* (sic: Erfurt, 1800), by the 'Gothic' novelist J. F. E. Albrecht, is a satirical *roman-à-clef* about Suvorov (Kakodämon), the Russian Marshall, notorious for his brutality, who died in 1800.

10 Jones, 155.

Common to both these self-perceived 'devils' is debilitating self-doubt and a sense of guilt that, at times, they find overwhelming. If De Quincey was obsessed by 'the fear of an imposed and unjust guilt',[11] Kafka carried such a (partly self-imposed) burden throughout his life; Josef K. in *Der Proceß* embodies it. The idea of De Quincey incurring, in the form of his addiction to opium, what he, in his 'Preliminary Confessions',[12] calls 'a captivity so servile', thereby fettering himself with 'such a sevenfold chain' of misery[13] in the form of a base, earth-bound addiction, is not only Gothic, but Gothic in a late Romantic, Kafkaesque way, for the 'yoke of misery' is self-imposed. Kafka, for his part, did not write under the influence of opium (or of anything else save his own suggestibility), and, given his associative style, could not have done so, for, as De Quincey put it in his comments on the *Confessions,*

> The *technical memory*, or that which depends upon purely arbitrary links of connexion, and therefore more upon a *nisus* or separate activity of the mind – that memory, for instance, which recalls names – is undoubtedly affected, and most powerfully, by opium. On the other hand, the *logical memory*, or that which recalls facts that are connected by fixed relations, and where, A being given, B must go before or after – historical memory, for instance – is not much, if at all, affected by opium.

Kafka's work is the product of 'technical' memory' in this sense. Hypnagogic imagery, the mind's natural form of expression when it is in semi-conscious mode, day-dreaming or on the edge of sleep, underlies the work of both men, who have strongly visual minds. It is naturally Kafka who makes fuller, more systematic and more knowing use of it, for he knew Freud's *The Interpretation of Dreams* with its account of the 'dream-work' by means of which thoughts are translated into pictorial images. Whether he availed himself of it or not, De Quincey had the opportunity, when at Bohte's in 1821, to read Schubert's *Die Symbolik des Traumes*, which, as we have seen, describes dreams in a proto-Freudian way.

Both men were preyed on by anxiety, haunted by existential dread and a sense of personal inadequacy. Kafka's brain was as 'phantom-haunted' (the epithet is De Quincey's) under the condition of sobriety as De Quincey's was under the effect of laudanum. They were both haunted by their Gothic selves. Aletha Hayter has written of the way in which the faces of those who dominated De Quincey's childhood 'surge up through the sea-waves of his nightmares'.[14] It is just the same with Kafka, in whose disguised autobiographical fragments the faces of his father, mother and governess, but above all of his self or selves, are similarly ineffaceable. These Ensor-like masks belong to dream and nightmare, for the work of these two introspectives, seemingly so different, is, in each case, an exploration, undertaken by tapping into the unconscious, of the interior life, a mapping of the landscape of the mind, in which childhood events and emotions, kaleidoscope-like, combine and re-combine in obsessive patterns. Both men wrote at night, when the mind, over-tired, lets down its rational defences and goes into hypnagogic dream or quasi-dream mode, in which ideas take the form of images. They both had a natural dreaming faculty, which they

---

11 Baxter, 180, quoting Robert M. Maniquis, 'Lonely Empires: Personal and Public Visions of Thomas De Quincey', in *Literary Monographs,* Vol 8, ed. E. Rothstein & J. A. Wittreich (Madison: University of Wisconsin, Department of English, 1976), 51.

12 In *Confessions,* ed. Hayter, 33.

13 I take this to be a perversion of the 'seven-fold gifts' of the 'Veni, Creator Spiritus'.

14 *Confessions*, ed. Hayter, 19.

sedulously cultivated, and were fascinated by the secret life of the mind of which dreams and nightmares afford glimpses; they lived in the world of their dreams. De Quincey shares with Kafka not merely a vivid, often 'Gothic' dream-life, but an increasing ability to go into dream-mode more or less at will, although there is no reason to suppose that he went as far as Kafka in this respect; he stressed that the *Confessions* was written with the purpose of 'displaying the faculty [of dreaming]'. It is hardly surprising, then, that his 'theory of dream mechanism'[15] points to Freud's account of the 'dream-work', and to Kafka's work, which illustrates it.

As transcripts of linked day-dreams or virtual dreams, works such as *Das Urteil* (*The Judgment*), *Die Verwandlung* (*The Transformation*), *Der Verschollene* (*America*), *Der Proceß* (*The Trial*) and *Das Schloß* (*The Castle*) can be compared with the work described by its author as 'the legend of some hideous dream that can return no more', the *Confessions of an English Opium-Eater*, which, as we have seen, is important for its elaborate use of Gothic convention, for its profound influence on the development of the autobiographical novel, and for its place in the history of dream theory,[16] claims which can equally well be made for Kafka's novels. De Quincey's pre-Freudian text presents the narrative of a life suffering from a disorder that inhibits the will and with it the steady generation of the narrative, so that the author is obliged to resort to *rifacimento* as a way of continually kickstarting his narrative, whereas Kafka's post-Freudian narratives have overcome a similar inhibition by using Freudian dream-theory to enable and encrypt the narrative. Kafka, able to go into dream mode more or less at will, was spared the intermittent nature of opium-dependent narration, in which 'inspiration' or the flow of hypagogic imagery comes not with the drug but in its aftermath. Kafka's work as a whole is the most consequential attempt to describe the author's dreamlike inner world in order to define himself; as such, it enables us to see De Quincey's dream-narratives for what they are, a large step in that direction.

De Quincey's mind, like Kafka's, was 'powerfully visual, translating words directly into pictorial imagery', something that happens most naturally when the mind, exhausted, slips into dream-mode. Already in 1803, Lindop writes, 'he was moving towards a conscious development of the „dreaming faculty" which would play a central part in his literary work' (L 106). Unlike Kafka, he initially resorted to opium to boost his stamina and stimulate his imagination, but, like Kafka, he developed (by 1817) the capacity to enter at will a state on the threshold of consciousness and summon up the hypnagogic images that are translated into his work, although he naturally made far less consistent and effective use of it than Kafka, who used the dream-work both to format his texts and to mask their meaning. There is in this respect a clear difference between De Quincey's dream-texts and Kafka's novels: in the former passages of oneiric imagery alternate (to their detriment) with straight (and to that extent flat) autobiography, whereas Kafka's disguised autobiographical novels are wholly dream-like, constructed throughout of images deriving from and structured by the dream-work.

It was in 1817 that De Quincey began to be troubled by 'a return of bright hypnagogic imagery such as he had not seen since childhood' (L 222). As he lay in bed, exhausted and

---

15 Hayter, 21.
16 Thomas, 11.

on the very edge of sleep, he would see 'vast processions' of figures forming 'friezes of never-ending stories':

> The images were partly voluntary: they could be visualized by an act of will, and [...] he experimented with this, until he found that [...] he had only to think of something and he would see it before him in the dark. Worse, as he fell asleep it would persist and develop [...] Sleep became an exhausting phantasmagoria of elaborate nightmares,the restless images bringing with them dreadful anxiety and feelings of limitless despair. He 'seemed every night to descend – not metaphorically, but literally to descend – in to chasms and sunless abysses, depths below depths, from which it seemed hopeless that [he would] ever re-ascend'. Terrible claustrophobia was accompanied by 'suicidal despondency' such as 'cannot be expressed in words'.
>
> Some of the dreams brought back with startling immediacy long-forgotten incidents from childhood [...] episodes of fear or humiliation [...] Everything he wanted to forget came at him in his dreams, grotesque and magnified [...] Dizzying distortions of time and space sickened him [...] He was reminded of the vast yet claustrophobic architectural extravaganzas of Piranesi. (L 222f.)

One of the 'fearful memories' that appeared in this way, when what Freud calls the 'doorkeeper' was off duty, is a dramatically heightened version of a traumatic experience dating back to the age of two:

> Once again [...] the nursery of my childhood expanded before me: my sister was moaning in bed; and I was beginning to be restless with fears not intelligible to myself. Once again the elder nurse, but now dilated to colossal proportions, stood as upon some Grecian stage with her uplifted hand, and [...] smote me senseless to the ground. (1: 49f.)

The 'elder nurse' acts as father-substitute in this Oedipal drama, performing the role of the Devil already described. Lindop is surely right to argue that these experiences were shaped as much by De Quincey's character as by the physiological processes of withdrawal from opium, for 'Always a vivid dreamer and visualizer [...] he was very prone to obsessive, repetitious thought carried to the point of mental fatigue' (L 223), and it is at that point that thought really becomes repetitious and obsessive, particularly when nightmare (or what Macnish calls 'day-mare') is involved. Freud's account of the 'dream-work' makes clear that it is precisely in a state of mental fatigue that the mind, on the edge of sleep, slips into hypnagogic dream-mode, thereby as it were completing the circle of De Quincey's phantasmagoric experience, of thought slipping beyond control.

Kafka, for his part, was far from abusing himself in De Quincey's way (as opposed to the psychological way in which he might be said to have done so by dwelling on imaginary shortcomings) and, though an *Augenmensch* (visual person), did not have the Englishman's 'photographic' memory to fuel them, but he nevertheless experienced and cultivated very similar hypnagogic visions. No less than De Quincey, he was concerned with 'involutes', the subconscious patterns that crystallize in the dreaming mind, or, hypnagogically, in the mind on the threshold of sleep. The difference is, of course, that Kafka was writing in the immediate wake of *The Interpretation of Dreams*, whereas De Quincey was writing almost a generation before Freud was born, a fact that makes his tracing of those involutes all the more remarkable. Macnish's work (the German translation of which, *Der Schlaf in allen seinen Gestalten* [1835], is listed in Bibliography A of *The Interpretation of Dreams*) and, with it, the *Confessions*, fed into Freud's analysis of the dream-work.

Both men's visions invite comparison with what De Quincey called Piranesi's 'dreams'. The *locus classicus* is the description, in the *Confessions*, of Piranesi's engravings of imaginary prisons:

> Many years ago, when I was looking over Piranesi's 'Antiquities of Rome', Coleridge, then standing by, described to me a set of plates from that artist, called his 'Dreams', and which record the scenery of his own visions during the deliriums of a fever. Some of these (I describe only from memory of Coleridge's account) represented vast Gothic halls; on the floor of which stood mighty engines and machinery, wheels, cables, catapults, &c., expressive of enormous power put forth, or resistance overcome. Creeping along the sides of the walls, you perceived a staircase; and upon this, groping his way upwards, was Piranesi himself. Follow the stairs a little farther, and you perceive them reaching an abrupt termination, without any balustrade, and allowing no step onwards to him who should reach the extremity, except into the depths below. Whatever is to become of poor Piranesi, at least you suppose that his labours must now in some sense terminate. But raise your eyes, and behold a second flight of stairs still higher, on which again Piranesi is perceived, by this time standing on the very brink of the abyss. Once again elevate your eye, and a still more aerial flight of stairs is descried; And there, again, is the delirious Piranesi, busy on his aspiring labours: and so on, until the unfinished stairs and the hopeless Piranesi both are lost in the upper gloom of the hall. With the same power of endless growth and self-reproduction did my architecture proceed in dreams. (3: 438f.)

This is, of course, another kind of *rifacimento,* a recreation from memory of another man's verbal account of a third man's engraved image(s). It is more a conflation and interpretation/translation, applying Piranesi's images to De Quincey's fear of the abyss, than a description of any particular engraving. That these are not 'Dreams' (the title presumably given them by Coleridge) but architectural drawings of *c.* 1745 entitled *Carceri d'Invenzione*,[17] is beside the point, as is the fact that these vast threatening spaces are, strictly speaking, not Gothic, in the historical sense of medieval, but classical. In the more important literary sense they are memorably Gothic, images of a Fall that is forever on the point of happening, which is exactly how De Quincey saw his life. At the same time 'poor Piranesi', forever unable to fall, is the Wandering Jew, with whom, as a symbolical brother of Cain, both Kafka and De Quincey identified. The same confusing, surreal internal geography reappears in Pollunder's Gothic mansion in Kafka's *Der Verschollene,* and his Castle has a shifting, indeterminate appearance that places it firmly in the same context.

Piranesi's powerful images of '*metaphysical prisons*, whose seat is within the mind, whose walls are made of nightmare and incomprehension, whose chains are anxiety and their racks a sense of personal and even generic guilt'[18] point to the heart of De Quincey's Gothic, for these imaginary prisons memorably involve space that is as awesomely vast as, there being no escape from it, it is claustrophobic (L 223): the human, reduced to puny contingency and thereby to insignificance by the presence of the transcendent (which includes what German writers would call the negative transcendence of the Fall), faces an abyss in which the imagination is afraid of losing itself. These prisons of the imagination, which leave the imagination with no way out other than the fall into death, are closely connected with Coleridge's Gothic Cathedral of Imagination in Chapter 13 of the *Biographia Literaria* (1817) and with De Quincey's *Confessions*, which describe architectural vistas 'in proportions so vast as the bodily eye is not fitted to receive', where

---

17 These images can be found in Jonathan Scott, *Piranesi* (London: Academy/St. Martin's, 1975).

18 Aldous Huxley, *Prisons* (London: The Trianon Press, 1949), 21f., 24f.

distance is 'amplified to an extent of unutterable and self-repeating infinity' (L 223). Piranesi's images embody the chasm of De Quincey's imagination that conveys not only a Gothic sense of unfathomable vastness in which depth after depth reverses Piranesi's image of height after height while retaining its giddying meaning, but also a Gothic sense of claustrophobia and incarceration. In other words, they represent the sublime of terror and point straight to the Pit that Poe was to describe, the 'cavern of death' and 'cavern of horror' of the Gothic popular novel, the emptiness that Shelley was afraid would swallow him, as indeed it did.

All these meanings come together in Kafka's *Der Bau (The Burrow),* which shows his mole-like persona, representing not only the creative artist-constructor trapped in his own construct, its elaborate defences pointless when the threat comes from within, but, more basically, the human animal imprisoned in its own consciousness, the victim of its own fear of death. Piranesi's images will also have carried a further, personal significance for De Quincey, who, ever conscious of his diminutive stature, hankered after a 'high literary name'. The Spectre of the Brocken (1: 52), whose colossal size is the mirror-image of the 'delicate little ghost' Thomas De Quincey, is the writer's Other. Unable to compete with Wordsworth, he deliberately cultivated the Gothic, which Wordsworth despised. Stressing his own high aims, by analogy with Karl Moor (Charles de Moor), he had a horror of failure, an abstract notion which the 'dream-work' depicts literally, as a fall. In the background therefore is an abyss of the nonentity, nothingness and non-significance of which he was afraid. That Kafka was afraid of it too is shown by *Das Schloß*, which turns on the semi-autobiographical protagonist's vain attempt to have his personal significance officially attested. The solitary human climbing to his fall, or actually falling as in Hubert Robert's *The Fall*[19] is a figure of nightmare. Robert's *The Fall* depicts literally the fall which so profoundly affected De Quincey's life and work.

If he had known it (and there is no reason whatsoever to suppose that he did), Kafka's attention would have been held by De Quincey's description of the dreamer:

> The dreamer finds housed within himelf – occupying, as it were, some separate chamber in his brain – holding, perhaps, from that station a secret and detestable commerce with his own heart – some horrid alien nature. What if it were his own nature repeated, – still, if the duality were distinctly perceptible, even *that* – even this mere numerical double of his own consciousness – might be a curse too mighty to be sustained. But how, if this alien nature contradicts his own, fights with it, perplexes and confounds it? How, again, if not one alien nature, but two, but three, but four, but five, are introduced within what once he thought the inviolable sanctuary of himself?

The idea of the 'inviolable' sanctuary of the self being challenged from within by a *Doppelgänger* in the form of an alien, Gothic self, and maybe by several, for who knows what lurks within those depths within depths within depths, what nanodemons, would have been all too credible to Kafka, familiar as he was with the concept and reality of another self, whose autoscopic antics he depicted in his major works, and indeed of a host of inner demons. One need only read *Confessions* and *Suspira de profundis* in tandem with Kafka's diaries and letters to see that here, in this most private of respects, there is another significant parallel between the two writers. A major difference between them is that the

---

19 Gaunt, Plate 30.

antogonistic double of which De Quincey writes arguably represents ‘a part of [his] self which he cannot or will not read and which he cannot replace’,[20] whereas Kafka is willing and able to read his Gothic self and seeks – albeit ‘unsucessfully’, for he knows that he could not exist without it – to replace it by writing about it.

It has been said that ‘In De Quincey’s economy of the self, in his offering of the self as prodigal, as perpetual transgressor, to a willing audience, a new, fundamentally modern form of subjectivity appears’.[21] Kafka, three generations later, seems to do much the same thing, but he is more fundamentally concerned with the problem of subjectivity, and more especially of the subjectivity of meaning and moral valuations from which De Quincey shied away, for the twentieth-century writer inevitably has fewer historical inhibitions than the nineteenth-century one. In *Das Schloß* he goes further in blurring the distinction between good and evil, thereby reuniting himself with an absent God by clinging to the no longer credible doctrine of original sin.

Although De Quincey occcasionally evinced a malicious streak that Kafka lacked, each of them was quicker to recognize his own shortcomings than those of others. Kafka went further than De Quincey in this respect too, for the Opium-Eater, quixotically, emphasized that his self-accusation in the *Confessions* did not amount to a confession of guilt, whereas Kafka’s self-accusations were all premissed on the unshakeable, Schopenhauerian conviction of his guilt: I am, therefore I am guilty. It is easy to misunderstand De Quincey: he meant, not that he was not guilty, but that he needed, psychologically, to cling to the guilt around which he had constructed his inner life and by which he defined himself; he could not afford to jettison it, for there would have been nothing left. De Quincey claimed, to my mind rather unconvincingly, to be writing to help others; Kafka was more certainly writing to help himself. De Quincey spoke of a ‘noxious umbrage’ that overshadowed and darkened his later years, when suffering ‘threatened to besiege the citadel of life and hope’; the last decade of Kafka’s life was overcast by a similar dark shadow, this being shown, not least, by the novel *Das Schloß*, which is about that very citadel being besieged by ‘ghastly phantoms’ similar to those described by De Quincey, represented in the novel by the swarms of crows swirling round the nondescript tower of a notably Gothic edifice. The ‘horror of a self-destructive, but self-defining tendency’ within himself that has been attributed to De Quincey[22] was familiar to Kafka, whose diaries reveal a clear self-destructive impulse; the two tendencies come memorably together in Josef K.’s dream of death at the end of *Der Proceß*.

If De Quincey is ‘a subtly self-effacing writer whose works virtually *are* his life,[23] so too is Kafka. Eaton’s verdict on De Quincey, that ‘even in this autobiographic mood – in his literary expression of it – he escapes us. Instead of looking from the inside out, he looks from the outside in’ (E 514f.), is strikingly applicable to Kafka, whose Castle, as such, is based, in part, on Schopenhauer’s statement that we can never arrive at the real nature of things from the outside, for in seeking to do so we should be like a man walking round a castle, looking in vain for an entrance.[24] What Lindop has said of De Quincey, that ‘Even in

---

20 Baxter, 129.
21 Clej, 11.
22 Baxter, 129.
23 Snyder, in *Bicentenary Studies*, xxi.
24 Schopenhauer, *The World as Will and Idea*, Vol. I, Book II, §17.

his most fantastic tales he could not really free himself from the autobiographical compulsion' (L 304), applies equally well to Kafka, whose fictions, like De Quincey's 'The Household Wreck', are largely made up of autobiographical fragments[25] 'translated' (and corrected!) from the diaries. The work of both men is fictionalized autobiography, an autobiographical masquerade, a series of masked confessions; both variously epitomize what has been called 'the gothicism of phantom-self autobiography'.[26] The narrator of the *Confessions* is a fictionalized autobiographical figure,[27] as are the protagonists of Kafka's novels, who likewise have not a little of the Gothic (Satanic) hero in their makeup.

If De Quincey introduces 'large slices of autobiographical material' (L 207) into his fiction, Kafka invariably introduces an autobiographical level of meaning into his. There are, however, marked differences between these two writers of masked autobiography. De Quincey writes autobiography so named, but also elaborated and thereby further falsified autobiography (no longer labelled as such, in the form of his dream-texts) or autobiographical fiction; even his essays on other writers include passages of autobiography. Kafka, for his part, writes nothing but disguised, fictionalized autobiography, both in the sense that all his autobiographical writing is fictionalized, and in the sense that he writes nothing else – even his diaries and the letters to his father have been subjected to some fictionalization (poetic licence, exaggeration). He simultaneously reveals and conceals himself and his meaning, going to endless trouble to do so via patterns of secondary meaning, so that permutations of meaning, built into his texts, turn them into a hermeneutic nightmare. He also plants within each of his three novels the deconstructive idea that what he is writing is a tall story. De Quincey, by contrast, who lived almost twice as long as Kafka, is a congenital rewriter, keenly aware of the problems surrounding the reliability or otherwise of the text in front of him, but making much less use of verbal ambiguity. The work of both men is multi-layered, the layering in question both remarkably similar and totally different. With De Quincey it is mainly a matter of different versions of the 'truth' that are generated successively; with Kafka it is very much a matter of simultaneous, mutually exclusive meanings that exist side by side.

To a large extent the reasons why Kafka does not write straight, undisguised autobiography overlap with the reasons why De Quincey produces only self-cancelling, mutually exclusive fragments of autobiography. Highly self-aware, they are both conscious of the fact that not only their work, but, through it, their self is contingent upon what is yet to come, so that autobiographical text-generation is rooted in falsehood as a shed (dead) self is described by another whose words become untrue even as they are written down, one of the reasons why biography is truer than autobiography. The text is thus a form of premature death, signed, sealed and delivered over to posterity. Both men are fully aware of the gulf between the text as written and read. There can be no absolute understanding of the text, which Kafka and, I suspect, De Quincey fears. The text-as-read may produce, as Baxter says,[28] a *semblance* of the text-as-written, but it is not a *vraisemblance*. In addition to this metaphysical and moral flux, there is also the linguistic one, for the 'unintentional opening

---

25 Baxter, 104.
26 Russett, 179.
27 See Lever, 332-4.
28 Baxter, 20.

left for double interpretations' that De Quincey[29] found in most people's words, was deliberately cultivated by Kafka, who turned it into the very foundation of his literary edifice. No wonder both men were dissatisfied with their work.

Autobiography is, of its very nature, what De Quincey calls *rifacimento*. It recreates or translates the past into terms intelligible and acceptable to the present self, a dubious procedure that by definition involves falsification, for 'If to impart truth is the purpose of the De Quinceyan text, then the only truth it can impart is that the autobiographical intervention is a lie, a necessary fiction'.[30] The original experience is a pre-text both in the sense of predating the text and in the sense of providing the occasion or excuse for a creative moment. Both De Quincey and Kafka know that in the final analysis there is only that fleeting moment: it is why they live for their writing. De Quincey, thinking of Rousseau's *Confessions*, writes scornfully of 'the spectacle of a human being obtruding on our notice his moral ulcers or scars' and then went on to do precisely that. Kafka describes those same scars, but goes to great lengths to disguise the fact that he is doing so. His work, equally confessional, consists of 'notes and memoranda' (*Aufzeichnungen*) addressed to the self, and is marked by precisely what Baxter, writing of De Quincey,[31] has called 'a striving towards a privacy and a precision which would be impenetrable if entirely realized'.

Both are aware, then, of the unreliability not only of language as such, that finite medium with the potential for infinite misunderstanding, but of the self as author. Masters of the art of echoing that confers a spurious reality on what is echoed, they hide behind their respective styles. As these show, Kafka was far from being the scholar-poet and man-of-letters that De Quincey so eminently was. De Quincey lacks Kafka's almost 'Japanese' genius for lapidary formulation. Kafka lacks the genius for digression that so often causes De Quincey to mislay or conceal his point. Stylistically, they are miles apart, for Kafka's ultra-plain language is far removed from the intricate, Latinate surges and billows of De Quincey's memorably idiosyncratic prose. De Quincey is studiedly rhetorical; Kafka eschews rhetoric, of which he had a horror. De Quincey's prose is, at its best, 'im-passioned'; Kafka's is dispassionate, but only because he is passionate about what he is doing.

---

29 See Baxter, 49.
30 Baxter, 49.
31 Baxter, 47.

Bibliography

Aguirre, Manuel, *The closed space: Horror literature and western symbolism* (Manchester: Manchester University Press, 1990)

Alexis, Willibald, *Walladmor*, 3 vols (Berlin: Herbig, 1824, repr. Leipzig: Edition Leipzig, 1967)

——— *Schloß Avalon*, 3 vols (Leipzig: Brockhaus, 1827)

——— *Erinnerungen*, ed. Max Ewert, new edn (Berlin: Concordia, 1905)

Andriano, Joseph, *Our Ladies of Darkness. Female Daemonology in Male Gothic Fiction* (Pennsylvania: Pennsylvania State University Press, 1993)

Apel, J. A., and F. Laun (eds), *Gespensterbuch*, 6 vols (Leipzig: Göschen, 1811-17)

Appell, J. W., *Die Ritter-, Räuber- und Schauerromantik* (Leipzig: Wilhelm Engelmann, 1859)

The Arabian Nights Entertainments [tr. from Galland] (London: T. Longman, 1763)

Archenholz, J. W. von, *Annalen der Brittischen Geschichte*, Vol. 19 (Tübingen: Cotta, 1799)

Bachmann, Frederick Wilhelm, *Some German Imitators of Scott*, Diss. Chicago, 1933

Baldick, Chris (ed.), *The Oxford Book of Gothic Tales* (Oxford & New York: Oxford University Press, 1992)

Bannerman, Anne, *Tales of Superstition and Chivalry* (London: Vernor & Hood, 1802)

Barruel, Abbé, *Memoirs Illustrating the History of Jacobinism*, tr. R. Clifford, 2nd edn (London: T. Burton, 1797)

Batt, M., 'Gillies and the *Foreign Quarterly Review*', *Modern Language Notes*, 17/3 (March 1902), 165-70

——— 'Gillies and *Blackwood's Magazine*', *Modern Language Notes*, 18/3 (March 1903), 65-69

Baxter, Edmund, *De Quincey's Art of Autobiography* (Edinburgh: Edinburgh University Press, 1990)

Beaujean, Marion, *Der Trivialroman in der zweiten Hälfte des 18. Jahrhunderts* (Bonn: Bouvier, 1964)

Birkhead, Edith, *The Tale of Terror* (London: Constable, 1921, repr. New York: Russell & Russell, 1963)

Black, Joel D., 'Levana: Levitation in Jean Paul and Thomas De Quincey', *Comparative Literature*, 32 (1980), 42-62

——— *The Aesthetics of Murder* (Baltimore: The John Hopkins University Press, 1991)

Blackall, Eric A., *The Novels of the German Romantics* (Ithaca & London: Cornell University Press, 1983)

Block, Andrew, *The English Novel 1740-1850* (London: Dawsons, 1967)

Botting, Fred, *Gothic* (London & New York: Routledge, 1996)

Börsch-Supan, H., *Caspar David Friedrich*, tr. Sarah Twohig (Munich: Prestel, 1974)

Breuer, Rolf, and Werner Huber and Rainer Schöwerling, *English Romanticism. The Paderborn Symposium* (Essen: Die Blaue Eule, 1985)

Bridgwater, Patrick, *Anglo-German Interactions in the Literature of the 1890s* (Oxford: Legenda, 1999)
—— *Kafka, Gothic and Fairytale* (Amsterdam & New York: Rodopi, 2003)
Brockden Brown, Charles, *The Rhapsodist and other uncollected writings*, ed. Harry R. Warfel (New York: Scholars' Facsimiles and Reprints, 1943)
Burwick, Frederick, 'The Dream-Visions of Jean Paul and Thomas De Quincey', *Comparative Literature*, 20 (1968), 1-26
—— 'How to Translate a Waverley Novel: Sir Walter Scott, Willibald Alexis, and Thomas De Quincey', *The Wordworth Circle*, 25/2 (Spring 1994), 93-100
—— 'De Quincey and the Aesthetics of Violence', *The Wordsworth Circle*, 27/2 (Spring 1996), 78-86
Caracciolo, Peter L., *The Arabian Nights in English Literature* (Basingstoke: Macmillan, 1988)
Carlyle, Thomas, *Critical and Miscellaneous Essays*, 4 vols (London: Chapman & Hall, n.d.)
—— *The Life of Schiller* (London: Chapman & Hall, n.d.)
Chevalier, Jean, and Alain Gheerbrant (eds), *The Penguin Dictionary of Symbols* (London: Penguin, 1996)
Christoph, Friedrich, *Über den Einfluß Jean Paul Richters auf Thomas De Quincey* (Hof: no publisher named, 1898)
Clej, Alina, *A Genealogy of the Modern Self* (Stanford, CA: Stanford University Press, 1995)
Clery, E. J., and Robert Miles (eds), *Gothic Documents: A Sourcebook 1700-1820* (Manchester: Manchester University Press, 2000)
Clute, John, and John Grant, *The Encyclopedia of Fantasy* (London: Orbit, 1997)
Coleridge, S. T., *Biographia Literaria* (London: Bell, 1876)
—— *Collected Letters of Samuel Taylor Coleridge*, ed. E. L. Griggs, 6 vols (Oxford: Clarendon Press, 1956-71)
Cooke, Margaret W., 'Schiller's „Robbers“ in England', *Modern Language Review,* 11 (1915), 156-75
Crowe, Catherine, *The Night-Side of Nature, or Ghosts and Ghost-Seers* (London: T. C. Newby, 1848)
De Quincey, Thomas, *De Quincey's Works*, ed. David Masson, 14 vols (London: A. & C. Black, 1896-97)
—— *Confessions of an English Opium-Eater*, ed. Richard Garnett (London: Kegan Paul, Trench, 1885)
—— *Confessions of an English Opium-Eater*, ed. Alethea Hayter (London: Penguin, 1986)
—— *Confessions of an English Opium-Eater*, ed. Grevel Lindop (Oxford: Oxford University Press, 1998)
—— *A Diary of Thomas De Quincey, 1803*, ed. H. A. Eaton (New York: Payson & Clarke, 1927)
—— *Niels Klim*, ed. S. Musgrove (Auckland: Auckland University College, 1953)
—— *The Peasant of Portugal*, ed. Edmund Baxter (London: Aporia Press, 1985)
—— *The Caçadore*, ed. Edmund Baxter (London: Aporia Press, 1888)

——— *Klosterheim*, ed. Jonathan Wordsworth (Oxford & New York: Woodstock Books, 1992)

——— *The Works of Thomas De Quincey*, ed. Grevel Lindop et al. (London: Pickering & Chatto, 2000-)

Doughty, Oswald, 'Coleridge and „The Gothic Novel" or „Tales of Terror",' *English Miscellany*, 23 (1972), 125-48

Duncan, Ian, *Modern Romance and Transformations of the Novel* (Cambridge: Cambridge University Press, 1992)

Eaton, Horace Ainsworth, *Thomas De Quincey: A Biography* (New York: Oxford University Press, 1936)

Essig, Erhart H., *Thomas De Quincey and Robert Pearse Gillies as Champions of German Literature and Thought* (Diss. Northwestern University, 1951)

Fiedler, Leslie A., *Love and Death in the American Novel* (Normal, IL: Dalkey Archive Press, 1997)

Fischer, Richard, *'Schloß Avalon', der erste historische Roman von Willibald Alexis* (Diss. Leipzig, 1910)

Foster, James R., *History of the Pre-Romantic Novel in England* (London: Oxford University Press, 1949)

Frank, Frederick S., *Guide to the Gothic: An Annotated Bibliography of Criticism* (Metuchen, NJ, & London: The Scarecrow Press, 1984)

——— *The First Gothics* (New York & London: Garland, 1987)

——— *Gothic Fiction, A Master List of Twentieth-Century Criticism and Research* (Westport, CT: Meckler, 1988)

——— *Guide to the Gothic II: An Annotated Bibliography of Criticism, 1983-1993* (Lanham, Md, & London: The Scarecrow Press, 1995)

Freud, Sigmund, *The Interpretation of Dreams*, tr. James Strachey, 3rd imp. (London: George Allen & Unwin, 1967)

——— *Art and Literature*, tr. James Strachey, ed. Albert Dickson (London: Penguin, 1990)

Galinsky, Hans K., 'Is Thomas De Quincey the author of *The Love-Charm*?", *Modern Language Notes,* 52 (1937), 389-94

Gamer, Michael, *Romanticism and Gothic* (Cambridge: Cambridge University Press, 2002)

Garside, Peter, and James Raven and Rainer Schöwerling, *The English Novel 1779-1829*, 2 vols (Oxford: Oxford University Press, 2000)

Gaunt, W., *Bandits in a Landscape* (London: The Studio, 1937)

Gillies, R. P., *German Stories*, 3 vols (Edinburgh: William Blackwood, & London: T. Cadell, 1826)

——— *Recollections of Sir Walter Scott* (London: Fraser, 1837)

——— *Memoirs of a Literary Veteran*, 3 vols (London: Richard Bentley, 1851)

Gleick, James, *Chaos* (New York: Penguin, 1988)

Goethe, J. W. von, *The Sorrows of Werter*, tr. Daniel Malthus [1789], ed. Jonathan Wordsworth (Oxford & New York: Woodstock , 1991)

——— *Goetz of Berlichingen with the Iron Hand*, tr. Walter Scott (Zwickau: Schumann, 1829)

Goldman, Albert, *The Mine and the Mint* (Carbondale & Edwardsville: Southern Illinois University Press, 1965)

Grosse, Karl, *The Dagger* (London: Vernor & Hood, 1795)
Guthke, Karl S., *Englische Vorromantik und deutscher Sturm und Drang* (Göttingen: Vandenhoeck & Ruprecht, 1958)
Haddawy, Husain (ed./tr.), *The Arabian Nights* (London: Davis Campbell, 1992)
Hadley, Michael, *The Undiscovered Genre. A Search for the German Gothic Novel* (Berne, Frankfurt a. M. & Las Vegas: Peter Lang, 1978)
Halbertsma, J. H., *Het geslacht der Van Haren's. Fragmenten* (Deventer: Lange, 1829)
Hale, Terry (ed.), *Tales of the Dead* (Chislehurst: The Gothic Society, 1992)
Hammer, Joseph von, *History of the Assassins*, tr. O. C. Wood (London: Smith & Elder, 1835, repr. New York: Burt Franklin, 1968)
——— (ed.), *New Arabian Nights Entertainments*, tr. George Lamb (London: Henry Colburn, 1826)
Hansen, Thomas S., with Burton R. Pollin, *The German Face of Edgar Allan Poe* (Columbia, SC: Camden House, 1995)
Heiderich, Manfred W., *The German Novel of 1800* (Berne & Frankfurt a. M.: Peter Lang, 1982)
Hitzig, Julius Eduard, and Wilhelm Häring, *Der neue Pitaval*, 67 vols (Leipzig: Brockhaus. 1842-87)
Hogle, Jerrold E. (ed.), *The Cambridge Companion to Gothic Fiction* (Cambridge: Cambridge University Press, 2002)
Hoffmann, E. T. A., *The Devil's Elixir,* [tr. R. P. Gillies,] 2 vols (Edinburgh: William Blackwood, & London: T. Cadell, 1824)
Hofmann, O., *Studien zum englischen Schauerroman* [Diss. Leipzig] (Halle a. S.: John, 1915)
Holmes, Richard, *Coleridge: Early Visions* (London: Hodder & Stoughton, 1989)
Huber, Werner (ed.), *The Corvey Library and Anglo-German Cultural Exchanges 1779-1799* (Munich: Fink, 2000)
Huxley, Aldous, *Prisons* (London: The Trianon Press, 1949)
Irving, Pierre M., *The Life and Letters of Washington Irving*, 4 vols in 3 (New York: Putnam, 1869)
Jack, Ian, *English Literature 1815-1832* (Oxford: Clarendon Press, 1963)
Johnson, Edgar, *Sir Walter Scott. The Great Unknown*, 2 vols (London: Hamish Hamilton, 1970)
Jones, Ernest, *Nightmare, Witches, and Devils* (New York: W. W. Norton, n.d.)
Kiely, Robert, *The Romantic Novel in England* (Cambridge, Mass.: Harvard University Press, 1972)
Klein, Jürgen, *Der gotische Roman und die Ästhetik des Bösen* (Darmstadt: Wissenschaftliche Buchgesellschaft, 1975)
Koch, John, 'Sie Walter Scotts Beziehungen zu Deutschland', *Germanisch-Romanische Monatsschrift*, 15 (1927), 36-46, 117-41
Koerner, Joseph Leo, *Caspar David Friedrich and the subject of landscape* (London: Reaktion Books, 1995)
Kohler, Hedwig Frida, *'Walladmor' von Willibald Alexis: Untersuchung des Romans in seinem Verhältnis zu Walter Scott* (Diss.Marburg, 1915)
Korff, Hermann A., *Scott und Alexis* (Diss. Heidelberg, 1907)

Laun, Friedrich, *Gesammelte Schriften*, introd. Ludwig Tieck, 6 vols in 3 (Dresden: Arnold, 1843)
Lee, Harriet, *Kruitzner; or, The German's Tale* (London: John Murray, 1822)
——— & Sophia Lee, *Canterbury Tales for the Year 1797*, 5 vols (London: Robinson, 1797-99)
Lee, Sophia, *The Recess: A Tale of Other Times* (London: T. Cadell, 1783-85)
Lever, Karen M., 'De Quincey as Gothic Hero: A Perspective on *Confessions of an English Opium-Eater* and *Suspira de Profundis*', *Texas Studies in Literature and Language*, 21 (1979), 332-46
Lévy, Maurice, *Le roman «gothique» anglais 1764-1824* (Paris: Albin Michel, 1995)
Lewis, M. G., *The Bravo of Venice* (London: J. F. Hughes, 1805)
Lindop, Grevel, *The Opium-Eater: A Life of Thomas De Quincey* (London, Melbourne & Toronto: J. M. Dent, 1981)
Lockhart, J. G., *Memoirs of the Life of Sir Walter Scott* (Edinburgh: A. & C. Black, 1851)
Ludz, Peter Christian, *Geheime Gesellschaften* (Heidelberg: Lambert Schneider, 1979)
Macnish, Robert, *The Philosophy of Sleep*, 2nd edn (Glasgow: W. R. M'Phun, 1834)
McDonagh, Josephine, *De Quincey's Disciplines* (Oxford: Clarendon Press, 1994)
Menhennet, Alan, *Schiller and the 'Germanico-Terrific' Romance* (Leeds: English Goethe Society, 1981)
Michelsen, Peter, 'Thomas De Quincey und Schiller', *German Life & Letters*, 9 (1956), 91-99
Michelsen, Peter, 'Thomas De Quincey und die Kantische Philosophie', *Revue de Littérature Comparée*, 33 (1959), 356-75
Miles, Robert, *Gothic Writing 1750-1820: A Genealogy*, 2nd edn (Manchester: Manchester University Press, 2002)
Miller, J. Hillis, *The Disappearance of God: Five Nineteenth-Century Writers* (Cambridge, Mass.: The Belknap Press, 1975)
Miller, Norbert, *Archäologie des Traums* (Munich: Hanser, 1978)
More, Hannah, *Strictures on the Modern System of Female Education*, 2 vols (London: T. Cadell, 1799)
Morgan, B. Q., and A. R. Hohlfeld (eds), *German Literature in British Magazines 1750-1860* (Madison, Wisconsin: University of Wisconsin Press, 1949)
Morrison, Robert, and Chris Baldick (eds), *Tales of Terror from Blackwood's Magazine* (Oxford: Oxford University Press, 1995)
Müller-Fraureuth, Carl, *Die Ritter- und Räuberromane* (Halle a. S.: Max Niemeyer, 1894)
Mulvey-Roberts,Marie (ed.), *The Handbook to Gothic Literature* (Basingstoke: Macmillan, 1998)
Murphy, John V., *The Dark Angel. Gothic Elements in Shelley's Works* (London: Associated University Presses, 1975)
[Naubert, Benedikte], *Herman of Unna*, 3 vols (London: Robinson, 1794)
Nelson, Lowry (Jr), 'Night Thoughts on the Gothic Novel', *Yale Review*, 52 (1962), 236-57
Oppel, Horst, *Englisch-deutsche Literaturbeziehungen*, 2 vols (Berlin: Erich Schmidt, 1971)
Otten, Kurt, 'Der englische Schauerroman', in *Europäische Romantik II*, ed. Klaus Heitmann (Wiesbaden: Athenaion, 1982), 215-42

Parnell, William, *Julietta, or The Triumph of Mental Acquirements over Personal Defects* (London: J. Johnson, 1802)
Parsons, Coleman O., *Witchcraft and Demonology in Scott's Fiction* (Edinburgh & London: Oliver & Boyd, 1964)
Patterson, Charles J., 'De Quincey's Conception of the Novel as Literature of Power', *PMLA*, 70 (1955), 375-89
Paulin, Roger, *Ludwig Tieck. A Literary Biography* (Oxford: Clarendon Press, 1985)
Pilkington, Mary, *The Accusing Spirit* (London: Minerva Press, 1802)
Pitaval, François Gayot de, *Causes célèbres et intéressantes*, 26 vols (Amsterdam: Chatelain, 1734-71)
Poe, Edgar Allan, *The Collected Works of Edgar Allan Poe*, ed. Thomas Ollive Mabbott, 3 vols (Camb ridge, Mass.: Harvard University Press, 1969)
Praz, Mario, *The Romantic Agony*, tr. Angus Davidson (London: Oxford University Press, 1933)
—— *The Hero in Eclipse in Victorian Fiction*, tr. Angus Davidson (London, New York, Toronto: Oxford University Press, 1956)
Price, Lawrence Marsden, *The Reception of English Literature in Germany* (New York & London: Benjamin Blom, 1968)
Punter, David, *The Literature of Terror*, 2 vols (London: Longman, 1996)
—— (ed.), *A Companion to the Gothic* (Oxford: Blackwell, 2000)
Radcliffe, Anne, *The Castles of Athlin and Dunbayne: A Highland Story* (London: T. Hookham, 1789)
—— *The Italian, or The Confessional of the Black Penitents. A Romance* (London: T. Cadell, Jr., & W. Davies, 1797)
Railo, Eino, *The Haunted Castle* (London: Routledge, 1927)
[Raspe, Rudolf Erich], *The Travels of Baron Munchausen* (London: Kearsley, 1786)
Raven, James, 'Cheap and Cheerless: English Novels in German Translation and German Novels in English Translation, 1770-1799,' in *The Corvey Library and Anglo German Cultural Exchanges 1770-1799*, ed. Werner Huber (Minich: Fink, 2000), 1-35
Reichart, Walter A., *Washington Irving and Germany* (Ann Arbor: University of Michigan Press, 1957)
Richter, Jean Paul, *Levana; or, The Doctrine of Education* (London: Bell, 1901)
Robbins, Ruth, and Julian Wolfeys (eds), *Victorian Gothic* (Basingstoke: Palgrave, 2000)
Roberts, J. M., *The Mythology of the Secret Societies* (London: Secker & Warburg, 1972)
Roberts, Marie, *Gothic Immortals: The Fiction of the Brotherhood of the Rosy Cross* (London & New York: Routledge, 1990)
—— *British Poets and Secret Societies* (London & Sydney: Croom Helm, 1986)
Robison, John, *Proofs of a Conspiracy against all the Religions and Governments of Europe* (Edinburgh: London: T. Cadell jun., & Edinburgh: W. Creech, 1797)
Robson-Scott, W. D., *German Travellers in England 1400-1800* (Oxford: Blackwell, 1953)
Rommel, Otto, 'Rationalistische Dämonie. Die Geisterromane des ausgehenden 18. Jahrhunderts', *Deutsche Vierteljahrsschrift*, 17 (1939), 183-220.
Rudwin, Maximilian, *The Devil in Legend and Literature* (Chicago & London: The Open Court Company, 1931)

Russett, Margaret, *De Quincey's Romanticism* (Cambridge: Cambridge University Press, 1997)

Schiller, J. C. F., *Merkwürdige Rechtsfälle als ein Beitrag zur Geschichte der Menschheit*, 4 vols (Jena, 1792-95)

——— *The Robbers* [tr. A. F. Tytler] (London: Robinson, 1795)

——— *The Ghost-Seer; or, Apparitionist, an Interesting Fragment*, tr. D. Boileau (London: Vernor & Hood, 1795)

——— *The Ghost-Seer*, tr. H. G. Bohn, ed. Jeffrey L. Sammons (Columbia, SC: Camden House, 1992)

——— *The Historical Works of Frederick Schiller*, tr. George Moir, 2 vols (Edinburgh: Constable, 1828)

Schopenhauer, Arthur, *The World as Will and Idea*, tr. R. B. Haldane and J. Kemp, 3 vols (London: Kegan Paul, Trench, Trübner, n.d.)

Schubert, Gotthilf Heinrich von, *Ansichten von der Nachtseite der Naturwissenschaft* (Dresden: Arnold, 1808, repr. Eschborn: Dietmar Klotz, 1992)

——— *Die Symbolik des Traumes* (1814, repr. Stuttgart: Belser Presse, 1968)

Scott, Jonathan, *Piranesi* (London: Academy/St Martin's, 1975)

Scott, Sir Walter, *Letters on Demonology and Witchcraft* (London: John Murray, 1830)

Sedgwick, Eve Kosofsky, *The Coherence of Gothic Conventions* (New York & London: Methuen, 1980)

Shelley, Percy Bysshe, *Zastrozzi and St Irvyne*, ed. Stephen C. Behrendt (Oxford & New York: Oxford University Press, 1986)

Smeed, J. W., *German Influence on Thomas Carlyle* (Edinburgh: The Carlyle Society, 1964)

Snyder, Robert Lance, '*Klosterheim*: De Quincey's Gothic Masque', *Research Studies*, 49 (1981), 129-42

——— (ed.), *Thomas De Quincey: Bicentenary Studies* (Norman & London: University of Oklahoma Press, 1985)

Spieß, C. H., *Biographien der Wahnsinnigen*, 4 vols in 2 (Leipzig: Voss, 1795-96; repr. Darmstadt: Luchterhand, 1976)

Stark, Susanne (ed.), *The Novel in Anglo-German Context* (Amsterdam & Atlanta, GA: Rodopi, 2000)

Stephen, Leslie, *Studies of a Biographe*r, 4 vols (London: Duckworth, 1898-1902)

Stockley, V., *German Literature as Known in England 1750-1830* (London: Routledge, 1929)

Stokoe, F. W., *German Influence in the English Romantic Period 1788-1818* (Cambridge: Cambridge University Press, 1926)

Strout, Alan Lang, 'Writers on German Literature in *Blackwood's Magazine*', *The Library*, 9 (1954), 35-44

Summers, Montague, *The Gothic Quest* (New York: Russell & Russell, 1964)

Symonds, Barry, 'The Stranger's Grave: Laying a De Quinceyan Ghost', *The Charles Lamb Bulletin*, 83 (July 1993), 105-107

Thalmann, Marianne, *Der Trivialroman des 18. Jahrhunderts und der romantische Roman* (Berlin: Ebering, 1923)

——— *Die Romantik des Trivialen* (Munich: List, 1970)

Thiergard, Ulrich, 'Schiller und Walpole. Ein Beitrag zu Schillers Verhältnis zur Schauerliteratur', *Jahrbuch der deutschen Schiller-Gesellschaft*, 3 (1959), 102-117
Thomas, L. H. C., 'The Literary Reputation of Willibald Alexis as an Historical Novelist', *Modern Language Review*, 45 (1950), 195-214
——— '*Walladmor*: A Pseudo-Translation of Sir Walter Scott', *Modern Language Review*, 46 (1951), 218-31
Thomas, Lionel [H. C.], *'Schloß Avalon'*, *German Life & Letters*, 10 (1957), 97-105
——— *Willibald Alexis. A Biography* (Oxford: Blackwell, 1964)
Thomas, Ronald R., *Dreams of Authority. Freud and the Fictions of the Unconscious* (Ithaca & London: Cornell University Press, 1990)
Thompson, G. R., *The Gothic Imagination: Essays in Dark Romanticism* (Pullman: Washington State University Press, 1974)
Tieck, Ludwig, and Friedrich Eberhard Rambach, *Biographien berühmter Schwärmer, Gauner, Mörder, Mordbrenner und Strassenräuber* (Hanover [no publisher named], 1797)
Tompkins, J. M. S., *The Popular Novel in England 1770-1800* (London: Methuen, 1932)
Trainer, James, *Ludwig Tieck. From Gothic to Romantic* (The Hague: Mouton, 1964)
Tromlitz, A. von, *Sämmtliche Schriften*, 24 vols (Dresden & Leipzig: Arnold, 1829-32)
——— *Sämmtliche Werke,* 108 vols in 46 (Leipzig: Arnold, 1829-42)
Varendonck, J., *The Psychology of Day-Dreams* (London: George Allen & Unwin, 1921)
Varma, Devendra P., *The Gothic Flame* (Metuchen, NJ & London: The Scarecrow Press, 1987)
Vaughan, William, *German Romanticism and English Art* (New Haven & London: Yale University Press, 1979)
Vulpius, Christian August, *Rinaldo Rinaldini, the Robber Captain*, tr. John Hinckley (London: Longman & Rees, 1800)
Ware, M., *Sublimity in the Novels of Ann Radcliffe* (Lund: Uppsala University English Department, 1963)
Warfel, Harry R., 'Charles Brockden Brown's German Sources', *Modern Language Quarterly*, 1 (Sept. 1940), 357-65
Webster, Nesta, *World Revolution: The Plot against Civilization* (London: Constable, 1921)
——— *Secret Societies and Subversive Movements*, 5th edn (London: Boswell, 1936)
Wellek, René, *Immanuel Kant in England, 1793-1838* (Princeton, NJ: Princeton University Press, 1931)
——— *Confrontations. Studies in the Intellectual and Literary Relations between Germany, England and the United States during the Nineteenth Century* (Princeton, NJ: Princeton University Press, 1965)
[West, Jane], *The Infidel Father* (London: Longman & Rees, 1802)
Williams, Ioan (ed.), *Sir Walter Scott on Novelists and Fiction* (New York: Barnes & Noble, 1968)
——— (ed.), *Novel and Romance 1700-1800: A Documentary Record* (New York: Barnes & Noble, 1970)
Willoughby, L. A., 'English Translations and Adaptations of Schiller's *Robbers*', *Modern Language Review,* 16 (1921), 297-315
Worringer, Wilhelm, *Form in Gothic*, tr. & ed. Herbert Read (London: Putnam's, 1927)

Index